Experiences of War

The British Sailor

KENNETH POOLMAN

Experiences of War

The British Sailor

KENNETH POOLMAN

ARMS AND
ARMOUR

'Not fare well,
But fare forward, voyagers.'
— T. S. Eliot, *The Dry Salvages*

First published in Great Britain in 1989 by Arms and Armour Press,
Artillery House, Artillery Row, London SW1P 1RT.

Distributed in the USA by Sterling Publishing Co. Inc., 387 Park
Avenue South, New York, NY 10016-8810.

Distributed in Australia by Capricorn Link (Australia) Pty. Ltd, P.O.
Box 665, Lane Cove, New South Wales 2066, Australia.

British Library Cataloguing in Publication Data
Poolman, Kenneth
Experiences of war: the British sailor.
1. Naval operations by Great Britain, Royal Navy. History
I. Title
359.4'0941
ISBN 0-85368-992-X

Designed and edited by DAG Publications Ltd. Designed by David
Gibbons; edited by David Dorrell; typeset by Nene Photosetting Ltd,
Northampton; illustration & camerawork by M&E Reproductions,
North Fambridge, Essex; printed and bound in Great Britain by
Richard Clay Ltd, Bungay, Suffolk

Contents

Acknowledgements

I wish to thank the following for their invaluable help with this book:
Alan Armstrong; Tom Bailey; A. Barlow; Dennis Bond; Neville Bradpiece; Gus
Britton; Jack Bryant; Chris Buist; Ivor Burston; William Capseed; Douglas J.
Cole; Eric Craske; Stewart A. Crawford; Howard G. Cunningham; Lieutenant-
Commander W. Curtis, RN (Rtd); Mick Dale, BEM; John E. Dodds, DSM;
Lieutenant S. Donovan, MBE, RN (Rtd); G. E. Denny; Bill Earp; Lieutenant-
Commander D. W. Elliott, RN (Rtd); L. W. Ellis; Peter Embleton; Lieutenant-
Commander F. N. Fieldgate, RN (Rtd); Lieutenant-Commander W. S. Filer,
RN (Rtd); R. G. Fletcher; S. France; G. H. Goodfellow; M. E. Grundy; F. Hall;
A. C. Harman; Lieutenant W. J. Heath, RN (Rtd); Norman Hollis; Lieutenant-
Commander A. Janman, RN (Rtd); W. Jeffery; Charles Jones; Lieutenant-
Commander Ben Kennedy, RN (Rtd); George Knight; Denis Langdale, BA; F.
Lee; W. G. Lambert, DSM; Lieutenant-Commander Richard Leggatt, RN
(Rtd); H. Liddle; Lieutenant-Commander F. Longman, RN (Rtd); Lieutenant-
Commander R. Lunberg, RN (Rtd); Sub-Lieutenant George MacPherson, RN
(Rtd); B. Male; J. Malin; Captain A. Mathison, MN; W. McCall; Lieutenant-
Commander A. J. McCulloch, RN (Rtd); George Monk; Lieutenant-Com-
mander H. A. Monk, DSM, RN (Rtd); L. W. Nelson; Iain Nethercott, DSM,
AIMEE; E. North; D. V. Oliver; Lieutenant-Commander P. Parsons, RN (Rtd);
G. Penny; Lieutenant-Commander C. E. Perry, RN (Rtd); J. J. Pinkerton;
Lieutenant-Commander F. C. Rice, DSM, RN (Rtd); E. S. Rickman; G.
Rogers; R. R. Rowbottom; David Satherley; S. S. Saunders; Les Sayer; Jack
Skeats; C. Shiels; Cliff Smith; Eric Smith; Lieutenant- Commander J. Francis
Smith, RN (Rtd); Philip Spencer; Alan Todd and Mrs Roma Todd; E. W. F.
Tyler; Captain W. B. Thomas, MN; Mark D. Wells; Nicola Windell; Rocky
Wilkins; Phil Wilton.

Kenneth Poolman, 1989

Introduction

The two oldest items of memorabilia in my attic are a white-enamelled water dipper six inches long and one and a half inches in diameter, and a seaman's scratched and battered clasp knife with a broad blade and a spike for splicing. The first was used in my father's lifeboat to measure the water ration (half-full, twice a day) after his ship, the AMC *Salopian*, had been sunk. When George Monk, late radio officer of SS *Auditor*, called on me recently he produced an identical object, relic of his own 13-day ordeal. George was the only radio operator to pick up the SOS from my father's boat, and probably saved his life. Both men's stories are in this book, along with many others.

The 'Pusser's dirk' is mine and tells a much less dramatic story. Its spike was never used for splicing (the only thing I ever spliced was the mainbrace), though it has punched holes in many a tin of fruit, and the blade has only sharpened pencils; but it was with me in a cruiser, a minesweeper and a destroyer, where I, an HO and amateur matlow, once served with real sailors, men like Tom Bailey, who joined the 'Andrew' (Royal Navy) in the Depression for 'three square meals a day and a pair of boots', and found he liked the life; Iain Nethercott, DSM, Sea Scout, hard destroyer man and submarine sailor; Mark Wells, who went from the footplate to the saucy *Arethusa*, and felt at home; Fred Lee, who tells salty tales in the manner of the late Robb Wilton; Dennis Bond, drafted from the South-Eastern Electricity Board and the Godalming Brass Band to face *Scharnhorst*, *Gneisenau* and *Prinz Eugen*; Eric Craske, DEMS gunner from a family of fishermen and lifeboatmen, who grew to love even a 'dirty British coaster'; Bill Earp, who never saw the OK Corral but watched the mighty *Hood* blow up and shadowed *Bismarck* until revenge was exacted – and made a smashing Red Riding Hood; HO Bill McCall, who signed on for twelve; David Satherley, smooth Combined Operator who slept with a sergeant-major (female); Ernie North, who lost his heart with *Chanticleer*; 'Vic' Oliver, with us still only because none of his mines went off; Fred Hall ('From Stock Exchange to Hooligans' Navy'), who did not faint at autopsies; Alan Mathison, who never got to drive his bus but steered tramps through dangerous waters; Bill Thomas, who fought weevils in rust buckets even U-boats ignored; Jack Dodds, DSM, who survived because of where he slung his mick; Con Shiels, to whom the Andrew was home – after the sad streets of Jarrow; Bill Filer, who knew the blue altitudes and the black depths . . . and there are the flying sailors of the Fleet Air Arm, the TAGs and rating pilots, whose company I tried to join, sadly too late, matlows with the hearts of eagles.

These men, and more, tell their stories in the pages that follow. These are the tales of ordinary men at war on the sea, which brought out the best in them – the nod to the need for discipline; the love of ships, especially their own, sentimental in the best sense; the sense of duty owed to ship and self (ideally identical); to messmates and to their great loved/hated guardian, the Royal Navy, which fed them, clothed them, paid them (in many cases when no one else would) and gave them ambition, a chance of achievement; above all, perhaps, the gritty grey humour at their lot – tested, sometimes, by heartless, thoughtless treatment, incompetent leadership, worn-out weapons, hard lying and the worst of weather – 'You shouldn't have joined if you can't take a joke,' they said, and 'Roll on my twelve!'

Kenneth Poolman

Senior Service

Ganges tea is tasty, *Ganges* tea is fine,
It's good for cuts and bruises
And tastes like iodine.

Ganges bread is tasty, *Ganges* bread is fine,
A loaf fell off the table
And killed a mate of mine.

VOLUNTEERS

Wiveliscombe lies in the green Vale of Taunton Deane, Somerset. Once over the Brendon Hills to the north it is less than ten miles to the Severn Estuary, and only a short day's yomp westward to Minehead and Porlock Bay, where the river is lost in the shining Bristol Channel. The little town once bred rugby players. Members of the Hancock family, who ran the local brewery, had captained England and Wales in the 1880s, and in the 1920s the place was still a bustling market town.

The Burstons kept the New Inn, frequented by both farmhands and sailors. Young Ivor Burston, his elder brother Chris, and his friend Alfie Slocombe used to sit entranced by the salty stories of old Bill Prole who had shipped before the mast when sail was still supreme, and ex-Petty Officer Shipwright Fronde Bellew, who had gone to sea with the old ironclad Navy, and served in the dreadnought battlecruiser HMNZ *New Zealand* in the battle of Jutland. Lubricated by a steady flow of ale on the house, the teak-faced old salthorse told tales of the *Shark*, with Loftus Jones steering steadfast for the enemy though mortally wounded, of great ships blowing up, gun flashes in the mist, Von Scheer's battlecruisers looming through the smoke, and especially of Jack Cornwell, VC. A hundred jingo-jangles and doggerel verses had painted the young hero in stirring primaries. In 1927 Chris joined the Royal Marines, and was soon in the King's Hundred, an elite group. Alfie was the next to go – to the old three-decker training ship HMS *Impregnable* at 'Guz' (Devonport).

GANGES

Ivor's turn came on 2 October 1928, when he presented himself with 32 other keen lads at 126 Victoria Street, Bristol, for medical and other examinations.

Only six boys passed, including Ivor, and were given 1/6d each to sustain them on their long journey to HMS *Ganges*, the training ship at Shotley near Ipswich in Essex. The Royal Marine Recruiting Sergeant took 6d of this for 'getting you lads into the Royal Navy', and '. . . we felt honoured to pay up'. In the smoky halls of Paddington they were met by 'a gentleman in a blue serge suit and a bowler hat' who led them, not by tube, but on the top of a bus to Liverpool Street Station so that they could see the sights of London, which were a wonder to them. They felt they were already at sea, and in the City there were 'big shiny models of ships in the windows'.

They disembarked at Harwich in the dark, then were led on the double to a waiting steam pinnace with shiny brass funnel, which took them, not to a ship, but to the bottom of a long flight of steps (the famous 'Faith, Hope and Charity', as they later learned), which led to *Ganges*, a 'stone frigate' training establishment. After a bath they were shown into the 'Nozzers'' (new boys') mess for a late supper of bully beef soaked in 'Alley Sloper's Sauce' and an aluminium bowl of cocoa layered with grease – the famous 'kye', which helped to keep the Navy afloat. They were kitted out and shown how to tie on the blue collar framed with three white stripes ('for Lord Nelson's three great victories – Copenhagen, where 'e "clapped 'is glass to his sightless eye", the Nile and Trafalgar), the black silk square ('black for 'is death') which folded into a narrow band to go under the collar and down into the jumper, and how to sew their names on every article of clothing. Here too they were taught how to march, and suffered various 'jabs'. Back in the main camp they became 92 Class, 35 Mess in the Short Covered Way, part of 5 Division; their Divisional Officer was Lieutenant H. W. Sharp, wicket-keeper of the Royal Navy cricket team.

They spent their days doubling between their mess (''Eave-o! 'Eave-o! 'Eave-o! Lash up and stow! Lash up and stow! Rise an' shine, the morning's fine, the sun'll burn yer bleedin' eyes out!'); on the vast parade ground for squad and rifle drill ('By the right, form Squad!'. . . 'Royal Salute, *pre*sent IPE!'); and in the classroom for seamanship – knots and splices, ship's time, shipboard duties and organization, signals and flags, the compass, navigation, Rule of the Road:

> Green to green, red to red –
> Perfect safety, go ahead.

Farting in gunnery class was punished by doubling up and down Laundry Hill carrying a 6 in 'projjy'; there was boat work in the harbour, pulling ('raw hands and sore bums') and sailing; and plenty of sport on the playing fields of Shotley, on which a war would be won. Ivor ran long distance and played rugger with their PT Officer, Lieutenant-Commander C. A. Kershaw, the famous England scrum-half.

Dominating all their activities was The Mast, the mainmast of the old *Ganges*, a Nelsonian three-decker, whose figurehead faced all new entries at the main gate. The Mast was visible everywhere, with its three long yards and high 'tops', a symbol of those old days of 'wooden ships and iron men', when the hands hung on by their fingernails as the yards rolled above high, raging seas, and many a man, his hands frost-bitten, plunged to his death on the hard deck or in the engulfing sea, his despairing shriek drowned by the howling wind. But it was more than a symbol, it was reality for these civvy lads. The greenhorns of 92 Class were not allowed to climb higher than the first top, and they could go up through the 'Lubber's Hole' if their courage failed them at the vicious overhang of the '(Devil's) Elbow', where ratlines inclined almost horizontally over their heads out to the edge of the platform. But they had seen the ceremony of 'Manning the Mast', where the ratlines and every yard were manned by boys linking hands or hanging on the very truck of the mast, on the flat, round Button, 150 feet above the concrete parade ground. Ivor's classmate Boy Hussell tried to scramble up the last stretch of mast to the Button, lost his hold, and as he fell grabbed one of the stays, which threw him clear of the safety net to his death on the cruel parade ground.

Life on the Lower Deck of HM Navy was still harsh. The torture of the lash had disappeared, but for being found with a 'tickler' (cigarette) in his hand in the 'heads' (lavatories) at Stand-Easy Ivor was awarded twelve cuts of the cane, stretched over a vaulting horse. 'To prevent crying out you got the top of your flannel (shirt) in your teeth and bit hard.' The finger-thick cane broke Ivor's skin and, unluckily, that night was swim night in the baths on the foreshore. The sour chloride found his cuts.

One relief from the harshness of the routine was to watch the practice runs of the seaplanes of the British 1929 Schneider Trophy team, based at Felixstowe. The *Ganges* mast was one of the markers for the trial course.

MARLBOROUGH AND MALAYA

Suddenly training was over and Ivor went to sea. It was a proud day when, with his best suit and seaman's bone-handled knife (replaced in World War II by an all-metal, cheaper version, the spike on which was more often used to open condensed milk tins than for splicing), he embarked in the tender *Harlequin* for the battleship *Marlborough*, an old coal-burning dreadnought in the Training (and Third Battle) Squadron.

The old 'battlers' took their coal from the colliers *John* and *Francis Duncan*, or alongside the coaling wharves in the Royal Dockyards. 'Coal ship day, although hard work, was good fun,' says Ivor Burston. 'Everyone could smoke, the Marine band played stirring music, there were great vats of lime juice, from which the coal dust had to be scooped off before your mug could be filled. At the completion of coaling, usually at 1,500 or 1,750 tons, the whole ship had to be cleaned. If we won the race to get our coal in, we had cake for tea on the following Sunday – but if you couldn't fight for it you didn't get any!'

Working 'part of ship' was hard too, and much the same as it had been in Nelson's *Victory*. 'The decks were well sanded, and each boy, with a holystone in either hand, knelt down and pushed them to and fro until the whole deck was grated, when it shone really white.'

One of their trips in *Marlborough* took them to Arosa Bay, Spain, across the Bay of Biscay in some of the roughest weather there in living memory. The Fleet tug *Jenny* was sunk with all hands, destroyers took waves over the bridge and down the funnels.

In May 1930 Ivor left the old *Marlborough* for HMS *Malaya* of the *Queen Elizabeth* class, which had represented an attempt by the British Government to regain a clear lead in the naval race with Germany by introducing 15 in guns before the latter had anything bigger than the 12 in, with a top speed of 25 knots, practically that of the German battlecruisers, and achieved by the new oil-fired propulsion. Before Ivor joined *Malaya* all the '*QE*s' had been reconstructed, with bridge and control towers rebuilt into more massive structures, anti-torpedo bulges added to the sides, extra AA guns, and the original two funnels trunked into one big one, which gave them their distinctive appearance. Some of them were to be further rebuilt in the late 1930s.

'A very happy ship,' noted Ivor, 'under the Captain, Hugh Shipway. We excelled at Regatta, boxing, running and rugby, with Lieutenant-Commander "Nutty" Halloran, an old Irish international, being a very hard taskmaster.'

Ivor became a 'hammock boy' for Midshipmen Custance, Moore and Warmington, for 2/6d a month extra to his 8/9d a week. 'Every evening I had to sling the three middies' hammocks outside the Gunroom, then unlash them, and prepare for sleeping, laying out sheet and blankets and pillow. Each morning I had to fold up the bedding, place it in hammocks, put on the lashing, seven turns of marling hitches, and stow it in the hammock netting.'

ROUGH DAYS AT INVERGORDON

As a Side Boy Ivor manned the gangway, 'a general dogsbody running messages for the Quartermaster'. He laughed when Midshipman Moore rammed the picket boat into the gangway at Invergordon . . . 'to my cost. The Commander was there, and Moore was placed on one lower boom shouting "I'm the middy who crashed the gangway!" and I was put on the other side, hollering "I'm the Side Boy who laughed at him!"'

Midwinter in Invergordon made this quite a harsh punishment for such a crime. It was in this bleak anchorage on the west coast of Scotland that the ratings of the Home Fleet had mutinied over the savage and senseless pay cuts proposed under the pressure of the Depression, sharpening the deep-rooted resentment at the privileges blatantly enjoyed by officers (who would suffer far less than the Lower Deck from the pay cuts) – a smouldering, sullen undertow which went back, even in 1932, in a matlow's folk memory to the mutinies at Spithead and the Nore and 'the same spirit which prevailed in 1914 as in the year 1797', and more immediately to the 'rumbling of discontent heard about the years 1916–17' (recounts Seaman Sydney Knock in his book *Clear Lower Deck*, 1932).

The Fleet at Invergordon had been prevented from sailing for 48 hours, while men like Able Seaman Len Wincott and Jack Copeman pleaded with the Admiralty to abandon the proposed cuts, which reduced the wages of the lower-paid ratings by 25 per cent from four to three shillings a day, with far smaller comparative reductions for officers. Wincott described them as 'the forerunner of tragedy, misery and immorality among the families of the Lower Deck'. Dismissed the Service he loved, Wincott joined the British Communist Party, which sent him to Soviet Russia in 1934 to run an international seamen's club in Leningrad. He spent the rest of his life, including ten years in a Stalin labour camp, in Russia, and when he died in 1984 a Royal Navy chaplain honoured his last request, via his widow, to scatter his ashes over Plymouth Sound.

UP THE STRAITS WITH THE BIG SHIPS

Ivor was soon in the Mediterranean again with the light cruiser *Calypso*, in Malta, island of 'bells and smells'; in opulent Beirut; the notorious 'Alex' (Alexandria), home of the Mediterranean Fleet; Naples, and a smoking Vesuvius; rugger in Rome for the Third Cruiser Squadron against the University; sitting near Mussolini for Italy versus Austria; back to Malta, for more Farson's beer at 2½d a half-pint, a jar of the local Ambit, 1/6d for 1½ pints; cricket, football, rugby and running – then Sliema Creek to join the destroyer *Basilisk*, on her first commission.

Ivor, now an Ordinary Seaman, youngest in his mess, was Spud Boy for the cook of the mess. They dined so much better than many of their families at home, on 'Straight Rush' (rib of beef, baked spuds, onions and vegetables), a 'Bugle' (shin of beef, carrots, celery, turnips, tomatoes and doughboys), 'Schooner on the Rocks' (joint of beef on a suet duff, with roast potatoes, fresh vegetables when in harbour), and 'Baby's Head' (individual steak and kidney pudding) at Corradino Canteen. *Basilisk* completed her commission in September 1933, and Ivor, now AB, was an established Salt, who had done a commission 'Up the Straits'.

Ship followed ship, 'big ships' and small – battleship *Barham* to Barbados and the West Indies, regattas in Scapa Flow, King George V's great Review at Spithead, the greatest assembly of naval power seen for several years. Ivor went ashore with brother Chris, now in the aircraft carrier *Furious*, cheered the King and Queen as the Royal Yacht steamed up and down the lines of warships, Dressed Overall, the flags of many nations flying. In *Queen Elizabeth*, champion ship of the Med Fleet in all sports, they just defeated HMAS *Australia* in the race for Seaman Cutters; patrolled the coast of Spain while the Civil War raged, delivering food to British embassies and consulates; cruised the Greek islands; and came home for the Coronation Review, attended by the German *Graf Spee* and the Japanese heavy cruiser *Ashigara*. Then it was marching aboard the new cruiser *Newcastle* to the Geordie tune 'Blaydon Races', and taking her to Glasgow for the World Fair.

'I was married on Boxing Day 1938 and came back to barracks to find that I had been loaned to the New Zealand Navy', complains Ivor Burston. 'The draft was a mixed blessing. The parting was hard but financially came just at the right time. My pay on marriage comprised 21/- a week as Able Seaman, with 3d a day for a Good Conduct Badge, 3d a day as a Seaman Gunner, 3d a day Kit Upkeep Allowance. I gave my wife 14/- a week, plus 7/6d a week Marriage Allowance. On secondment to the New Zealand Navy my pay was trebled, and my wife's allowance went up to £3 a week, which helped to buy a double bed, though I slept in a hammock for 18 months.' He joined HMNZS *Achilles*, a new *Leander*-class light cruiser, and as a 'Lamp trimmer' (keeping all emergency lamps in trim, in case of main electrical failure), he received another 3d a day.

'We sailed late in 1939, for the Far East, via Gib, Suez, the Red Sea (where our Walrus spotter plane crashed, a total write-off); the bazaars of Aden, Colombo, Kandy and the "Temple of the Tooth"; Singapore, where we played hockey and rugby, and beat the Raffles Hotel Select Water Polo team, who did not even give us a drink afterwards, though we made up for that in the "Happy World"; then Bali, a lotus land with silver bells, and finally Auckland, "City of Sails", on 8 May 1939.

'This watery city was warm and friendly. I called on some people from Wiveliscombe, who made me welcome. We cruised to Fiji, Samoa, the Friendly Islands, Ellice, Tonga and Pago, everywhere greeted by Hula-Hula dancers, bands, streamers and flowers, but back in Auckland we had the worst blizzards in years, and the buzz went round that war was in the wind. On 29 August the Captain cleared lower deck and told us that hostilities with Germany were expected. *Achilles* sailed for a destination and a destiny that would bring her within sight of a certain "pocket battleship" which I had last seen decked with flags at Spithead, but the only flag she would be wearing this time would be a battle ensign!'

THE NEW PRESS GANG: ESCAPEES FROM DEPRESSION

> We went and joined up,
> We went and joined up,
> We went and joined Fred Carno's Navy,
> Three meals a day,
> Promotion and pay,
> Number for a holystone
> And scrub your life away . . .

Ivor Burston had answered a traditional call, the lure which for a century and more had made young British lads 'run away to sea' with romantic visions of tropical seas, snowy awnings, gaudy regattas and the Isles 'neath the Wind – 'Join the Navy and see the World'. But there was another tradition. A new Press Gang was active in the Britain of the 'Thirties – the pale horsemen of the Depression.

Chris Buist was born in Fife, Scotland, not far from Rosyth, the naval base, and was used to seeing warships of all kinds plying the Firth of Forth. He left school in 1933, a time when unemployment was rife all over Scotland. His father, who had fought in 'The War', was a tram-driver trying to keep four children on his meagre wages. Chris wanted to contribute to the family income. He got clothes from the Salvation Army, but there was no work anywhere. He tried the shipyards, but the only ships moving were His Majesty's. Like many other young workless men, he went to the Navy recruiting office. The only thing on offer was the Royal Marines, and Chris signed up, remembering all the yarns his uncle had spun about his Navy days in the War.

'To have food and new clothes was heaven to me. The discipline was nothing. I soon settled in, but some could not take it, and bought themselves out for £90. All I had was my 14/- a week pay, 5/- of which had to be saved for train fare to go on leave at the end of training, and we bought toilet gear, Blanco, Bluebell, etc out of what was left. With five bob a week for cleaning my mate's equipment I used to have just enough for a run ashore in Plymouth, a couple of beers at the Long Bar or the Snake Pit.'

Chris spent seven months at 'Guz', was sent to 'Pompey' (Portsmouth) for sea service training as a gunner, and then shifted to his home base, Chatham, on draft to the heavy cruiser HMS *York*, which he joined in July 1939, and sailed for the West Indies. Chris and his mates did not have very long to enjoy the rum and sunshine of their tropical paradise before war was declared, and *York* sailed flat-out for Halifax, Nova Scotia, to look after the first convoys.

In the autumn of 1938 Tom Bailey was one of the great army of unemployed, 'mother dead, father vanished into the night', walking the streets of Preston, Lancashire. 'One afternoon I found I had just enough coppers in my pocket to treat myself to the pictures. The film was "Boy from Barnardo's", in which Mickey Rooney, as a sailor boy on one of the latter's sea training ships, showed Freddie Bartholomew how to put on and tie the Royal Navy sailor's collar.' Afterwards Tom was walking home when he stopped at the Royal Navy Recruiting Office. 'If it had been the French Foreign Legion I would have still gone in.'

Tom joined the Navy, subject to having one tooth filled, and finally arrived at Guz, Royal Naval Barracks, Devonport, otherwise HMS *Drake*. He had never seen a warship before, except in the movies, but at Guz the barrack roads all sloped down to the shining sea, where grey ships of all types were to be seen, and a fresh offshore wind always blew in off the Channel.

'What a day!' he wrote. 'Joined for three square meals a day and a pair of boots. Now I've got *two* pairs!'

The 'tiddie oggies' (Cornish pasties) in the canteen were succulent and juicy, generous with the meat and potatoes, and soon Tom felt in his element. 'Squad drill and seamanship were meat and drink to me, and I devoured it all!' He was usually the one to get the class 'fell-in' ready for their PO Instructor, and he was made class leader, with the privilege of shore leave every night. He thrived on the life, passed out top of the class, and was presented with a bosun's 'call' on a silver chain. During gunnery training aboard the destroyer *Brazen* the news came in of the tragic sinking of the new submarine *Thetis*, off Liverpool. The destroyer at once landed a very thoughtful bunch of trainees and steamed back out to help rescue attempts.

After training they moved to Grenville Block and were allocated to various working parties. 'Life was good, a few bob a week spending money, good old Navy ticklers (tobacco) 1/3d a tin, a couple of bars of Pusser's Hard (soap) once a month, 3d for the barracks cinema, and of course the good old NAAFI for a cup of char and a sticky bun. I always found the food to my liking, and you could always make a meal out of a couple of plates of Pusser's soup – I have never yet come across soup to match it.' A familiar jibe at his expense was 'You're all for it, Bailey!'

'During those days a mobilizing exercise was carried out, but us youngsters didn't realize the state of the world. I was happy and courting a local girl, and that was my main concern.'

At the start of the week before war was declared, 'Clear lower deck!' was piped, and Tom fell in with the hundreds of other ratings on the parade ground. Then it was 'From here to the left – one pace forward MARCH!' 'We all wanted to go to small ships, but the "Andrew" had other plans. We were drafted to HMS *Renown*, a battlecruiser. With bags and hammocks packed we entrained at the barracks platform for Plymouth and our destiny.'

The Fleet Air Arm

> Eager and ready, the crying lone flyer
> Whets for the whale pathe the heart irresistibly
> O'er tracks of ocean;
> > *The Seafarer* (From the Anglo-Saxon)

In 1910 Eugene Ely had flown his Curtiss biplane off a forward ramp on a US cruiser, and later landed on a platform over the fantail of a battleship. A year later Lieutenant Charles Samson, RN, was launched in a Short S.27 biplane fitted with flotation bags from the battleship HMS *Africa*. British sailors were learning to fly.

A Naval Wing of the new Royal Flying Corps was formed, and a collier was converted on the stocks into HMS *Ark Royal*, to carry ten seaplanes. Just before war broke out in 1914 the Naval Wing of the RFC broke away to become the Royal Naval Air Service. A small converted passenger/mail steamer, HMS *Engadine*, made a pioneer sortie at the battle of Jutland; another, HMS *Ben-my-Cree*, launched the first aerial torpedo attack in history, at Gallipoli, and supported the Army in Asia Minor.

Further progress was made with HMS *Campania*, an old liner fitted with a 'flying-off deck'; HMS *Furious*, a redundant 'light battlecruiser' with an 18 in gun, also incorporating a 'flying-on deck'; HMS *Argus*, 14,450 tons, with the first stem-to-stem flight deck, repeated in HMS *Eagle*, 22,600 tons, a converted battleship which also featured a bridge 'island' to starboard (copied later in *Furious*); in the small, purpose-built *Hermes*, 10,950 tons, launched in 1919; and by *Furious*'s sister battlecruiser conversions *Courageous* and *Glorious*.

TELEGRAPHIST AND AIR-GUNNER

Telegraphist Jackie Heath first saw sea service in the coal-burning battleship HMS *Emperor of India*, but was then switched from the old Navy to the new with a two-and-a-half year commission in the aircraft-carrier *Eagle*. He remained in carriers, moving on to HMS *Furious*, which he had already seen in the Mediterranean when *Eagle* had operated with her and the new *Courageous* in mock strikes against other warships.

He had watched the little Fairey Flycatcher biplane fighters leap out of *Furious*'s lower hangar, and the Fairey IIIFs and Blackburn Ripon torpedo-bombers sedately sail the air.

He wrote home, 'If I'm going to be in aircraft-carriers I might as well be an air-gunner.' As a telegraphist he could volunteer for duty as a Telegraphist/Air-Gunner. In those early days TAGs were not recognized as a branch in their own right. So that they never got out of touch with their Branch, they spent no more than two years with the Fleet Air Arm, then returned to General Service as shipborne telegraphists for a year.

Telegraphist/Air Gunner was the only flying job open to ratings at that time. In April 1918 the old RNAS and RFC had amalgamated to form the Royal Air Force. Thirty per cent of FAA pilots were RAF officers, observers were naval officers, and the Navy had operational control at sea; but for sixteen years equipment, air stations and ground crews were under the neglectful direction of the Air Ministry. The FAA was regarded as a backwater for promotion. It did not receive the latest aircraft, and its personnel were generally treated as 'dirty-fingernail types'. At that time controversy raged as to whether bombers could destroy a battleship, and the carrier replace it as the capital ship of the future. The old battleship *Centurion* was used as a target, but results were not conclusive. In the USA trials favoured the aircraft, but US Army Air Corps General Billy Mitchell was court-martialled for propagating such heresy.

Jackie was accepted for AG training, spent twelve weeks at RAF Gosport on aerial telegraphy, then went to RAF Eastchurch for the Air Gunnery course. At the end of that time he was kept on for a further month to do the Bomb-Aimer course. In a Fleet exercise a combined striking force of aircraft from *Courageous*, *Furious* and *Glorious* had scored 21 hits out of a possible 32.

'You had to find the direction and speed of the wind, and on a sort of little computer put the temperature at that height, the airspeed and wind speed. That gave the speed at which your aircraft was travelling over the ground. You lay on the cockpit floor to instruct the pilot to turn left or right, in the meantime watching the red and green on your compass. When your two aircraft pointers reached the target you released a bomb and plotted it on your chart.'

When Jackie landed after his first bombing sortie, 'There was a reception committee on the tarmac. I thought "What have I done? Have I hit the Mess or something?" They asked to see my bombing chart, then told me I had broken the RAF record by dropping eight bombs in a 16-yard diameter 25 yards from the target!'

From Eastchurch he went to No 820 Squadron and *Courageous*, Flagship of the first Rear-Admiral, Aircraft-Carriers. As a Home Fleet carrier, she often exercised in the most savage Atlantic weather. While flying in a gale off the Scottish coast one of her aircraft hit a 5 ft square wooden target with a bomb from 6,000 ft. In a mock squadron torpedo attack on four new *Southampton*-class cruisers, half the 'mouldies' found their targets, while in an exercise in the Mediterranean *Glorious* scored nine hits with her strike force of fourteen TSRs (torpedo/spotter/reconnaissance aircraft). In 1936 Heath was aboard *Eagle* once again, on the China Station. War in Europe broke out just as the troopship returning him to England left Aden, and as a Leading Telegraphist he took over the ship's wireless office. He was on leave when recalled for a course on the ASV (Air-to-Surface-Vessel) version, not yet in production, of the new Radio Direction Finding (RDF), or radar, weapon.

SAILOR FIRST, AVIATOR SECOND

Norman 'Blondie' Hollis joined the Navy in 1930, becoming Boy 2C No 3987 on the books of HMS *St Vincent* ('or was that my mother's Co-Op number?').

'In 1922 my parents took over a farm, a co-operative inasmuch as Father, Mother, Brother and Sister all had their allotted jobs to do, up and about early every morning milking, feeding the animals, delivering milk twice a day, and all for one shilling a week, which was handed over to Mother. Not having a great interest in farming, and with a scarcity of other jobs when I left school, unless parents were able and prepared to pay for an apprenticeship, I answered an advertisement in the *Daily Express* for boys of 16 years of age to train in the RN as telegraphists. Mother asked me to promise her one thing. I asked her what that was, thinking that I was going to be warned off bad women and the Demon Drink, but no, all I had to promise was *not to get tattooed*!'

'Had supper on arrival,' he wrote in his diary, 'macaroni cheese, quarter of a loaf, pot of margarine and a dip – aluminium sugar bowl – of tea. (I haven't eaten macaroni cheese since.) Out of bed 0500, taught how to make up one's bed, then into Mess Room for two ship's biscuits and dip of greasy cocoa. Had thoughts of going over the wall and back home to Mum.

'12 April 1932. Joined HMS *Rodney* . . . 1,500 men and boys. We have a mess of our own and are in the charge of a PTI who has a pair of eyes tattooed on his backside! There was more gold braid aboard her than in Pusser's stores. It took ages to find your way around her, and to scrub whiter than white those acres of foredeck. When she put to sea we discovered that she had a very slow, ponderous roll, the worst sort of motion for *mal de mer*, and when she fired her broadside she smashed all the crockery in the messdecks.

'But I had a soft spot for the ugly old girl, perhaps because I was rated telegraphist aboard her, and my pay shot up to 28/- a week. "What wealth!" I wrote in my diary. "Perhaps I can afford a girlfriend!" Yes, she had her points, they didn't sing "Roll on the *Rodney* . . ." for nothing.

'From dignity to impudence. After *Rodney* I picked up the destroyer *Broke*, which had just been loaned to Gaumont British to make the film "Forever England". She was practically rebuilt with papier mâché to become "HMS *Rutland*." For a fortnight we and a couple of tugs fought the Battle of Eddystone Light. We were paid 5/- a day by the film company, who came aboard every morning with hampers bulging with food and drink which they invariably left untouched, thanks to *Broke*'s lively motion.

'After *Broke* came another of the "boats", the modern *Defender* of First Flotilla. At Singapore we exchanged her for HMS *Wren* and Captain (D) Warburton-Lee, later to win a posthumous VC in the Norwegian Campaign. We thought *Defender* was lively, but the *Wren* could stand on her bow and stern in quick succession! There was a popular Radio Music Hall song called "Red Sails in the Sunset" at the time, sung by comedienne Susette Tarri. We changed the words:

> Red sails in the sunset
> Out over the sea,
> Out doing manoeuvres
> With Warburton-Lee.

'It must have been about this time that I set my mind to getting out of boats. I'd met a telegraphist/air-gunner once in hospital. That was the life! Living at RAF stations! Flying pay of 2/6d a day! I never thought that dive-bombing, dogfighting and aerobatics could be a helluva sight rougher than *Wren* in a gale!'

Wren was half of a destroyer sub-division. Sub-Divisional Commander in *Wishart* was Lord Louis Mountbatten, and goodwill trips with him were mostly to the French and Italian Rivieras. 'Wherever we went we were followed by his private yacht with his wife and other members of his family. At Nice we were met by his Rolls with its distinctive radiator cap – a silver signalman with his flags held in the "4/6" position.'

In early August, Norman joined fourteen other budding aviators aboard HMS *Victory* to begin the telegraphy part of the new AG's course. It was a significant ship in which to begin a flier's life. Where was the link with the Old Navy? Indeed, was there a link at all? If sailors had been meant to fly . . . But it was always stressed 'A naval airman is a sailor first, an aviator second'.

Flying training was in Blackburn Sharks for radio procedure and the art of streaming and towing drogue and flag targets. 'Should you lose a target you had to borrow a bicycle and pedal around the countryside looking for it, and be prepared to pay a 5/- reward.' At RAF Northcoates in Westland Wallaces – the aircraft which had conquered Everest – they learned the intricacies of the Lewis gun, 'how to strip, rebuild and fire it'; and dogfighting, 'that is if you had remembered to operate the cocking handle on the climb to prevent it freezing'.

On 8 October 1937 he joined No 811 Squadron in *Furious*, with Swordfish, and went to Donibristle on the Firth of Forth – 'a small RAF station, beautifully maintained, a dining room with *tablecloths* on the tables, smashing food cooked and served by WAAFs' sited on a small grassy plateau overlooking Dalgety Bay, close to the Naval base at Rosyth.'

MALTA, ALEXANDRIA AND THE SPANISH CIVIL WAR

Jack Skeats was a countryman whose life was changed by the Depression. 'Aylesbury was a small market town of only 13,000 souls and as my school-leaving date approached it became apparent that there were no jobs of any kind to be found. My father had nine children of whom six were still at home. The situation was quite galling to me since I had won a scholarship to Aylesbury Grammar School, but on 18 December 1933, I joined the Royal Navy as a Boy Seaman on sixpence a day. Discipline was unreasonably harsh, the food was pitiful and I am still of the opinion that My Lords were showing the lower deck that the last had not been heard of Invergordon.

'A year later I went to sea, seventeen years of age, Boy Seaman First-Class and a fifty per cent rise to ninepence a day (old money). I took passage on the *Hood* to Gib, passing on the way *Nelson* stuck on Hamilton Bank. The Press made much of this – "History Repeats Itself", etc. At Gib I was shifted to *Ajax* for onward passage to Malta and *Revenge*, known affectionately as the *"Rev-en-gee"*, which carried the Flag of the C-in-C, Med Fleet. Before long the Fleet sailed to Alexandria – gunboat diplomacy – to show our Government's disapproval of the Italians' conduct of the Abyssinian war. The Maltese disapproved also; a large part of the population depended upon our ships, partly for employment but mostly for food. All the garbage was sifted by the gasheens who kept watch at the rubbish chutes and sorted it out into food and other desirables which were then sold down at the Marsa. It may have been uneatable to us, but the poor Malts loved it and missed the Fleet no end. They felt the pinch so badly that regular collections were held to alleviate their distress. At Alex I enjoyed all the pleasures of Sister Street, the gilly-gilly boys and so on.

'There followed two commissions in the "boats" (destroyers) and I volunteered to become an Air-Gunner. It had always been my ambition to fly – as a child I was never without a model aircraft and I used to go to Hendon each year, to see the Air Show. It was then 1936 and we were soon snarled up in the Spanish War. We were in Gib when the *Jaime I*, flagship of the Spanish Navy, nosed its way up to the breakwater asking for water. The lower deck was in command, all the guardrails were missing, and we were told that the officers had been rolled up in them and thrown over the side. Life became more interesting, we did a little cloak and dagger work and evacuated some British from Huelva. A distress call was received from "Potato" Jones who was famous for shipping spuds into Spain, running the blockade. He was not alone since he had the *Scheer* for company, the German "pocket battleship".

'The situation was tense, she trained one of her turrets, we trained torpedo tubes. "Auf Wiedersehn" she said, and left. Either side bombed us at will and on one occasion, after speeding all night to rescue the survivors of the Spanish cruiser *Canarias*, we had the hell bombed out of us while slowly circling the wreckage to pull seamen out of the oily sea. A whaler lowered by one destroyer suffered an almost direct hit which killed one crew member. And it wasn't even our war. We looked a mess with vertical black bars of oil from hauling up survivors standing out against the light blue paint of the ship's side.

'Still no news of becoming an Air-Gunner. Then I was told that I had been under observation for several years as a possible officer. The truth being out, I was shipped to Pompey Barracks to commence an Upper Yardsman course. Hardly were matters on the run when I was in front of the Commodore, wondering what on earth I had done wrong. Here's me with one foot in the wardroom door and up in front of His Nibs. "Skeats," he said, "I have a piece of paper here calling you for training as an Air-Gunner, I presume you wish me to tear it up?" "No, sir," I said. He stiffened. "Are you telling me that you would sooner be an Air-Gunner than a Naval Officer?" "Yes, sir," I said. He gasped and pointed to the door.

'During flying training at Eastleigh war seemed a certainty. Ralph Richardson and Laurence Olivier appeared as pilots and I gathered Rafe's autograph in my flying logbook and "Lolly Olly's" on the back.' 'What a lovely wife he had in Vivien Leigh,' remembers Doug Cole, another TAG trainee, 'who was so very kind to many of us young lads. She walked on water as far as we were concerned.'

BECOMING A RATING PILOT

In the House of Commons the Government announced that the Fleet Air Arm was to be returned wholly to the Navy, although basic flying training would remain in RAF hands. The formal take-over was to be on 24 May 1939. One result was the publication in June 1938 of an AFO asking for volunteers to train as Rating Pilots. *Ab initio* training was in Avro Tutors at Short Brothers, Rochester, followed by No 1 FTS at Netheravon, Wiltshire, and armament training at RAF Catfoss, Yorkshire. In January 1939 the first Rating Pilots joined No 811 Squadron, 'Like the TAGs they were treated as nonentities,' says Norman Hollis, 'ringless hacks considered to lack the "moral fibre" to make a torpedo attack'.

Freddie Longman's early life was spent in Potters Bar, in those days not much more than a village, partly in Hertfordshire, partly in Middlesex, but famous as the place where the Zeppelin *L31*, shot down by Lieutenant Wulstan Tempest, RFC, in his B.E.2c on 2 October 1916, had crashed in flames. The blazing airship hit an oak tree a glancing blow as it fell, which Freddie and his pals used to go and look at, and which stands today in a garden in Tempest Avenue. He was one of five children, money was very tight, and in 1931 he joined the Lanes & National Sea Training School in Wallasey, Cheshire. 'The school trained young lads for both the RN and MN, and the competition was always on to be one of those selected for the RN.' Freddie joined *Ganges* in November 1932. From there he went to the cruiser *York* and was paid off in October 1936, an AB and Seaman Gunner.

'The *York* carried a Fairey IIIF, catapulted off and hoisted back inboard by crane. The aircrew, Lieutenant "Ting" Little (pilot), Lieutenant French (observer) and Leading Telegraphist Basil Gill, were my heroes. The highlight of my day was to be on the end of the "wing tip line" getting the aircraft back on the catapult. *The bug had bit!*'

He passed for Leading Seaman, and in the brand-new light cruiser *Southampton* became Turret Captain.

'*Southampton* carried two Walrus, two hangars and a catapult, and by now I wanted to be a pilot! After a final board during a day at sea in HMS *Courageous* during the Munich crisis and one more ship as a salthorse I was called back early from Easter leave in 1939 and sent to HMS *Pembroke*, Chatham Barracks, for flying training with No 4 Rating Pilot Course, first at Short's, Rochester, in Avro Tutors, then at No 7 FTS, Peterborough, on Hawker Harts. I won my wings in August 1939.'

In 1932 Eric Monk was at Grammar School 'with little hope of matriculating as my French was poor and one had to pass six subjects at one go, Maths, English, Science, History or Geography, Foreign Language, with Physics, Chemistry, or English Language. My family were market gardeners, lots of hard work and small returns. Just before half-term one of my form mates showed me an advertisement "Boys required for the Royal Navy".'

At 5.30 p.m. on a cold wet February night in 1933 he was shivering in the fore-peak of a steam pinnace on his way to *Ganges*. On the fourth day there, as a special treat, they went swimming. 'It was still freezing, and we were ordered to put on one of a row of white canvas "duck suits" which had been hung up wet, and were frozen stiff. Non-swimmers were sent to the deep end of the pool and flung in, the others had to climb to the top board and jump in.'

The great mast held no special terrors for Eric and his mates. 'J-class yachts used to race off Shotley, and after the p.m. muster there was a race by "spare" boys for the seat on the truck. The worst part was getting from the bare pole at the top on to the button. I'm pleased to say I managed it, and clung to the lightning conductor for an hour'.

'The final event was to point and graft clews and lashings for one's hammock, the only friend you took to sea. It was decided that we were to do the rope-climbing display for the RN at the Royal Tournament. Chatham boys would then go to the cruiser *Sussex*, which was to take the Duke of Gloucester to Australia for the Melbourne Centenary on a year's exchange with HMAS *Australia*.

'We picked up the Duke at Marseilles and sailed blue summer seas to Oz. We Boy Seamen (under 18s) were invited to spend leave at the Scout Training Camp at Pennant Hills. As a result, several of us joined the Deep Sea Scouts and spent many happy evenings and days with shore-side Scouts and Cubs in Australia and also during our tour of New Zealand. We also had a happy Rover crew in the ship, and it was not long before our shipmates gave up remarking when we went ashore in Scout uniform.

'In the Solomon Islands I heard of the drive to recruit Air-Gunners, and set myself to reach the standard of 16 words per minute in Morse to qualify. At Tulagi I and other volunteers were each taken up in the ship's Osprey floatplane by Lieutenant Evans (later Admiral Sir Charles Evans) which gave me a vivid memory of the island, its bright green coconut palms, brilliant white coral beaches and pale blue shallows darkening to tropical blue deep water further out, basins of coral alive with sharks. That was my first flight.

'Back in the UK I transferred to the even newer Rating Pilot course. On my first exercise I was lucky to fly early in the day, and the target was into sun. As I opened fire I could see the sun glinting on my bullets going down so I ignored my gunsight and "hosepiped" my bullets into the target. I often wondered if my score of 68 out of 100 helped selection as a fighter pilot.

'We qualified as deck-landers aboard *Courageous*. Each pilot did 30 landings, and Jack Hadley finished up in front of the bridge, tail up, nose down, port wheel in the range-finder seat, and the fin broke the glass screen of the compass platform. This was the end of training and Jack and I were sent to No 800 Squadron, *Ark Royal*. We joined the "*Ark*" at Portland only to find that 800 were at Worthy Down changing their Ospreys and Nimrods for Skua fighter/ dive-bombers, the first monoplanes for the Navy. A bird book I consulted described the Skua as a gull which folded its wings and dived into the sea.

'The working-up period soon went by and towards the end of June 1939 we were the RN Display Squadron at the opening of Birmingham and Derby Airports, after which we moved to Lympne for leave in early August. War seemed imminent.'

Ron Lunberg would never have settled to a land-lubber's settled existence. Many years later, when he could look back on his life in the Navy as 'the absolute fulfilment of a career to the extent that I enjoyed even the black spots', failing School Certificate seemed to have been fate. There was no work to be had on Merseyside in 1931, but there was still employment at sea. He signed on as Pantry Boy aboard the freighter SS *Aquila*.

For 12/6d a week he slaved from 0445 in the forenoon to eleven at night, with one stand-easy of two hours every other day. 'I was fed and that was about all.' He found out that a probationary Writer (clerk) in the RN received 17/6d a week on joining and 25/- at the end of six months' training, and after just six weeks in the Merchant Navy he made the switch, and signed up for twelve years. He was in HMS *Vernon* after training when he read AFO 848/38 calling for Rating Pilots.

'To me the AFO was electrifying!' He applied instantly and his name was forwarded, subject to passing the ET2 exam. With his strong motivation, this proved easier than School Certificate, and in May 1938 he reported to RAF Leuchars in Scotland with the nineteen others, including Eric Monk, on Course No. 41.

'We looked forward to exercising a lead when we were in a position to do so. In Rating Pilots this was frowned upon. Commissioned aircrew generally treated us as equals as far as flying went but there were one or two who did not approve of us until we showed a good degree of competence and skill. Unfortunately I was involved in a flying accident on what was almost my first flight as a newly qualified pilot.

'I had joined the cruiser *Glasgow* in place of a lieutenant pilot to fly one of her Walruses. With sister ship *Southampton* we were escorting King George VI and Queen Elizabeth to Canada. I had never been catapulted in charge of a Walrus, and had never made the normal seaplane touch-down in the "slick" of a ship's wake as she turned, when *Glasgow* was ordered by *Southampton* to "Exercise slick landing with junior pilot". *Glasgow* queried the wisdom of the order but the SO in *Southampton* insisted. So off I went.

'The first touch-down, after three dummy runs, was so much of a resounding *crunch* that I decided to go round again. After all, it was fairly choppy. The next attempt resembled the first but I decided to stay down. This time the starboard wing float broke off and the aircraft cartwheeled with the starboard wing in the water. The TAG who had come with me, to hook on to the crane when hoisted inboard, and I were picked up after about 10 minutes but he died on board of shock. You can imagine how I felt!'

Merchantmen to Militarymen

> There's steam on the capstan,
> Smoke in the stack,
> The boys on the fo'c'sle are hauling in slack,
> We're slipping the buoy now, the ocean to plough,
> I wonder, my darling, who's loving you now . . .
> HMS Keith, 1939

Other boys had begun life at sea in the Merchant Navy with more luck in their first ship than Ron Lunberg. It was not surprising that a boy brought up in Hull should go to sea. Alan Mathison's stepfather was a steward in the Bell Line, his grandfather a ship's carpenter in various tramp steamers, though on leaving school at 14 he became an errand boy on 5/- a week for a shipping chemist supplying medical items to ships for their medical cabinets as required by the Merchant Shipping Acts. 'The contents of a ship's medical cabinet were meagre in those days – a few rolls of bandages, a bottle of iodine, Black Draught for constipation, Cough Linctus, tins of Stabichlor for purifying doubtful "fresh" drinking water, jars of zinc ointment for scratches and abrasions, a jar of mercurial ointment for "crabs", aspirin, toothache tincture, and a couple of lances for boils.' Alan's job got him cycling down to various ships in Hull Docks, and his interest in the sea really started then. As a joiner's labourer at Brigham & Cowan's ship repair yard he talked to sailors about their voyages. 'It was then that I decided that I would like to go to sea and see for myself all "Those faraway places with strange-sounding names, far away over the sea". My parents knew somebody in a Ship Agency office, and he got me a job in a tanker as an Ordinary Seaman in April 1932.

'The *Saranac* was owned by the then Anglo-American Oil Company (later the Standard Oil Company, and finally Esso). She was at that time the world's largest tanker, at about 17,000 tons deadweight. After three years as Deck Boy and Ordinary Seaman, I qualified for Able Seaman and joined *Saranac*'s sister ship *Cadillac*, but I did not see eye to eye with the Chief Officer, who was a slave-driver, and I was logged, for the first and only time in what was to be 45 years at sea, for "swearing at the Chief Officer", which appeared in my Discharge Book as the only blemish in 96 separate voyages.'

After only two voyages in *Cadillac*, he was in several ships as AB, the last prior to the outbreak of war being the worst, the *Llandilo*, a Cardiff-owned tramp:

'The diet was almost a starvation one, the seaman and fireman were treated like dirt, and you only had running fresh water if you ran along the deck to the engine room for a bucket of hot water from the condenser hotwell, and even that was rationed if the duty engineer felt bloody-minded.

'In March 1939 I decided enough was enough and found myself a job ashore. I became seasonal bus conductor with the East Yorkshire Motor Company, which lasted until the start of hostilities, when the Ministry of Transport ordered me to report for seagoing duties as I was registered as a seaman. "Failure to report", they said, "will result in your being re-classified for service in the Armed Forces," and no doubt they meant the Royal Navy.

'I had every respect for the Royal Navy, but the two seagoing duties are poles apart, and besides it is better the Devil you know. On reporting to the Shipping Federation I was asked to volunteer for a course in gunnery run by the RN at the closed-down Earl's Shipyard. Being full of jingoistic ideas, I jumped at the chance to learn to hit back at the enemy. The course only lasted twelve days, and from later experience I realized that twelve days was as good as useless, especially when the gun crews of German submarines and raiders were probably the best trained in the world at the outbreak of the war. Immediately I came out of the gunnery school I was sent to Barry to join a ship called the *Stangrant*, which I did on 28 October 1939, an AB with an additional 6d (2½p) per day for my gunnery certificate.'

Mark Wells had started his seagoing career in the Merchant Navy. Born in Dover, when his father's business moved them to Leeds he spent all his holidays back at Dover with his grandparents. A distant relative was the Radio Officer on the Southern Railway steamer *Canterbury*. Mark wandered all round the docks all day looking at ships, and met *Canterbury* when she came in. 'At the age of ten I knew I just had to go to sea. All and sundry tried to talk me out of it but it fell on deaf ears. I drew ships at school on the back of exam papers. I guess I just loved ships.'

At 13 he joined the old wooden wall TS *Arethusa* at Greenhithe on the Thames, and from her got the job as deck boy with the Federal Steamship Company, part of the New Zealand Shipping Company, joining the former German SS *Cambridge*, bound for Auckland, New Zealand. 'I was going to sea!'

Mark saw a lot of sea, and chipped a lot of paint. They were three weeks in the Pacific without sighting another ship. In New Zealand waters they went round both islands unloading, then round again loading up. 'I found in my travels that seeing places was fine yet I was always glad when we were at sea. Somehow I never ever tired of it. I loved the sound of the engines clanking away, the solitude of wide-open seas, and us on a little island, as it were, desperately trying to maintain 15 knots or so.

'Back home again it was bad news – the ship was to lay up. It was a bad time for shipping. We paid off at Falmouth, and I noticed in the River Fal ships, ships and more ships, even liners, all rusting away, with no work. Up in London I walked the docks looking for vacancy signs on gangways, though it was usually "No Hands Wanted". Then one day I was offered a steward's assistant's job on MV *Orari* at Falmouth, loading for Australia. My duties consisted of endless washing up. After we had finished picking up cargo from coastal ports I told the

Chief Steward this wasn't for me and said good-bye to *Orari*. She was a nice ship and I loved the luxury of sheets and bedding. In the *Cambridge* you had one blanket, a mattress and a pillow and that was it, no radio, nothing, yet somehow we were a happy, contented crowd.

'Work of any kind was hard to get. I sold and delivered papers and other odd jobs, and worked in a factory, hating it, still pounding the docks at week-ends. Railways had always been another love of mine. Someone in the family remembered this and got me a job in the Locomotive Department at King's Cross, and there I started my days cleaning and training for the footplate. By the time 1938 came round I was well established on the footplate and I felt the exhilaration that I had at sea, and must say I enjoyed the footplate life and thereafter never bothered to go to the docks looking for work, though I often went to see the ships, went aboard many of them and enjoyed the seafaring chit-chat. It was still a part of me, deep down.

'1938 brought Munich. If there was going to be a war I would have to be at sea, and I registered. But by October 1939 I had heard nothing so I went to the nearest Recruiting Station and registered for the RN.

'At HMS *Royal Arthur*, Skegness, the uniform was very familiar to me, and I showed the others how it was worn. In time fancy "eye-shooting" bows appeared on caps, copying mine, U-fronts on jumpers, concertina trousers, bell bottoms. The old Chief said, "Well, you *look* like sailors, even if you aren't."

'When it came to choose which branch we wanted to go into, somehow I didn't feel I'd be happy in anything but the Engine Room Branch, it seemed right for me, leaving railway engines – I did know something of steam. Also down below you work in a small team. It's more confined than any other branch. I was surprised at how few had the same idea. Most of them wanted to be seamen, signallers, cooks.

'I was shipped off to Chatham, which I found the most depressing place I had ever been in. The training really was basic, no talk of damage control, emergency procedures, even what a ship was like. It was there that I saw my first naval ship close-up. It didn't impress me like the old P & O liners and Cunarders. Still, it was after all a war machine, not meant to be a thing of beauty. After end-of-course leave I was given a draft chit to HMS *Arethusa* – my second *Arethusa* – a modern light cruiser.

'She looked so small after a merchant ship. There was only a handful of stokers, mostly regulars. Two RNR men had been at Jutland. But they were all friendly, and we settled in. There were two boiler rooms, A and B, each with two POs, one in charge, one a watertender, and two stokers. I was in B. We were shown how to flash the burners and how to change them. Everything seemed to be run by the POs and Chiefs, with ERAs the background of the Engineering Department, in contrast to the Merchant Navy, where the Engineers were always there and for the most part did most of the work. It puzzled me why so many men were required to do anything. Even on deck it took so many more than the five forward and five aft in a 16,000-ton merchantman.

'We sailed, and started our watchkeeping, four hours on, eight hours off. At sea you could wear whatever you wished, more or less, but in the Engine Room it was underpants and a boiler suit, and a sweater if you went on deck, never a cap. Upper deck men called us "dustmen", and we called them "dabtoes", "shell pushers", "crab wallahs" or "gorillas". They seemed to think we were a little below them.'

SEA SCOUTS GO TO SEA

Iain Nethercott from Canvey Island in the mouth of the Thames was one of the few Grammar School boys to enter the Royal Navy pre-war as a 'common-sailor'. He had been in the Sea Scouts from the age of eleven, and both his uncles owned old yachts on which Iain spent 'a lot of time, energy and skin off my hands'.

'In those days Sea Scouts used ex-naval Montague whalers for sailing and pulling, and old naval picket boats with petrol engines fitted to replace the old steam engines. By the age of 12 you were expected to know all the boat drill and how to pull an oar for at least a couple of hours. All the lads were mad keen on the sea in those days. They were a rough and ready crowd from working-class homes, quite a few with their dads on the river in tugs and barges. We learnt the International Code, semaphore, Morse light signalling, buoys and lights, fog signals, with hours of rope work and splicing in the winter evenings, and by the age of 14 we were fully conversant with the arts of boats and sailing. Most of the boys joined the Navy as Boy Seamen or Boy Signalmen, going to either *Ganges* or *Wildfire*, although quite a few of my friends went to sea in the Merchant Navy, mostly with the old Orient line.

'Every year at Easter all the Sea Scouts on the Thames went to a big meet at Cookham, near Richmond, up the river. As we sailed up the river from Barking with two naval pinnaces towing whalers and gigs right the way down the line to dinghies and kayaks, we used to meet up with the lads from Sheerness, Southend, Leigh, Gravesend and Tilbury, Purfleet and Rainham, and so on up-river with all the Central London troops, and then the posh lads from Putney, Mortlake and Chiswick.

'At Cookham we used to camp in bell tents in the river meadows, and over the week-end we battled it out at whaler racing and canoeing. At night we sat in our thousands round a huge camp fire singing till about two in the morning, and believe me the songs we sang in those days were not the ones sung at the "Gang Show". "The Harlot of Jerusalem" and "Nobby Hall" were good examples, although we all knew the old sailing ship shanties like "Blow the Man Down" and "Shenandoah" and all the others.

'Yes, in those days our boy sailors were dead keen and very easily satisfied. All that was needed was an old boat to muck about in, plenty of sausages cooked on the stove and plenty of sea or river to swim in. They were probably the happiest days of my life, and for most of my companions. It was a good thing they were, because within ten years most of them were dead.'

Iain joined the Navy and early in 1939 came back from a commission in the Mediterranean in the destroyer *Hotspur*, 'browner than Alexander'.

'The barracks was no rest home for seamen then, but full of Gestapo in belts and gaiters and whistles looking for deserters from Coaling Party. They whistled, bellowed at you and sang out "What are we, then?" It was best to keep your reply simple. "Football Party" was a good answer. For patrolling two-ringers, "Anti-gas Fumigation Party" or "Hygiene Manipulative Yeoman, sir!" were recommended, probably confusing the poor man, who would bellow "Well, put your cap on straight, then!" But all this palaver grew wearing. I decided to blend into the landscape. No one ever notices a man pushing a broom. And no one would do the job from choice, would he? Every day I worked my way slowly round the barracks, free as the birds of the air. But it was all very boring and ridiculous, and I longed to get back to sea.

'In July the Reservists were called up and I got my longed-for draft chit. It was to HMS *Keith*, a flotilla leader of the "B" Class destroyers, then in Reserve at Chatham. The Reservists, bewildered tobacconists and hotel doormen, were kitted out, inoculated, vaccinated, those with teeth given corned dog sandwiches and an apple and many mugs of Pusser's bromided tea, and we were all sent on our way rejoicing to the Dockyard, found our ships, sorted out our messes and settled in. I did well, I was an Iron Deck man and bowman in the motor boat. Lovely! And I found a good slinging billet up by the paint shop.

'*Keith* was similar to *Hotspur*, though five years newer, one of the Admiralty-type Destroyer Leaders (others were *Kempenfelt* and *Duncan*) included in the 1928 Estimates; keel laid October 1929, launched 10 July 1930, completed 9 June 1931 by White's of Cowes, Isle of Wight, the oldest builder to the Navy.

'There were certain domestic improvements – a bathroom about 12 ft by 8 ft with six basins for 130 men. No taps, no water. You took your precious personal bucket (also used for dhobi-ing) along the Iron Deck, filled it at the freshwater pump, proceeded to the leeward side doors of the coal-fired gallery, and begged a bucket of "hotters" in exchange for your bucket of cold, hoping the chef was in a good mood. If the weather was rough, and Chiefie presiding over a great sliding mass of Straight Rushes, potmesses (Irish Stew), and Pusser's peas leaping out all over his boots, he was not sympathetic to the toiletry needs of a hairy-arsed AB.

'My Action Station was No 2 (trainer) of the Port 2-pounder pom-pom. This made sense as I had shown no aptitude for gunnery (*far* too noisy), and had never seen a pom-pom before. Ours must have been used in the Boer War. The belts holding the shells were made of canvas, which swelled up in seawater and heat and jammed the old cannon, whereupon one clouted the breech with a sodding great mallet, supplied for the purpose. The gunlayer was as ignorant as I was, and the Gunner's Mate not interested in our little gun. His love lay in his 4.7s, the TS (Transmitting Station) and the Director. Our weapon was fitted with two ring sights, calibrated for 100-knot aircraft – Stukas, Heinkels and Ju 88s would of course slow down for us!

'The ship was sailed to Weymouth in August for the King's Review – an antiquarian collection of "V" and "W"-class destroyers, Great War vintage, old "C" and "D"-class light cruisers, and a heterogeneous gaggle of ancient battleships including Jellicoe's old coal-burning *Iron Duke*, de-militarized.

'We polished up all our brightwork – then painted over it, fitted warheads to the torpedoes, put ready-use ammo in the shell racks near the guns, unshipped and landed the Captain's furniture and chintz curtains, took on board a ton of Pusser's peas and two crates of Ally Sloper's Sauce, and HMS *Keith* was ready for war.

'On 3 September at about 1130 in the forenoon we sailed, leading our ancient flotilla of Vs and Ws out to sea from Plymouth Sound for a sweep up the Welsh coast looking for any U-boats already in position there.'

Bill Thomas began his seafaring career as an Ordinary Seaman in the coastal steamer *Avon Gwilli*, sailing out of Llanelli in August 1932 with coal for Continental ports and bringing back general cargoes to the UK. In November of that year he was apprenticed to the Cardiff tramp ship company Evan Thomas Radcliffe on world-wide voyages in the steamship *Vera Radcliffe*.

'Conditions in tramps were tough in those days; there were still sailing ships around, and our senior officers were all ex-windjammer men who insisted on treating us in the traditions of sail. Fresh meat stores were kept in an ice chest on deck, the contents of which melted as soon as we hit the tropics, a week out from the UK. From there on, until our next port of call our only fresh meat was "Weevil", picked out of our morning Burgoo (a sort of porridge). Our staple diet became salt beef and pork, which was quite tasty, much preferable to the rotting remains of fresh meat which the steward always tried to give us.'

In 1936 he qualified for a Second Mate's ticket and served in the Llanelli pilotage service until 1938, when he went back to sea as Mate in coasters. Aboard the steamer *Stronsa Firth*, taking a cargo of ammunition from Saltash to Loch Swine in Scotland, he heard Mr Chamberlain declare over the radio that Britain was at war with Germany.

To War at Sea

When I went down to Devonport
My face was cold as slate,
They gave me a number for my name
As I went through the barrack gate.

Charles Causley, Signalman HMS *Glory*

In the early hours of Wednesday, 30 August 1939, the draft for HMS *Renown* arrived at Portsmouth Station. 'There was a lot of skylarking unloading the kit from the train and on to lorries,' Tom Bailey noted, 'then away to the dockyard to join my first ship!

'What a sight! Thirty-odd thousand tons, six 15-inch guns and twenty 4.5s plus pom-poms and machine-guns!

'"Pick up your hammocks and turn in anywhere!" was the order, then after Reveille we had kippers for breakfast! We had kippers for breakfast *every* Wednesday all the time I was on board *Renown*.

'Frantic hours of work then, storing and ammunitioning ship and the wonderful experience of buying a packet of Duty Free Woodbines for 4½d!' Tom, who had joined for 'three square meals a day and a pair of boots', was well pleased with life, though like most of his messmates he had really wanted a small ship, a dashing destroyer for preference. The significance of all this urgent labour was lost on them. 'Us youngsters didn't realize the state of the world.'

They were at sea heading north when the signal came in: 'Fuse all shell. Ship all warheads'.

'When we left Pompey on Saturday evening, 3rd September, my first duty was SSO Messenger.' Later that evening Tom carried a sealed envelope to the Captain, little knowing that it contained the disturbing news of the sinking, 250 miles west of Ireland, of the 13,581-ton Donaldson liner *Athenia*, bound for Montreal with 1,400 people on board, by a German submarine, with heavy loss of life, including many women and children. After Divisions on Sunday the Admiralty made the war at sea official with the terse: 'Commence hostilities with Germany'.

The torpedoing of *Athenia* revealed that U-boats had taken up war stations before the event. For the old Reservists it was *déja vu*. Once before the U-boats had almost beaten the Royal Navy and almost starved Britain into surrender. In fact, there were no more than ten German submarines at sea as yet, but there was a big building programme. The German surface fleet was also far inferior in numbers to that of the old Imperial German Navy, and to the 1939 British Fleet, but most of the latter's ships were ageing relics of the Great War, whereas Hitler's warships were all modern: the three 11 in Panzerschiffe, called 'pocket battleships' in Britain, *Deutschland*, *Graf Spee* and *Scheer*; two powerful, fast battlecruisers, *Scharnhorst* and *Gneisenau*; three new 8 in heavy cruisers; with two huge 50,000-ton battleships, *Bismarck* and *Tirpitz*, under construction, not to mention the revival of another potent First World War weapon, the armed merchantman commerce raider, with her fast speed and hidden guns. All these sea wolves were to be unleashed on Allied merchantmen.

THE SINKING OF *COURAGEOUS*

When all the Royal Navy's ships in reserve had been reactivated and crewed, there was still a serious shortage, particularly of cruisers, which was not helped by the early loss of an important unit of the Fleet.

'In order to bridge the gap', records Winston Churchill, 'of two or three weeks between the outbreak of war and the completion of our auxiliary anti-U-boat flotillas, we had decided to use the aircraft-carriers with some freedom in helping to bring in the unarmed, unorganized, and unconvoyed traffic which was then approaching our shores in large numbers.'

One night, in very dirty weather, the new destroyer leader HMS *Kelly*, commanded by Captain (D) Lord Louis Mountbatten, was investigating a possible submarine contact off Land's End when an SOS came into her wireless office from the carrier *Courageous*. Aboard the carrier, in No 821 Squadron, was PO Tel/AG A.G. 'Murgy' Brown. 'There was no "phoney war" as far as the Navy was concerned – Admiral Dönitz and his U-boats saw to that. *Courageous* sailed from Plymouth with a destroyer escort, and started operations in the Western Approaches right away. Our Skipper was "Salt Horse", not an aviator (though he had a lot of time for aircrew) and the ship's company were mostly RNR, some very senior citizens among them, who should have been ashore, digging their allotments.

'We were flying day and night anti-submarine patrols, and one night, in poor visibility, one of our aircraft returning from patrol missed the ship – they flew right overhead, turned back and failed to see us. The Skipper had to make a difficult decision: accept the loss of his aircraft and crew, or break W/T silence (to give them a bearing) and fire a star shell, giving our position away. He chose to try to save the crew – without success – and the Germans had us pegged. About 8 p.m., on 17 September, two torpedoes from Otto Schuhart's persistent *U-29* hit us on the port side, and we keeled over. I was below, having a shave when it happened. Dropping everything, except my precious Rolls razor, I made my way to the upper hangar. The lower hangar was on fire, and a young Marine hangar sentry was operating the sprinkler system and trying to lower the fire curtain. "Bit too late for that, now, Royal," I said. "She's going soon," and grabbing two Mae Wests from the nearest aircraft I chucked one to him and told him to follow me up top. "No," he said, "I must wait until the Sergeant tells me to leave." And he stood fast. I've always admired the Marines, and never more so than at that moment.

'On deck, I helped a seaman hack a Carley float loose, and after a struggle we managed to drop it into the sea – and it was promptly seized by a group of swimmers and paddled away. I slid down the ship's side, hitting every ring bolt with my backside on the way, and into the water. Looking up as I drifted past the stern, a huge propeller ticking over a few feet from my head, I saw a Marine officer calmly smoking a fag as he ditched his confidential books over the side, before diving in. Suddenly a huge wall of water loomed up, higher than the ship's side, and I went under. When I eventually surfaced, lungs bursting, *Courageous* had gone – taking more than 500 of her company with her.

'The destroyers, including *Kelly*, were bustling around by now, dropping depth-charges all over the place; no joke for those of us in the drink – it was like being kicked by an elephant when they went off. I swam towards one of the destroyers, but never seemed to get any nearer. It was dusk by now, and I'd nearly had it, when I spotted a merchantman nearby, an old tramp bound for Liverpool from Sierra Leone. I made for her and managed to reach her as darkness fell. I was a good swimmer, and surprised that I was so exhausted – until I realized that I hadn't inflated my Mae West! Apart from being frozen stiff, I was all right, but others, who had seemed OK in the water, had first-degree burns – and begged to be put back when they had been pulled out.'

At midnight the tramp steamer's passengers were transferred to the destroyer *Inglefield*, which had come alongside, looking for survivors. 'We then searched the area until morning,' says Murgy Brown, 'picking up a few bodies, and continued patrolling for another two days before we were put ashore at Plymouth. Some survivors had been picked up by an American liner, and been given the full VIP treatment by the passengers – fitted out with civvies, hob-nobbing with film stars, and all set for a run ashore in the USA. They got a shock when Mountbatten turned up and took them aboard!'

In *Kelly*'s crowded Sick Bay 'Poultice Mixer' PO Sick Berth 'Tiffy' Bert Male made his patients as comfortable as possible. 'They were all exhausted, and had bad burns, lacerations, shock, and internal damage from gulping the oil.' One man, a stoker, was carried below to Gordon Rogers' mess. 'He had slid down the ship's side when she had heeled over and the barnacles had torn his back and his buttocks and hands and he was in a very bad way. The gash bucket in the mess was full of tealeaves and scrapings off our supper plates. When the poor sod saw the bucket he fell on his knees and stuck his hands all torn and bloody right into it. "Don't do that, old matey," I said, and tried to pull him back, "you'll get blood poisoning or something." "I don't give a shit," he said, "it's cool, cool, cool". . . When I looked closer I saw that he was pissed as a newt. The Yanks had poured a bottle of whisky into him, and they had given them thick blankets and warm clothes.'

For Murgy Brown it was back to *Daedalus*, and fourteen days' survivor's leave. 'My wife was waiting at the gate – she had been waiting there for days. All too soon our leave was over. We were lined up for a pep talk by Admiral Bell Davies, VC. "Cheer up, lads," he said enthusiastically. "The sea is His, He made it . . ." ". . . and He can keep it," muttered someone behind me. My sentiments exactly.'

For Tom Bailey in *Renown* and the other big ship matlows, 'Scapa Flow was a time of exercises, AA control and Damage Control, days at sea and plenty in harbour, working party ashore helping to build the new canteen'.

'What a time! Take your tin mug ashore to drink your beer, a mess kettle for enough pints to take back for your mates. And still kippers for breakfast every Wednesday!'

NORTHERN PATROL

As well as defending British seaborne trade against German submarines and surface raiders, the Navy had the important job of blockading Germany by stopping her merchant ships, of which there were many scattered round the globe, from reaching the Fatherland. Old 'C' and 'D'-class light cruisers, and occasionally one of the most modern ships, had revived the World War I Northern Patrol, which stretched a thin net from John O'Groats to Greenland, but they were too few, and the 'C's and 'D's were 'showing the flag' ships, not intended for the wild weather of these seas. There were too many gaps in the net.

These were to be filled, as in World War I, by Armed Merchant Cruisers (AMCs) – liners and cargo/passenger ships with a fair turn of speed, armed with old 6 in guns, crewed by Merchant Navy sailors on the special T124 articles (known in the RN as 'rockies'), officered mainly by Royal Naval Reserve Merchant Navy men ('cargo-shifters'), and commanded by Royal Navy captains brought out of retirement – some of it enforced by the pruning 'Geddes Axe' of the Depression. Their job was Contraband Control, the stopping and searching of ships suspected of being disguised German blockade runners. They were meant to take on German raiders.

On 29 September the first AMCs steamed into Scapa Flow. The Admiralty had previously earmarked 50 of these ships for conversion in time of war, when they had reckoned they would be 75 regular cruisers short for their commitments. Ships were 'stiffened' to take the weight and operating stresses of 6 in and 4 in guns, pedestals and mountings.

On 26 August the Royal Mail Line's big 22,098-ton *Asturias* had steamed up Southampton Water fresh from a Mediterranean luxury cruise, disembarked her passengers with brusque haste, and cast off for Belfast and a change of role. Young Geoffrey Penny had been a shipping clerk in the City, and now found himself 'to my amazement' a paymaster sub-lieutenant RNR in an Armed Merchant Cruiser fitting out for war.

'*Asturias* was stripped of most of her rich fittings. Dockyard mateys took away all the lovely mahogany and walnut furniture from the saloons, lounges and smokerooms, the golden wickerwork chairs and beautifully carved cedarwood tables from the Winter Garden, which was so bright and sunny, done out in the Spanish style. The First-Class Smokeroom was to be the new Wardroom, and the Grinling Gibbons carvings there were not touched, likewise the marble Adam fireplace in what was to be the Anteroom to the Wardroom.

'The ship's big forward funnel was sliced off at deck level with oxy-acetylene torches, then lifted in one piece by a giant crane on to the dockside, and we were fitted with eight old 6in guns, some smaller ones, searchlights and a primitive fire control system. The only ack-ack guns we had at first were two Great War Lewis machine-guns, which jammed when they were tested.

'When the conversion work was finished, the dockyard foreman said to me, "We've made a nice mess of your beautiful ship" – some of the truest words ever spoken. Our sister ship, *Alcantara*, got the same treatment at Southampton.'

One of the older generation serving in AMCs was 50-year-old Bert Poolman from Bath, Somerset – my father. He had spent most of his life close to water – river, sea and ocean. As a young man in the long, golden Edwardian summers, he had rowed on the Avon, won cups and medals in regattas, competing against the heavyweight farmers' crews from Evesham, while apprenticed to the firm of Stothert & Pitt, crane-makers. As a Territorial he was sent to France in 1914 but with his engineering experience was released to work on submarine trials from Newcastle-on-Tyne, which he found 'a bloomin' sight more dangerous than the trenches', in spite of the experience of having his old boyhood friend literally blown to pieces as he handed him a dixie of stew on the dugout steps.

Watching the big ships come and go from high up on a gantry while installing cranes in Southampton Docks had given him – to lace the Romany blood he had inherited from his mother – a longing for ocean travel which his experiences in submarines had not killed, and after the war he went into the Merchant Navy as an engineer, serving in 'dodgy old tramps' like *Bosworth* ('We used to have bets on which half we'd be in when she broke in two'), and graduated to the Bibby cargo liners *Somersetshire* and *Dorsetshire*. Beached in the Depression, with a wife and son to feed, he suffered the harshness of the dole, the indignities of the Means Test, but eventually got an engineering maintenance job with the pork butchers Spears of Bath. But his heart was still away at sea. He taught me to swim and row on the near-derelict stretch of green, tree-lined river which he himself had once adorned as a young lithe oarsman, took me on paddle steamers in the holidays at Weston-super-Mare ('Weston-super-Mud') or Weymouth, where we collected warship photographs.

Just before the Second World War started we both went aboard the destroyers *Fortune* and *Firedrake*, moored just downstream from the old Bristol Bridge. My father talked earnestly to an engine room artificer of impending war, as they gazed down into the grease-green pits of the huge pistons in the engine room. When war did come, he got the train to London on the very first day of hostilities, and came home a Sub-Lieutenant (E), RNR. Too old to sign T124 articles, he had been let in on a 'gentleman's agreement', and a few days later my mother and I saw him off in his darkened train at the Midland Station for Birkenhead, on the Mersey, and the Armed Merchant Cruiser HMS *Salopian*. Appropriately for him, the ship had originally been the Bibby liner *Shropshire*, loading in August 1939 for Rangoon and Colombo, but the county nickname 'Salop' had been used to manufacture a new name to avoid confusion with the County-class heavy cruiser HMS *Shropshire*.

When my father saw her she too had suffered a sea-change. 'The first thing I noticed was that she had lost two of the four masts that had made the old Bibby boats stand out. She'd had her black hull, white upperworks and pink funnel all daubed over a dirty grey. She looked proper down in the mouth. The men call her "Sloppy Anne". There is a sprinkling of RN ratings (captains of guns, gunlayers, key men), and the Captain is Sir John Alleyn, Bart., RN. He was a Great War hero (navigator of *Vindictive* at Zeebrugge) and is a re-tread like me and we hit it off being in the same age group.

'The ship is ballasted with pig-iron and her holds and 'tween decks are filled with thousands of empty 15 to 50 gal sealed oil drums for extra buoyancy in case we are "tinfished", though I don't think they would make much difference. The guns stick out like great lumps.'

Asturias, Aurania, California, Chitral, Rawalpindi, Salopian, Scotstoun and *Transylvania* were the first AMCs to reach the Flow. 'We were surprised to find such a huge area of water with all kinds of warships dotted about,' wrote Geoff Penny, 'all blinking away with signals and a great number of ships' boats all going the rounds.

'We in *Asturias* are quite green in RN procedures. It is my job to make sure that the ship's company is properly clothed to face patrols up beyond the Arctic Circle. The ship's stores, which had been one of the first-class passenger suites on C Deck, sells thick vests and longjohns, shirts and shoes, sheets and hussifs, and I have managed to "borrow" heavy fur coats, seaboot stockings, leather seaboots (much prized) and oilskins from the naval stores in Kirkwall.

'None of us are sufficiently worked up to go on patrol, and it is too rough outside the Flow to make a start; in fact it has been too bad *inside* to take on stores.'

The AMCs were trapped in Scapa, and the old 'C' and 'D'-class light cruisers of the 7th and 12th Cruiser Squadrons continued to maintain the Northern Patrol, 'straining our rivets', described Roy Coles, a young ERA in *Diomede*, 'and old engines in mountainous seas, with lookouts peering through snowstorms and driving sleet, boats, booms, bridge screens and guardrails smashed, lifelines permanently rigged on the upper deck, broken messtraps washing about in six inches of water below decks, and no way of keeping dry, even with oilskins over our hammocks, or shaving without serious risk of cutting your throat. High seas made it impossible to man the guns.'

On 2 October there was a flurry of excitement in the Flow. During the First Dog Watch the Commander-in-Chief hoisted a flag signal, addressed to *Ark Royal* and *Renown*, ordering them to raise steam for full speed by 1800. On the previous day survivors from the steamer *Clement* had reached the South American coast and reported that their ship had been sunk by the pocket battleship *Admiral Scheer* on 30 September. The Admiralty immediately organized a number of hunting groups to track her down, of which *Ark Royal* and *Renown* formed one – Force K.

The stranded AMCs were badly needed to plug the Denmark Strait gap, between Iceland and Greenland, where low fuel endurance made it impossible for the old cruisers to patrol. Through this gap homeward-bound German merchantmen and contraband neutrals were sailing with impunity, except when the odd modern Home Fleet cruiser could be released. But even the new *Sheffield* could only spend two days there, though *Belfast* bagged the German Hamburg-Sud-

Amerika Line's cargo/passenger liner *Cap Norte*, disguised as a Swede, on 9 October.

It was the time of the 'Phoney War', a muddled period of uncertainty when signals like the following were exchanged:

Admiralty to Destroyer X: 'Proceed with all despatch'
Destroyer X to Admiralty: 'Request destination'
Admiralty to Destroyer X: 'Aden repeat Aden'
Destroyer X to Admiralty: 'Am at Aden'

'A very eerie, cold and stormy time,' noted young *Salopian* boarding officer Bill Jeffery, in the Flow, 'chaotic, uncertain, anxious and bewildering'. It was desolate aboard the big, gutted liners, cavorting at their cables. 'Vast areas of the ship are just open spaces where scores of passenger cabins have been torn out. Meals are eaten amidst piles of the old furniture.

'At least we were safe inside the "impregnable" Flow, or thought we were. Various gates, nets and booms kept submarines out, and German bombers, with no aircraft-carriers to transport them across the North Sea, could not reach us . . .'

But just after one o'clock in the dark hours of the middle watch on 14 October they were all awakened by the deep underwater explosions of torpedoes. 'The impossible had happened, there were U-boats in the Flow.' Soon all the sleeping ships were awake, 'up-anchoring and zigzagging round the Flow in near-panic'.

Oberleutnant-zur-See Günther Prien – the 'Bull of Scapa' – had found a weakness in the defences at Kirk Sound, crabbed his *U47* inside, and got out through the same hole, leaving behind the 29,150-ton battleship *Royal Oak* capsized at her anchorage after four torpedo hits, with the loss of 830 men. If he had made his daring move twenty-four hours later he would have found no way in. The hole at Kirk Sound was known to the Admiralty, and a blockship was to be sunk there the very next day.

All the big ships were ordered to sea out of harm's way. There were no immediate repetitions of the sinking, but four days later two squadrons of Junkers Ju 88s flew over the anchorage and bombed those ships still there, hitting Jellicoe's old *Iron Duke*, doing duty as a base ship and floating coastal defence battery; she was damaged underwater by near misses and had to be towed into shallow water and beached.

The nine AMCs which had gathered in the Flow had left the day before, 17 October, passing a patch of oil below which the submerged tomb of *Royal Oak* lay. 'It could so easily have been one of us,' reflected Geoff Penny. *Rawalpindi*, *Scotstoun* and *Transylvania* had managed, not without difficulties and hold-ups, to complete their working-up, and were despatched at once to the Denmark Strait. *Asturias*, *Aurania*, *California*, *Chitral* and *Salopian*, although not properly worked up, were allocated mostly to more southerly patrols, with *Asturias* taking a convoy across to Halifax, Nova Scotia.

There was frequent trouble with the old guns, some of which had been made in 1898. *Rawalpindi*'s 6 in were 1901 and 1909 models, allowed to rust for decades, with bores, pivots and mountings worn by firing in the First World

War, and even when the Gunner's Party and the engineers managed to get moving parts to move, 'proper maintenance is impossible,' reported Petty Officer Shipwright Peter Winiatt of *Rawalpindi*.

'On the open decks the mechanisms (and the crews) are exposed to the severity of the weather. Water penetrates the moving parts, and some of the guns can only be trained with the help of two or three of the gun's crew pushing on the barrel.'

On 21 October a ship brought in to Kirkwall the crew of the Norwegian *Lorentz W. Hansen* with the news that the latter had been sunk by *Deutschland*. This confirmed the suspicion that there was more than one pocket battleship at large. On 22 October the German raider captured the American SS *City of Flint*.

Meanwhile the weather was the worst enemy. *Scotstoun*'s four forward guns were unworkable sculptures of frozen spray, gales cut her speed and ice stove in her forepeak, though she still managed to apprehend *Eilbek* of Hamburg. *Laurentic*'s guns jammed, her boats were holed. On 12 November the Norwegian *Tvirfjord* was brought into Kirkwall for examination, and her captain told the Contraband Control boarding officer that on 4 November they had been stopped by *Deutschland* 700 miles west of Ireland – he had forborne to radio the information for fear of reprisals by the Germans. On 20 November *Chitral*, after gun practice on an iceberg, caught the clumsily disguised German SS *Bertha Fisser*. 'This ship – no good,' said her captain when taken aboard the AMC, 'Our big ships come tomorrow. They take us away.'

The weather was so rough on the night of 21 November that *Chitral*'s boarding boat, returning from the scuttled German SS *Tenerife*, could not be re-hoisted. *Laurentic* did not even try to board the '*Flora* of Amsterdam' (actually the Hamburg-Amerika Line's *Antiochia*) and sank her with gunfire.

Also patrolling in the freezing northern waters was the 'saucy *Arethusa*'. 'Once in the Arctic,' says Mark Wells, 'we were told to wear the heavy-duty clothes issued, and no one was to undress, so we slept just as we were for duties below. It got very cold, the condensation dripped from the overhead pipes and bulkheads, everywhere was damp and cold.

'It was a joy to be on watch in the boiler room. However, as we worked in air pressure there were huge fans up top which spun round at 15,000 revs and sucked in the freezing air. At one stage there were icicles hanging down from them a foot long – and this was in the boiler room! At one stage there was ice all round the ship, when I went up top, and the ship was almost stopped. There was no wind and the sea quite calm, and I couldn't get over the silence everywhere, punctuated by the odd crunch of ice. As I tried to sleep off-watch, every half hour or so the speakers would wake me with "Port watch stand by to fend off ice aft" or some such thing, and so it went on!'

First Taste of Action

She's a tiddley ship, o'er the ocean she'll flit,
She sails it by night and by day,
And when she's in motion she's the pride of the ocean,
You can't see her arsehole for spray.

Side, side, *Achilles'* ship's side,
Jimmy looks on it with pride –
He'd have a blue fit if he saw someone spit
On the side of *Achilles'* ship's side!

CRUISER *ACHILLES*

The ancient Maori name for New Zealand is Tiritiri o te Moana – The Gift of the Sea. Her two islands lie like a division of ships in the blue South Pacific, and she is an ocean trader, relying heavily on the sea for her prosperity. The present-day Maoris' ancestors came to Tiritiri in great oceangoing canoes with names like *Tainui, Te Arawa, Aotea, Takitimu, Tokomaru* in 1350 from Tahiti and the Marquesas. For four centuries the sea god Tangaroa protected them from the greed of white plunderers, helping them to repulse Abel Tasman in the Jade Sea; but rapacious whalers and sealers swindled, robbed, kidnapped and abused the Maoris, aided by escaped convicts from Australia, decimated them with their European diseases, and sold them guns to accelerate their decline by inter-tribal war. There was some retaliation: in 1809 everyone aboard the ship *Boyd* was killed and eaten. But the Bay of Islands north of Auckland became an important trade centre for flax, wood, European-introduced potatoes and maize, and ship-victualling. 'The Gift of the Sea' was grabbed eagerly for its equitable climate, lush grasslands, virgin commercial potential and wide open spaces, backed by grand mountains and warmed by hot springs from the centre of the earth. Colonization was secured by the Maori wars and by the time the novelist Trollope visited her shores, New Zealand considered herself to be, he thought, 'the cream of the British Empire'.

Colony became Dominion, and sent over 100,000 men overseas in World War I, who suffered 58,000 casualties, including 17,000 dead – greater than Belgium, the central battlefield, with a population six times greater. New Zealand paid £1,698,224 for the honour of having a battlecruiser of her own, HMS *New Zealand*, which took part in all the big North Sea actions, sank the cruiser *Köln* at

Heligoland, finished off the battlecruiser *Blücher* at Dogger Bank, and swamped the enemy's rate of fire at Jutland, scoring many hits on the German battle-cruisers. HMS *Dunedin* joined the New Zealand Division, followed by her sister ship *Diomede* on 21 January 1926. In February 1936 she went home and secured at Sheerness astern of her replacement, the new *Leander*-class light cruiser *Achilles*, 7,030 tons (9,740 fully loaded), and armed with eight 6 in guns in four turrets.

Sparker Jack Harker from Governors Bay, Lyttelton Harbour, was one of the New Zealand ratings who moved their gear over to the new ship. He had inherited a love of the sea from his father 'who sailed before the mast for 21 years and never set foot on a steamship'. After the cramped old *Diomede*, *Achilles* was 'unforgettable; no longer stooped under low deckheads, we stood straight and looked up at a wealth of overhead space. Individual lockers took all our kit with room for more; mess-tables spread expansively, clean and new. We felt we'd boarded the *Queen Mary* . . . The W/T department had an operating room 'as large as *Diomede*'s complete outfit!'

For the next two years they cruised the sunny South Pacific, fighting mock battles with a force of elderly V-and-W destroyers led by HMASS *Canberra* and *Sydney*. *Achilles'* sparkers kept a listening watch for missing Amelia Earhart's plane, picked up a weak, despairing SOS, and searched in vain for her as long as fuel would allow.

Just before Christmas 1938 they berthed at Tahiti, and were soon wondering how Bligh had managed to get *anyone* back aboard the *Bounty*. 'Night warmed to the tempo of the tamure; smoke, beer and champagne dispersed caution; sailors whisked barefooted pretty young vahines out into the parks off Rue Pomare and Rue de Jeanne d'Arc.' It was also a temporary farewell to the Pacific; they were on their way back to England.

At Portsmouth they saw cranes hovering like vultures over *Hood*, fitting more (but not enough) armour, and other cruisers and battleships being modernized, before the New Zealanders went off for a return visit to 'The Big Smoke'. When they returned they found new faces on the messdecks. Their Imperial quota had been replaced by new hands, of whom Lamptrimmer Ivor Burston from Wiveliscombe was one.

In late February 1939 *Archilles* rolled her way to New Zealand again. Kiwi Pete Trant from Christchurch joined as telegraphist/air-gunner for the Walrus, only to get the blame when the aircraft's pick-up from the water went wrong, and it sank.

They arrived in Auckland on 8 May and tied up alongside the Naval Base at Devonport, NZ, some 13,000 miles from Devonport, England. 'Some journey!' wrote Ivor in his diary. One of his first calls ashore was on the Hatswells, from Wiveliscombe, who made him most welcome, as did some friends of T.V. Pearse, the Wiveliscombe solicitor.

As events in Europe went from fraught to frightening, *Achilles* took the Governor-General of New Zealand, Lord Galway, for an island cruise, with the hands betting on the colour of his daughter's panties, trying discretely to observe her true colours as she negotiated ladders.

The ship continued to be hard on aircraft. Her new Walrus was launched to overfly Aitutaki and its cheering islanders; it returned to *Achilles* and made a good slick landing. Pete Trant climbed up on the centre-section while craneman Jackie Alder swung the grab down for Pete to clamp through the lifting eye . . . but the grab didn't grab, the plane was dragged on its side by the tricing wires, and capsized, taking Pete down with it. A huge air bubble shot him to the surface, to see the rescue whaler punch a hole in the 'Shagbat's' hull, and finally sink her by tearing a long gash in the wing.

From leave they were urgently recalled to store ship. Bunting-tosser Colin Malcolm 'drew money from a Devonport bank and paid all debts . . . drank in the "Mon Desir" with the old crowd . . . went down to the old home and broke down when our cat "Old Fat" came running out to see me . . .'

On Tuesday, 29 August, *Achilles* left to join the West Indies Squadron, commanded by Commodore Harwood in sister ship *Ajax*. As she left, Colin Malcolm used the 18 in searchlight to say good-bye to his Auckland girl friends, and wondered when, or if, he would see them again. Imperial Lamplighter Ivor Burston did the rounds of his charges. They might be needing them soon.

As they were battling rough seas on the way to Balboa, Telegraphist Neville Milburn, from Bradford, Yorkshire, England, received the signal: 'Britain has declared war against Germany'.

Their destination was changed to Valparaiso, Chile, to patrol the west coast of South America, looking after British ships, and looking for German vessels trying to sneak homewards, most of them hugging the neutral harbours until they saw what the situation was like at sea. At Valparaiso two German merchantmen, *Dresden* and *Dusseldorf*, were marking time. All foreign ships there were bound by the laws of neutrality, but for *Achilles* the rules were stretched, and she was allowed to fill to capacity with 1,385 tons of Chilean crude, and stuff her stores with Argentine beef, greens and spuds. Her departure was spectacular, with her Marine band in white topees, uniforms of blue, gold and red, playing them out with 'Heart of Oak'. This was partly to entertain the Chileans, partly for the watching captains of *Dresden* and *Dusseldorf*.

In Chilean ports German crews jeered them. They passed the spot off Cape Coronel where Craddock's old cruisers *Good Hope* and *Monmouth* had gone down in 1914 before the guns of Von Spee's earlier *Scharnhorst* and *Gneisenau*; but they saw no Germans at sea, and were handicapped by their lack of an aircraft. At night on 18 September they heard of the loss of *Courageous*.

On 30 September the British steamer *Clement* was sunk by a German pocket battleship which identified herself as the *Admiral Scheer*, 70 miles off Pernambuco, Brazil. Like the *Deutschland*, she had obviously taken up her war station before the actual outbreak. Survivors reported her when they reached the Brazilian coast. *Achilles* was ordered south, to round the Horn and refuel in the Falklands. Her sailors were reluctant to leave the local girls, who were 'very free with love,' Jack Harker says. Some men drank with German cadets off the training barque *Priwall*, at the German cafe 'Neptune's Bar', and saluted 'the dead already' when they were told that a U-boat waited for them outside the harbour – when they left on Friday the 13th. Ivor Burston remembers how 'The flagship of the Chilean Navy, *Almirante Latorre* (the Royal Navy's old battleship *Canada*), signalled when *Achilles* left "Goodbye to the millionaire love ship".'

BATTLE OF THE RIVER PLATE

On 22 October *Achilles* was lying in bright sunshine in Port Stanley harbour. The German raider had sunk the tramp *Newton Beach*, freighters *Ashlea* and *Huntsman* off Ascension Island. The next day *Achilles* cruised north and met the heavy cruiser *Exeter* off the River Plate; the latter then went south for a rest, and County-class *Cumberland* took her place. An owl which had perched on *Achilles'* mainyard was killed by an albatross, which the men took as a bad omen. New Zealand coders howled with rage when they translated a signal promising only a 9d per day rise in pay instead of the promised 3/-. 'Miserable bastards!' was the mildest comment.

On 10 November *Achilles* entered Rio de Janeiro, the men bored with endless drills. Two of them deserted, and another was found dazed minus his wallet. The ship returned to the Falklands to refuel, with *Cumberland* and *Exeter* watching the Plate. A buzz went round, correct for once, that a pocket battleship calling herself *Graf Spee* was in the Indian Ocean. The Admiralty deliberated. *Two* pocket battleships south of Capricorn? The German had stopped a small tanker, *Africa Shell*, found her empty, and sunk her. *Achilles'* men worked off their frustrations in sport, 'resulting in hockey-stick shin-bruises and deck abrasions, black eyes from low-flying chucks'. Off Natal *Achilles* was identified by planes as the pocket battleship she was hunting, and was then ordered south at full speed to Montevideo. A raider had sunk the *Doric Star*, the frozen meat ship *Tairoa* and the freighter *Streonshalh* on the Cape Town–England route. On 10 December *Achilles* rendezvoused with Commodore Harwood in *Ajax*, and on the 12th *Exeter* joined them off the Plate, where Harwood was convinced one of the raiders was heading.

The sun had just risen when on the 13th the alarm rattlers sounded for Action Stations. 'Everyone fell out of their hammocks and grabbed their clothes and scurried away to their Stations,' recalls Ivor Burston, his own station being on the 0.5 in gun on the bridge.

AB 'Pusser' Hill was No 6 on P2 4 in AA. 'More bloody evolutions!' He watched the geyser of spray flung up by a shell. 'Blimey, that's a bit near for a throw-off. Christ, it's the bloody *Scheer*!'

To loud Kiwi cheers the New Zealand ensign soared to the peak.

Captain Parry had his binoculars on the unmistakable shape of a pocket battleship's control tower. 'Open out to four cables from *Ajax*, Pilot, and keep loose formation. Weave when she fires.' The three cruisers diverged so as to split '*Scheer*'s gunnery, as . . .

> . . . the German gunlayers stationed
> Brisk at their intricate batteries – guns and men both trained
> To a hair in accuracy, aimed at a pitiless end –
> Fired, and the smoke rolled forth over the unimpassioned
> Face of a day where nothing certain but death remained.

'*Scheer*' also had the 'Seetakt' gunnery radar set, one of the first German warships fitted with this 50 cm type, while the British ships had none, and had to make do with the old optical range-finding system.

The German concentrated on *Exeter*, which had opened fire and straddled '*Scheer*'. A screaming 11 in salvo landed close aboard, splinters killing most of *Exeter*'s torpedo tube crew. 'B' turret took a direct hit, which knocked it out and killed its crew and most on the bridge, also destroying engine-room communications. Wounded, Captain 'Hooky' Bell dragged himself to the after control position. *Exeter* hit '*Scheer*' near her funnel, and hit again. '*Scheer*' made smoke and altered course.

Achilles went to full speed and opened fire. An 11 in shell dropped in her wake, 100 yards off, as the Panzerschiff engaged the two light cruisers. *Achilles*' guns began to overheat, jammed on recoil. 'Gunners with heavy boots' kicked the breeches, and they slid forward. 'What a lovely ship the '*Scheer*' is', thought Commissioned Gunner Watt irrelevantly as she came for them through the early morning sun. Six columns of black smoke rose between *Ajax* and *Achilles*. In 'A' turret Bill McKenzie said, 'Lads, you are now closer to the enemy than anyone else on board'. Gunlayer Stacey said, 'I can think of places I'd rather be'.

'*Scheer*'s 5.9s have the range now, shells swish overhead. *Exeter* draws the German's fire away from the two lighter ships, and once more takes heavy punishment. The 6-inchers strafe her, she hesitates, then replies. Men in *Achilles* can see her hull waver like a thundersheet from near-misses. Old hands joke to steady the younger ones – 'Blimey, I bin done – but I was done *first!*'

Exeter is a mass of smoke and flame, her aerials fall. The *Leanders* lay a saturation barrage. *Ajax* launches her Seafox seaplane. '*Scheer*' turns on *Achilles*. Near-misses fling red-hot splinters at her. In the W/T office Neville Milburg is hit, collapses; alongside him Frank Stennett's head is bloody. Milburn coughs and dies. Marine Sergeant Trimble sits in Control, rigid and deadly pale, badly hurt, glasses still on the enemy. The sightsetter sits dead at his wheel, young OD Rogers takes his place, to control range correction for all turrets, and immediately obtains hits. AB Harry Beesley on P1 4 in says, 'Come on, Ian, get behind the bloody gun before we catch those bloody splinters'. OD Ian Grant coughs as a steel splinter kills him. Harry carries a wounded man out of danger. Captain Parry hangs on to the binnacle, legs torn and bloody; his continued manoeuvring saves the ship.

The two light cruisers make smoke, then double back through it, guns blazing. In the boiler rooms the stokers are deafened already by the roar of forced-draught fans. Are those distant booms ours or theirs? *Ajax* is hit aft, knocking out 'X' and 'Y' turrets, killing their crews. *Exeter* has only 'Y' turret left, makes to ram the enemy, who eludes her, making smoke. Below, damage control parties cut holes to free men trapped by fire. The sea pours in through a great hole on the waterline below the fo'c'sle. *Exeter* lists, down by the bow. '*Scheer*' steers towards her to finish her off. The *Leanders* distract her again with their popguns; she swings both turrets to engage them, only five miles off.

'Attack with torpedoes!' *Ajax* hoists. As she fires hers, she is hit aft, and 'X' and 'Y' turrets fall silent. '*Scheer*' combs the tracks as an *Achilles* salvo falls along her upperworks. She in turn swings and fires torpedoes, but Lewin and Kearney in the Seafox spot them, alert *Ajax*. A hoist in her 'B' turret jams. Men replace it with a human chain.

In *Achilles'* turrets, still all on the line, something strange is happening. Their crews work almost joyously as they swing loaded trays towards open breeches, ram 100-pound shells up the barrel, shove in heavy cordite bags – men like Mexican Bandidos with belts of firing tubes round their waists clip them into the gun. The air grows hotter. The men fight their guns almost naked, drenched with sweat. This clamorous metal box becomes detached from normal time, the action is like some highly charged rite, though it is only ordinary men doing their jobs. They push and heave and grin at one another, knowing that any second might bring black oblivion to this almost hysterical euphoria . . . *Load! Ram! Correct for aim! Fire! Load! Ram!* . . .

If it's hot in the turrets, it's hell in the boiler rooms. Furnaces roar, fans howl. At any time a shell from *'Scheer'* could turn this hellish place into a flaming, scalding horror . . .

Worried about shell shortage, Harwood decides to break off and shadow till nightfall, then go in with torpedoes. In black funnel smoke he turns east.

'Scheer' does not follow. She too has had enough, for now, but a parting salvo near-misses *Ajax*, her maintopmast and aerials fall. The German steams west at reduced speed towards the Plate, a black hump in the sun. *Exeter*, an 18-knot shambles, is ordered to the Falklands. *Cumberland* abandons her refit to replace her.

Just after 10 a.m. *Achilles* noses within range of the enemy. Instantly bright flashes twinkle on the black hump and 11 in shells splash athwart the cruiser's bows. Exhausted men taking a breather on the upper deck drag themselves below, where young Milt Hill of P2 gun sits in his desolate, ruined messdeck, thinking 'We're bloody lucky. We could have been the *Exeter*.' *Achilles* drops hastily back again. Surgeons Pittar and Hunter turn back to their patients.

The pocket battleship suddenly transmits, giving the call-sign 'DTGS'. The duty coder says 'She's not *Scheer*, she's the bloody *Graf Spee*!' His announcement is met with indifference, but under the green domes of the Admiralty the First Sea Lord once again speculates: *'Graf Spee* as well? Where is *Scheer*? Or is this just one raider sowing confusion?' While he deliberates his aide brings another signal reporting Harwood's order to *Exeter* to leave the battle. What happens if *Graf Spee* re-engages? With 'X' turret out, 'Y' jammed, one 'B' gun useless, *Ajax* has only three 6 in working . . .

Achilles sights another ship to starboard. In a gun-happy daze lookouts identify her as a *Hipper*-class cruiser . . . then the sun picks out the bulk of a merchantman . . . A great sigh rises from the cruiser's decks.

Three hours pass. Damage-control parties clear away debris, restore communications. If *Graf Spee* comes out again, *Achilles* will have to take the weight. Harwood edges them closer, torpedoes cleared away, but the German captain has read his mind. A salvo straddles *Ajax*. She makes smoke and drops back.

In the dying sun *Graf Spee* stands out sharp against the land, where car headlights flash. *Ajax* steers to cut off the German if she should suddenly alter course to escape between the sandbanks. *Achilles* clings to her, raising great muddy following waves in the shallows. *Graf Spee* suddenly opens up, shells drop close. *Achilles* replies, and starts a fire aboard the German. On the New Zealander's bridge Torpedo Officer Davis Goff, former boy seaman, urges Captain Parry to get in 'close enough' to let loose his 'kippers'.

He will never get the chance. *Graf Spee* enters Montevideo, and Harwood takes his battered light cruisers out to patrol the mouth of the Plate. *Cumberland*, the nearest support, races up from Port Stanley. *Ark Royal* and *Renown*, Counties *Shropshire* and *Dorsetshire*, light cruiser *Neptune* and three destroyers converge. Force K had called at Rio, where, says Tom Bailey, 'in *Renown* we spent a whole day scraping the barnacles off the waterline, while being buzzed by a tiny aeroplane, a Pou du Ciel (the midget "Flying Flea", popular just before the war). The Skipper did not think it worth while manning the guns! And there were still kippers for breakfast on Wednesdays!'

Four days go by, *Cumberland* arrives. Then from the snooping Seafox comes the signal: '*Spee* is blowing herself up!'

It is over. There has been only one pocket battleship at large in Harwood's parish, and now she is gone, scuttled by the Führer's orders. Captain Langsdorff shoots himself. In *Achilles* Lamplighter Ivor Burston, who has had no chance of getting his little 0.5 into action, records 'The sad job of preparing our dead for burial at sea was being completed, and when all was ready we "Cleared Lower Deck" and paid our last tributes to our pals . . .'

The cruises of the two Panzerschiffe, particularly that of *Spee*, had disrupted the movements of Allied shipping in the Atlantic, and made the positional chart in the Admiralty out of date.

PRESUMED SUNK BY *GRAF SPEE*

Former Hull shipping chemist's errand boy, tankers' decky learner, tramp steamer AB and East Yorks Motor Company bus conductor Alan Mathison had joined the steamer *Stangrant* on 28 October 1939 as an AB with an extra 6d (2½p) per day for his hastily acquired 'as good as useless' Merchant Navy gunnery certificate, and was yet again disappointed in his ship.

'The *Stangrant* turned out to be a wreck of a ship, which should never have been allowed to sail in the state she was in. Her engines and boilers were worn out, though her hull was sound enough. It was only on the third attempt to sail from Barry for Santos, Brazil, with a full cargo of coal that she managed to get to Milford Haven for an outward-bound convoy. But she could not even keep up the speed of a slow convoy, and ultimately we were given instructions from the Commodore of the convey to *proceed alone* to Rendezvous X, some 1,000 miles out in the North Atlantic, thence to proceed as conditions allowed towards our destination.

'It is interesting to note that despite the wartime slogan "Careless talk costs lives", it was the dockers at Barry who told us where we were bound. That was not an isolated case. I found on several occasions later that the dockers in Britain could tell the crews of ships where they were going, when it was all supposed to be hush-hush.

'The convoy steamed away from us, and when they had finally disappeared over the horizon, we felt very, very alone. Hardly a day passed without the ship having to stop for some fault or other in the engine room, many of the stoppages being for several hours, during which we were a sitting duck for any enemy sub or raider that should be around. Our guardian angel must have been with us on that passage; in the 32 days it took us to reach Santos we only had two incidents which put the wind up us. Of course we were a darkened ship at night, and one particular night, fine but cloudy, we saw silhouetted against a very low moon, just above the horizon to the west of us, a warship, which we later found out was the *Graf Spee*. As we were down-moon from her, against the dark horizon to the east, she apparently did not sight us. She was steaming to the south at a high speed from the way she quickly passed the moon's face. Had she spotted us that would have been our lot.

'I had expected that gun drills would have been the order of the day, but each time I asked the Chief Officer if we could hold a gun practice, the reply was that there was work to be done on deck. It would appear that deck work was more important than training to defend your ship and the lives of the crew should the occasion arise. Personally, I would have held a gun practice every day, weather permitting, so that in the event of us having to defend the ship, we could at least have put up a stiff opposition against a submarine.

'The only other person we had aboard who knew anything about a 4 in gun was a retired ex-Royal Marine, who had volunteered for service in merchant ships for the duration of the war. He was in fact in charge of the gun party, as the gunlayer, and I was the trainer. My job was to train the gun on target, open and close the breech, insert the firing cartridge.

'The rest of the gun crew had to be made up from the other Able Seamen. Prior to leading the gun to fire a practice round, we went through the procedure, giving precise instructions as to what each man was to do – one man to pass the shell to the loader, and then help to ram it into the breech, one man to take the cordite charge from the case and pass it to the loader and ram it into the breech, whereon when they were clear, I would close the breech-block and train on to the target.

'The stupid seaman who was to pass the cordite charge decided that he needed a cigarette and promptly lit one while he was bent down over the open full cordite charge case. Sparks were flying in the wind, from his cigarette. I just happened to look round and see him cradling a charge to his chest, the end of which was about an inch away from the glowing cigarette end. I screamed at him "Put that f★★★★★g fag out you stupid bastard!" Needless to say, he was not very chuffed at my outburst and asked me who the hell I thought I was, or as he put it, "I'm only an AB, same as you."

'I was not an expert at explosives, but I did know that at each end of the cordite charge there was a gunpowder bag, and I also know that gunpowder can be ignited by a cigarette. Had that charge touched his cigarette, I dread to think what the consequences would have been to all of us on that gun platform. And that was the one and only gun practice we had while I was in the ship. With friends like that, who needed an enemy!

'On reaching Santos, we were informed that we had been given up as missing, presumed sunk by *Graf Spee*, as we were over a week late arriving there. After discharge of the coal cargo, we sailed down to the River Plate to Montevideo, and there in the river was the wreck of the scuttled *Spee*, still smouldering.'

DODGING THE U-BOATS

Second Mate Bill Thomas, used to the rougher realms of Merchant Navy life in tramp steamers – 'weevils in the burgoo, 'roaches in the milk' – as AB and apprentice, delivered *Stronsa Firth*'s sensitive cargo of shells and depth-charges at the secret MN hideaway of Loch Swine in north-west Scotland immediately after the outbreak of war.

'We were supposed to lie at our destination at anchor, to await naval vessels replenishing their magazines from us after a major battle with the enemy. There were five or six of us, large ships and small, lying off the village of Taviallic. As there was no naval battle in the vicinity, I became bored with the daily routine of picking blackberries and assisting the cook in the gruesome business of slitting the throats of mountain sheep. Both these activities were designed to brighten up our menu. Seeking more interesting work, I travelled home, later to join a Cardiff tramp as Third Mate.

'As convoys had not been properly organized at that time and as our engines had a tendency to break down, we sailed across the North Atlantic on our own. Without meeting the enemy, we tied up safely at Houston, Texas, to load a cargo of scrap iron for Glasgow. When I enquired at the Post Office about the price of an airmail stamp to the UK, I was surrounded by customers who wanted to know how I had travelled to Houston without getting bumped off by German submarines. As this was Texas, I decided to give my audience a line of their own bull. I became enthusiastic as I described my hair-raising escapes from packs of U-boats and completed the story by giving an impression of Errol Flynn emerging from the grasp of Captain Morgan's pirates. To my surprise, my listeners were spellbound, and they competed with each other for the honour of entertaining me during my stay in port.

'I came near to paying for my duplicity en route to Glasgow, when one of those U-boats surfaced half a mile away and her officers watched us through binoculars. We had stopped as usual to effect engine repairs and as we had not yet been issued with a gun, we prepared to abandon ship. The submarine suddenly dived and was seen no more, no torpedo came our way, and when our engine restarted we continued the voyage.'

The Little Ships

We're the little ships that Churchill clean forgot
And goodness knows we didn't ask a lot,
A few more spells of leave would do us all a lot of good,
We haven't got the comforts of the *Rodney* or the *Hood*,
When it comes to week-end leave there's none for us –
We're always shoving off to do our stuff.
Now the other ships get swingtime,
All we get is f★★★★★g sea-time,
We're the little ships that Churchill clean forgot.

THE COLLISION OF *BARHAM* AND *DUCHESS*

Fred Harman was a counter hand in a wet fish shop in Clacton in 1939. He had lived near the sea all his life without ever thinking of making it a career, other than through its products; unlike his best pal, Roy Ralmer, who was mad keen to join the Navy, and 'he twisted my brain'. At the recruitment exam Fred passed, Roy failed. 'Good lad,' said the Recruiting Petty Officer, 'that's another half a dollar for me'. In initial training much was made of a matlow's need to be able to swim, and life was made a misery for an oppo of his who could not. 'He was drafted to the *Hood*, and if he had been the best swimmer in the world it would have done him no good!'

Fred himself went to *Barham*, a *Queen Elizabeth*-class 'battlewagon' lying in Alexandria at the beginning of August. Fred was put initially on 4in AA guns with automatic breeches ('I'd never seen anything like them at Whale Island'), and ended up on a 6in in the port battery. When war came, Captain 'Hooky' Walker, later to command a task force in the hunting down of the last Japanese warships in the East Indies, informed them that they were off to join the Home Fleet at Greenock, as the 'Med' looked like being quiet.

Barham was with the Fleet off the Orkneys at 0427 in the morning watch on 12 December, carrying out the usual zigzag, with the destroyer *Duchess* on her port side, when a change of course to starboard was given. Instead of waiting for the executive signal, *Duchess* turned straight across the battler's bows and was struck amidships.

'A shudder went through *Barham*. I had just come off the middle watch and was having a cup of kye and a smoke before turning in.'

In *Duchess* Lancashire lad Jack Dodds, a former cruiser man, late of 'Whited Sepulchres' *Cumberland* and *Kent*, had also just come off the graveyard watch and was in his hammock aft of the messdecks in the canteen flat – the passageway from the messdecks on to the upper deck at the break of the fo'c'sle. 'A position', says Dodds, 'which I have always believed saved my life. The *Barham* hit us with such a loud crash that I was sure that we had either hit a mine or been torpedoed. I leapt out and dragged my mate out of his hammock as I ran for the upper deck.

'The lights were still on so I could see where I was going and what I was doing. Just inside the break of the fo'c'sle we had the coal bunker (we had not been changed to oil fires) and as I passed this I was aware of the coal falling out just behind me. By the time I reached the deck the ship was heeling over to port. I saw a couple of lads climbing over the guardrails so I ducked under the motor boat and joined them. By then the poor old *Duchess* was lying right over on her side, so we just walked down the ship's side. By the time I reached the bilge keel she gave a lurch and turned turtle, lying completely upside down.'

Fred Harman in *Barham* had 'rushed up on deck when we heard our engines put hard astern. Everyone on deck thought we had hit a submarine. All you could see was the upturned hull with the Asdic dome, which in the darkness looked like a conning-tower. It drifted down our starboard side and a few of her crew stepped off the hull on to our starboard 6in gun deck.'

One of these was Jack Dodds. 'By this time *Barham* had heaved to, and we were lying alongside, all sorts of lights were shining down on us. Some lines, which turned out to be hammock lashings taken from the midshipmen's hammocks, were thrown to us. No way could we climb up these as they were too small to hold on to, so we secured them to the Asdic dome, which was standing up like a big bollard. On these lines we all five of us swung across hand over hand, to drop down into the arms of the Chief G.I. and so on up on to the *Barham*. We were taken into the after screen and given a tot of rum – well, I call it a tot, it was a cupful, and a Pusser's cup in those days was a half-pint measure. I have often wondered if I was supposed to drink it all or not, but I did, and this is probably the reason why I can't remember anything till later on that morning when I woke up in one of the WO's cabins.'

Most of Jack's mates were still trapped inside the doomed destroyer or struggling in the black choppy waters. 'The screams of men in the freezing water and others with their faces at portholes not big enough to get through was terrible. She drifted just astern of us and then her depth-charges exploded. After that all was dead silent, no one could believe what had happened. When we went ashore in Greenock no one wanted to talk to us, as if it was our fault.'

A total of 117 men were lost out of 140 in *Duchess*. After leave Jack Dodds was drafted to HMS *Havock*, and was 'a wee bit worried for a while about joining another destroyer. But I soon got over that, and soon settled down in a very happy ship!' Another destroyer followed, HMS *Tyrian*, which took him East.

KEITH TO THE RESCUE

For nine months the destroyer *Keith* put in week after week of seatime, voyaging from mid-Atlantic to Cherbourg, up the Channel to Dover and Harwich . . .

> We're cold, hard and hungry, nothing to eat,
> No winter clothing, no boots on our feet.

Our hammocks are soaking, the messdecks awash,
We're living on potmess and biscuits and hash.

'We did our share', says Iain Nethercott, reluctant gunner (too noisy) at his jam-happy pom-pom, 'of picking up burnt and dying merchant mariners in the Atlantic, and such things as attempting to save the survivors of the *Gipsy*, blown in half by a magnetic mine in the Harwich approaches on a black and snowy night, with half her crew trapped in the fo'c'sle and no escape through the scuttles, which were too small, and all the gun hand-ups jammed . . .

'We were inspected by poor, sick George VI at Dover when we were leader of the Dover Patrol. We came in with the dawn one freezing morning in January 1940, and we were bustled out on to the Prince of Wales pier, still in seaboots and oilskins, and standing in a blinding snowstorm while this poor chap walked down our ranks!'

They lost two blades off their port propeller on Devil's Point, Plymouth, at 2a.m. in a snowstorm, crept back to the Dockyard 'and then had the satisfying thought of dockyard mateys being turned out of their beds at 3a.m. to get us into drydock. Unfortunately they couldn't work without a tiddey oggie inside them, and it was nearer six o'clock before we were on the chocks.'

'And so into Harwich, not before time,
Twenty more sea days and a gutfull of brine,
Let's get down the messdeck and drink up our tots,
We're sailing at seven and I'm on First Watch.'

'The only leave we normally had was 48 hours' boiler-cleaning leave to each watch alternately, occasionally evening leave till 10p.m. if we came in before 6p.m.; but we had to watch the ship from any pub we were in, and a black flag and a gun fired got us back in a panic. A Pusser's oilskin didn't keep out the terrible temperatures of that first war winter, we had no lammy coats or gloves (they went to the battlewagons swinging round the buoy at Scapa). The only heat in the seamen's mess came from the "fish and chip shop", the steam capstan engine sited on the seamen's messdeck on the older destroyers, with removable wooden covers but because of leaky joints always leaking steam into the messdeck accompanied by hissing and bubbling noises. It was a good place to crash down when off watch, always warm, but wet.'

Once, faced with towing a merchantman broken down in mid-Atlantic, they passed the towing strop round the mounting of 'Y' gun, the only thing which might take an 8,000-ton strain. At about 2 knots they struggled homewards, with one-hour tricks at the wheel, 'as the ship was a cow to steer with this dead weight veering all over the ocean, astern'. The 3½in towing wire was hanging by one thread when they got in, and the strain had started the gun mounting, but two years later Iain received £37 salvage money – 'a fortune for me'.

There were small comedies:

Keith to *Shikhari* (in full Atlantic gale): 'I can see your dome.'

Shikhari to *Keith*: 'Don't be so indelicate!'

At the beginning of May they were lying at Sheerness with a dozen other destroyers and the light cruisers *Arethusa* and *Galatea*. On the 10th Hitler invaded France.

Things grew rapidly worse across the Channel. On 23 May Boulogne was in imminent danger as the panzers had almost reached the coast. The destroyer *Verity* was acting as guard ship in the harbour there, and another V and W, *Vimiera*, was lying off the port. Two battalions of Irish and Welsh Guards, hastily shipped over from Wellington Barracks, were holding the town, while a big demolition party had been sent from Chatham to destroy the docks.

Keith led four of her V-and-Ws and arrived off the port in the late afternoon. In the roadstead were five French destroyers, all firing at the wooded heights to the south of the town. Fire was being returned from the shore but there were no clear targets for the British ships' 4.7s.

'The Skipper took us up the channel to the harbour, with *Vimy* astern, and *Vimiera* at the entrance to maintain visual signal contact with the rest of the flotilla. As we sailed in, a wood on the port side of the channel came alive with rifle and machine-gun fire. The bullets were whistling and pinging on the Iron Deck. Looking at the heights behind the wood, several German columns could be seen moving down towards the town. We opened up with HE at about 3,000 yards and started scoring hits immediately. Jimmy Wallis, my gunlayer, suddenly spotted several files of German infantrymen taking up position on the boulevard on the north side of the harbour. He gave me a yell and I spotted them immediately and brought the gun round. We gave them several long bursts, and brought down the portico of a hotel behind them. By now we were coming up to the centre of the harbour and had to turn to bring the ship port-side on to the Quai Chantzy.

'We were under a lot of small arms fire, mostly machine-guns, and were taking casualties. As we came alongside the jetty and made fast it was a scene of indescribable chaos. Hundreds of soldiers who appeared to be in a blind panic immediately rushed the ship. Lots of them were drunk, very few had rifles. The Skipper up on the bridge was going crackers. He ordered the torpedomen armed with rifles and bayonets and the Gunner T to "Clear all that rabble off the ship!"

'There were dozens of wounded on stretchers on the jetty and from where I was on the gun I could see them being trampled on by other soldiers who were staggering about with wine bottles. Although the Skipper refused to take off any of the French civilians who pleaded with him from the jetty, we took aboard a large party of French schoolgirls in the care of several nuns. These were stowed away on the messdecks, as the wardroom was full of dead and wounded!

'In the middle of all this activity we spotted a German Storch plane which flew over the hills and towards the harbour. The ships outside opened up on it but the pilot flew on and suddenly dropped a white flare. From then on all hell broke loose. Hundreds of German troops came pouring over the heights on both sides. We came under terrific fire and trench mortar bombs started dropping on the jetty and then on to the port side of our Iron Deck by the break of the fo'c'sle. My gunlayer was hit in the chest; the loading numbers put shell dressings on him and took him below. I took over the gun, as a large force of Stukas had appeared overhead and had just started their dives. Their bombs fell over the jetty and right alongside the ship, killing our sentries on the jetty. I got a long burst on one and blew away most of his nose, and he crashed into the harbour.

'The Captain had been shot dead on the bridge and they carried him down and put him alongside the CO of the Chatham demolition party who had been killed earlier. I had been hit in the shoulder by some of the splinters from the Iron Deck, and had been well clouted in the face with lumps of concrete from the bombs on the jetty, so I was bleeding like a pig and swearing like hell.

'Guardsmen on the jetty were repulsing an attack from motor-cycle troops, and when the dust had cleared a bit on the jetty I managed to sweep along a line of these bikes, and then blew down a dockyard crane from which I'm pretty sure the German machine-gunners who had killed the Skipper were firing. The *Vimy* next to us was in a bad way. Like us, her decks were full of dead and wounded soldiers. Her Captain was also dead on the bridge. It was a bright and sunny afternoon. A good afternoon to die.

'The *Whitshed* came steaming into harbour, her Skipper directing the guns on to targets with a hand megaphone. It was Lieutenant-Commander Conder, a man of character, who was now Senior Officer. Our First Lieutenant, who had been wounded, took over the ship. *Whitshed* signalled us and the *Vimy* to cast off and proceed to Dover with our troops, while he called in *Vimiera*, leaving *Wild Swan* and *Venomous* outside as back-up.

'*Whitshed* was engaging tanks on her port side, so on the way out we joined in as we had the guns in local control, with the TS hit. Both pom-poms were jammed and the OA and his assistant were frantically working on them. In those days rifles and cutlasses were provided at all guns, so we opened the boxes of 0.303 and carried on with rifles. There were loads of targets as German infantry were everywhere, so everyone on the upper deck including the more warlike of our soldiers kept up a barrage of rifle fire until we had passed out of the harbour mouth. We'd have used those cutlasses too.'

Iain went below and had a piece of shrapnel removed by an Army doctor.

'It hadn't penetrated very deep and after a good wash and a tot of neaters I was back in business. Off the Varne lightship we stopped engines, and the ship's company assembled on the upper deck. It was sunset, Jimmy read the Burial Service and we lowered the Captain, followed by the other captain, into the sea, to be followed by the others. It was very sad, and whenever I sail over the waters today I always pay my respects to my old shipmates.

'They sent us to Chatham Dockyard as the ship looked like a colander and all the boats were riddled with rifle bullets and shrapnel and needed changing. We were there for two days. They whipped out our old pom-poms and replaced them with two new ones with articulated belts. They removed our after set of tubes and put in a 3in HA gun. The worst of the holes were welded up, but they didn't have time to repair all the bullet holes in the funnels and upperworks. Mind you, we got *two nights* undisturbed sleep in our hammocks and we all managed to slip ashore and sink a few pints.

'We sailed down the river to Sheerness on the third day under the command of a new skipper, Captain Berthon, and with replacements for our dead and wounded. I had been made permanent gunlayer on the new port pom-pom, and the First Lieutenant had called me down to the Wardroom and let me know that I should put in for Leading Seaman. I couldn't believe, it, I was only just nineteen. I could see the war was going to improve my chances of promotion beyond my wildest dreams. The trick was obviously going to be how to stay alive to take advantage of these new conditions.

'We loaded up with extra ammunition at Dover. I met my first HOs on the messdeck. They were ODs who had been sent as replacements and the poor little chaps hadn't got a clue, they really thought that they were on a pleasure cruise. They didn't live the week out. Our new Skipper cleared lower deck and gave us a Noël Coward-type speech, and thus fortified, we sailed for Dunkirk.

'The earlier part of the evacuation, as far as we observed, was reasonably simple, as most ships, which included the big cross-Channel ferries, could get alongside the mole, and it was a simple case of troops marching down the mole and on to the ships without getting their feet wet. The drawback was that the German long-range artillery kept opening up on the mole and the harbour. Up the coast towards Nieuport they had an artillery spotter balloon which was obviously ranging the guns on to the targets. In my opinion we could have spared a few Spitfires to upset this little game. In the event, except for a Coastal Command Hudson, which was shot down on the beach, I never saw any RAF planes during the whole time I was out there.

'We carried back our load of troops in this way for a few trips, being fired on from the coast on a few occasions during the time when we ran parallel to the coast in the swept channel. I must admit that it looked very fearsome over there. The oil storage tanks were burning and the pall of black smoke covered the whole area for miles. The German planes spent most of their time bombing the beaches, though every now and then we were attacked. My new gun worked perfectly, but we had to economize on ammunition.

'On about our fourth day we were taken off evacuating troops and carried out bombardments of the German-held coast, shooting up tanks and other transport and infantry. We came under heavier and heavier air attack. At night we crept along in the main channel well to the east of the beaches, looking for E-boats which were infiltrating the evacuation fleet. One of them had sunk *Wakeful* with terrific loss of life.

'We were closed up at Action Stations all the time, and were existing on corned beef sandwiches and cups of tea. We catnapped on the guns but were getting more and more tired and especially at night it was getting hard to concentrate. The harbour was closed now with sunken ships, the big ships had gone for good, most of the modern destroyers had been withdrawn, and the soldiers were being taken off the beaches at night using small boats, and taken out to the old V-and-W destroyers and Fleet sweepers . . .'

> Oars in the darkness, rowlocks, shadowy shapes
> Of boats that searched. We heard a seaman's hail,
> Then we swam out, and struggled with our gear,
> Clutching the looming gunwales. Strong hands pulled,
> And we were in and heaving with the rest,
> Until at last they turned. The dark oars dipped,
> The laden craft crept slowly out to sea,
> To where in silence lay the English ships.

'We had by now been taken over by an admiral, Admiral Wake-Walker, who was in charge of the beach operations out there. As dawn came up on the "Glorious First Of June" we were cruising slowly in the roadstead off Dunkirk flying our Admiral's flag and our battle ensigns. We were very tired after days and nights without sleep, tired right through to our bones. The continuous bombing and artillery fire flung at us had made us all very jumpy, and the sight of so many ships bombed and sunk and all the bodies floating around, made us more and more depressed. An MTB came alongside and told us that the cross-Channel ferries had all sailed for Southampton, as the crews refused to sail to the beaches any more, and reported the buzz that *Verity*, one of our flotilla, had practically mutinied and was now moored at Dover and wouldn't sail. The news cheered us up no end.

'As dawn came up we were lying off Bray Dunes in company with *Basilisk* and some Fleet sweepers. At about 8 a.m. I spotted a large formation of Stukas coming up from the south. Most of them went round with the 3 in firing at them, out of range of our guns. Suddenly they dived from ahead, up-sun. I was firing long bursts at the first one, who pulled out just over the bridge and I saw his bomb come away, then another and another. We had full helm on and it was difficult to keep the gun trained. I thought that the bombs were going to hit the stern but they seemed to fall in the water right under our tail. The ship reared up and kept swinging, steering jammed. I saw the next formation of planes starting their dive, just as the ship straightened up. I got a long burst in on the second plane and carried on firing as he shot overhead and I blew all the wireless aerials down. I could see one bomb coming straight for the ship. It went down the after funnel and exploded down in the boiler-room. Clouds of smoke and steam poured out of the engine and boiler rooms and the ship slowed to a stop and started to list to port. An MTB came alongside and took off the Admiral, and shortly afterwards the Captain ordered "Abandon Ship". The Carley rafts were launched and most men were jumping into the water and hanging on to the rafts. The port whaler was lowered and filled with wounded, and everybody started making for the *Skipjack* and *Salamander*, which were steaming close to us. The *Basilisk* had just been sunk, I could see her going down to starboard.

'The Stukas came back and once again we got the gun into action, although the list on the ship made it difficult. I suddenly spotted several Messerschmitts flying low towards us and managed to open up on them. They opened fire on our survivors and seemed to be killing everyone in the water around the whaler. The sea around them was red with blood and I could hear the shouts and screams from where I was.

'Another wave of Stukas came diving down on us and I couldn't elevate the gun high enough to range on them because of the list. We were badly hit in the engine room and she carried on listing. Bomb splinters had killed several of our loading numbers on the gun deck, and it was time to sort them out. I noticed that *Skipjack* out to port had been hit and suddenly she turned over with all the soldiers on board thrown into the sea, but a Stuka had come down in the sea, and I wondered whether I had got him or whether it was the *Skipjack*'s gunners. Several small boats and a large tug, *St Abbs*, were alongside the starboard bow taking off the wounded and some of the soldiers. There were only two of us left on the gun deck; all the dead were piled up in the corner by the ready-use lockers. There was only myself and Paddy Dunbar, the trainer of the starboard gun, left.

'The ship was wallowing deep now and listing well to port. The cox'n saw us from the signal deck and gave us a yell to abandon ship, so we went up on to the fo'c'sle and helped to get the last of the wounded on to *St Abbs*.

'Eventually she pulled away. By then I thought my *Keith* would turn over any second, but it wasn't necessary as suddenly more Stukas appeared and dived on her. The bombs landed all over her and she just rolled over and sank. The *St Abbs* was pottering around picking up survivors of the *Skipjack* so I went up for'ard where someone had got a jar full of rum. I managed a tot, and a few minutes later a Stuka hit us with a stick of bombs. I was blown clean into the water, and bobbed up in my whaler's lifejacket, looking for the ship. She had gone. There didn't seem to be many survivors, and I felt myself going east with the tide. The water was very cold but there was no oil on the surface. There was an old merchantman lying bombed ahead of me, so I made a big effort and eventually caught a dangling boat's fall, worked my way along her side and climbed up a rope ladder on to her well deck. There was soon a crowd of about a dozen on board, including Captain Berthon. We were rummaging around when we were suddenly attacked by bombers. When they'd gone we found plenty of tinned food in the galley and had a feast of tinned salmon and some tinned rice pudding.

'The Skipper had examined one of the lifeboats which was still on the falls, and decided that we could use her to row back to England. We stocked her with corned beef and tins of pears and plenty of water. I rummaged around in the after locker and came up with the boat's sails. We couldn't find the mast or any spar that would suffice, but I told the Skipper that I could easily use two oars and rig up a jury rig. I hadn't been a Canvey Island Sea Scout for nothing! However, while I was working on this, a small motor lighter with a naval crew passed by in the deep water channel. After much yelling they noticed us and came alongside, and sailed on down the coast back towards Dunkirk with all of us on board, and transferred us to a Sheerness cement carrier, which took us home.

'I was bloody annoyed, after all that work.'

LIGHTING UP THE CHANNEL

If the RAF was not in evidence over the cratered and body-strewn beaches, the Fleet Air Arm was.

The urgent evacuation did not stop at dusk, but continued all through the night. To prevent U-boats from getting through to the rescue fleet in the friendly darkness, someone was required to hang a string of lights down the Channel in the night sky. The request went out for Navy air-gunners who could work a drogue winch.

TAG Jackie Heath of *Emperor of India*, *Eagle*, *Furious* and late lamented *Courageous*, star bomb-aimer, was one of those who volunteered. They were flown to Detling in Kent and he was told that his job was to 'light the Channel north of Dunkirk' so that U-boats attempting to interfere with the retreat there could be bombed. The process entailed letting the drogue out to 500 ft, with a stopper at a certain distance along the wire. A specially treated flare was then sent down the wire, and the jerk when it reached the stopper detonated the flare, which burned for about ten minutes as it was towed along; then another flare was put on the wire, and the routine repeated. 'It wasn't the Blackpool Illuminations, but it stopped Dönitz from destroying an errand of mercy.'

Norwegian Waters

Norway's a shadow; sullen the cliffs at midnight,
Stagnant the streams. Stare out beyond those fisted
Rocks; whose features stung by disease and hatred
Now rise from the mother sea, the moth-winged silence;
What calm, what certainty?
Great cities crumble, ocean to ocean cries,
All falls.

Recruits entered *Ganges*, Guz, Chatham, *St Vincent* and Eastleigh in a steady stream through the early months of 1939, to be turned into seamen, stokers, flying sailors, Sick Bay tiffies, Jack Dusties, submariners and Marine seaborne soldiers – the Regulars, the 12- and 22-year men who would take the weight in the first weeks and months of war, and pass on their knowledge and example to the green HOs who were to flood through the barrack gates.

NEW CARRIER *ARK ROYAL*

In the spring of 1939 Geoff Denny joined the Sussex Division of the RNVR at Hove, and thereafter drove down from his home in Horsham twice a week on drill nights.

'It was a reaction to the Government booklet issued to arouse the patriotic enthusiasm of suitably aged young men to join the reserve forces. I thought that my modest facility to read and send Morse and semaphore would be of use in the Signals Branch of the Royal Navy. I felt very proud of the round cap, and bell-bottoms, and enjoyed the elementary seamanship, including bends and hitches, which I was also able to cope with easily as a result of my years in the Boy Scouts, and the dreaded swimming test in a duck suit held no terrors for me as I was a county league water polo player. Inevitably, at the end of August the buff envelope dropped through my letter box. Within a couple of hours I had packed my kitbag, said goodbye to my parents, handed in the key to the office safe, and was on my way to help the Navy sort out Hitler.

'It was a beautiful golden August morning as the train took me through the achingly familiar Sussex countryside to Pompey to swell the ranks of all the other Reservists who had been activated. They didn't lose much time in deciding that I was urgently wanted at sea. On the boat across from Scrabster to Scapa Flow we looked in the turbulent waters of Pentland Firth for U-boats but got into the great anchorage safely and awaited the arrival of the Home Fleet. The next afternoon we had the unforgettable sight of the *Nelson*, *Rodney*, cruisers, and destroyers coming in to anchor. When they had all dropped their hooks, we, 40 RNVRs from the Clyde, Sussex and Ulster Divisions, were taken in a drifter to join our ship – the great new carrier HMS *Ark Royal*.'

The new carrier was not everyone's idea of maritime beauty. As she began her sea trials in 1938, she had made the signal to a nearby destroyer: 'How do I look?' The 'ocean greyhound' replied: 'Go back to Loch Ness'.

'The immense size was quite staggering when viewed from the waterline – seven decks up to a flight deck 800 feet long with two hangars carrying 72 aircraft, fighters and bombers.' She cost £3,000,000 and the contract lightened the weight of the Depression at Cammell Laird's on Merseyside.

The new all-welded system of construction used in *Ark Royal* led to some murmurs of 'jerrybuilding', and Lady Maud Hoare, wife of the First Sea Lord, Sir Samuel, took four attempts to smash the bottle of champagne against her bows at launching – traditionally a bad omen – but when the crack No 820 Squadron landed their Swordfish aboard '*Ark*' for the first time on 12 January 1939 they found her big deck welcoming. 'A change from *Courageous*,' according to one rating pilot, 'which was not the easiest carrier to work from – you had to do a round-down creep or the airflow over the stern came at you like a waterfall and the hot gases from the funnel could whisk you up just when you wanted to sink down'.

There was trouble with No 803 Squadron's brand-new Blackburn Skua fighter/dive-bombers. They were the first all-metal monoplanes in the FAA, with mod cons like dive flaps, two-pitch airscrews and retracting undercarriages, but their engines were under-powered and light, and had been shifted further forward than intended, unbalancing the machine. 'Bloody hell, this *is* an old tank!' said PO Brian Seymour, No 803's Senior TAG, after his first flight in the CO's L2873.

Geoff Denny's VR 40, the first non-active service ratings to join the '*Ark*', had been given a pierhead jump specifically for flight deck duties and to release the existing rangers back to their duties as pom-pom crews.

'We spent the first few days finding our sea legs, being seasick, exploring the ship and learning our duties from the Flight Deck Officer, the "batsman". We were allocated jobs as chockmen, on the signal booms, manning the fire-fighting equipment, besides working part of ship as appropriate. When there was no night flying we had the privilege of an "all-night in" with no middle watches, but on the other hand had to get used to a very early start to get the first aircraft range off an hour or so before dawn. When we were in the South Atlantic from October 1939 to February 1940 this was no great handicap, and the sight of the tropical dawn breaking over a calm ocean is a very pleasant memory, but at the end of November, we started a patrol in the "Roaring Forties" south of the Cape. Here, in a bleak and foggy sea, it was too rough to fly and we were glad to get back to sunnier areas.

'*Ark Royal* was a happy ship, and I like to think that the ranging parties soon became an efficient team. When the aircraft landed, the job was to get the hook disconnected so that the plane could taxi up to the forward end of the flight deck beyond the crash barrier as fast as possible. This involved two wind-buffeted rangers hanging on to the wingtips.

'We had one Skua miss the arrester wires and skid over the bows, one Swordfish broke up on the catapult as it was being launched, and its depth-charges exploded under the ship, causing a bit of a panic.'

HUNTING THE DORNIER

One of the untypical moves in the relationship between officers and men in the '*Ark*' was the commonsense announcement by junior commissioned flying officers that they would rather be led by experienced rating pilots than lead themselves.

When the Fleet, with *Ark Royal*, was at sea on the early morning of 26 September the Luftwaffe sent out a flight of Dornier Do 18 flying-boats to shadow the carrier and the battleships. 'Unfortunately', says the then PO Monk, 'the C-in-C allowed the Dorniers to fly round the Fleet, and for a long time only one was attacked'.

Lieutenant McEwan, with the Senior TAG of No 803 Squadron, Petty Officer Brian Seymour, who did not normally pair off, were the crew involved. Seymour had been 'busy right up to the last minute organizing the other TAGs and myself. A TAG's work was never done, even at the best of times, let alone in this mad rush. I was responsible for getting all the information on the positions of ships in the vicinity, the call-signs and codes of the day, and for looking after the observers' gear. It was also my job to maintain my wireless set in first-class working condition – if it failed in the air, the TAG was on the bridge in front of the Captain when he got down. That was as well as manning the aft-mounted Lewis gun, of course. And there was no special hot meal laid on for us before a patrol, like the commissioned aircrew had. The Admiralty knew as much about flying as Nelson did – with slightly less excuse'.

They took off and strained their eyes through the mist and murk. Suddenly they sighted a dark, mottled shape low on the water, indistinct because of the clever camouflage in blue, green and grey – but definitely a Dornier. McEwan opened up with his four forward-firing Brownings, then Seymour raked the German with his Lewis, with the Dornier firing back all the time. After a second attack the Dornier went down and flopped into the water like a shotgunned duck. The Germans broke out their rubber dinghy, and the flying-boat sank. It was the first enemy aircraft of the war to be shot down by any Allied force. It was also the '*Ark*'s' first aircraft victory, and for the officers there was a Black Velvet party.

'Later', Monk reports, 'Lieutenant Finch-Noyes, Lieutenant Spurway and myself were allowed off but we were limited to only one attack each on our Dornier 18. I was last to attack and the Dornier's slipstream was visible on the sea so I ignored my reflector sight and watched my bullets from the four machine-guns making ducks and drakes all over the Hun. He must have been riddled like a colander but his "fans" kept turning and I often wondered if he reached home. That was my first action and very disappointing too. After landing on, I went out on to the lower weather deck to walk down to the mess for a late lunch. That was the instant the bombs from Leutnant Francke's Heinkel exploded alongside the port side. I was drenched and wondered why one bomb made black smoke and the other white.'

The upthrust of water from the huge 2,000-pounder completely obscured the '*Ark*' from Francke's sight. Later in the day German aircraft mistook the British Second Cruiser Squadron for the whole fleet, could not locate the carrier, and reported her sunk. When the '*Ark*' returned to Scapa an all too familiar voice was heard over the broadcasting system:

> '*Gar*many calling . . . *Gar*many calling . . .'
> It was Lord Haw-Haw, the Irishman William Joyce.
> 'Where is the *Ark Royal*?'

The question was repeated throughout the following weeks by Goebbels' propaganda ministry. He sank *Ark Royal* every day, like some venomous Walter Mitty. Newspapers printed the episode in red, Goering decorated Francke with the Iron Cross. Even after Captain Allan G. Kirk, United States Naval Attaché in London, had visited the carrier and reported to Washington 'No ship was hit by the bombs during that attack and no casualties received', Germany went on demanding 'the truth about the *Ark Royal*'.

Francke contemplated suicide, and for Geoff Denny 'The subsequent propaganda and refutation did much to make us the *Daily Mirror* ship for the rest of *Ark*'s life – in competition, of course, with Mountbatten's *Kelly*. When I later appeared before a CW (commission) selection board in Portsmouth I was asked about the efficiency of the Navy in general. I replied that I thought the Fleet Air Arm the strike force of the future, and that naval gunnery left something to be desired as witness all the Home Fleet failing to hit one Heinkel. I was not recommended.'

FLYING WITH THE FAMOUS

With No 803 Squadron, which was moved to the air station at Wick, then just a field on the east coast of Scotland a few miles from John O'Groats, was TAG Alan Todd. Alan had intended joining the RAF as an apprentice but succumbed to the 'life of sea and air at the same time' promised on a Fleet Air Arm recruiting poster. The boring round of training at *Ganges* was not what he had signed on for. 'Where's the flying part', he naively asked, though he was an athlete and the dreaded mast presented no problem. He asked the same question when scrubbing the decks of the old coal-burning *Iron Duke*, though he had been pleased to be selected for the Boys Gun's Crew from *Ganges* for the Royal Tournament. He remained 'in a shanghaied state of mind' aboard the old battler for six months, and was then drafted to HMS *Barham*, aboard which he saw his first aircraft, a Swordfish on floats. He was only an OD but put in for Air-Gunner. Part of his training took place in the back seat of a Shark flown by Lieutenant (A) Ralph Richardson, who drove his beloved Harley-Davidson motor-bike well enough, but, according to Alan Todd, such notables 'were not the Navy's best pilots. They were really the products of the pre-war civil flying schools, which were gentlemen's clubs. Things like oil pressure gauges, temperature gauges meant little to them'.

Alan was flying with the future theatrical knight one forenoon when the engine suddenly burst into flames. Richardson crash-landed the aircraft just outside the village of Hursley near Winchester. 'The kite went up on its nose, burning merrily. I ended up under the pilot's seat, head-first, out stone-cold. I remember coming to, and someone was urging me "Get out of here quick!" I thought I was in my billet and people were shaking me – *Why don't they leave me alone and let me get on with my kip!* I could smell burning – *Good, the stove's on* . . . Then I did a double-take . . . *Christ, we're on fire!* I was out of that plane like a jack-rabbit. It didn't put me off flying, it just made you think. I wrote in my diary "Well, it isn't all a bed of roses, this!"' Shortly afterwards Alan received a letter from Richardson. Richardson crashed twice more, the second crash killing the trainee TAG, and shortly after that both Richardson and another actor, Lieutenant (A) Laurence Olivier, were returned to the world of Show Business, where it was felt that they could be of greater value to the British public.

After training, Alan joined No 803 Squadron at Hatson – 'in theory the fighter defence of Scapa Flow. That was the biggest laugh ever. The Skua was called a "fighter-bomber", but in fact was neither. It did not have the proper engine, its Bristol Perseus sleeve-valve job being grossly underpowered. The RAF had all that was going in those days, the Navy got what was left. If it had had the proper uprated Perseus it would have been a faster and better fighter, with a better bomb load.

'Two days later, 12 April, my mother's birthday, I was shot down over Bergen. We went across the hogwash to attack general shipping, and in the dive we caught one. The engine just faded away, we heaved ourselves over a small hill and went straight down into the fjord at 100–120 knots, just slithered along the calm water and came to an almighty splashy stop. We got the dinghy out of the tail stowage and got ashore. We made our way to a little house, where the family dried us off, then their local Dr Hansen took us down to the fjord to the US tanker *Flying Fish*, but they threw us off as soon as they found out who we were, fearing the hostility of the Germans. The Skipper said, "Give yourselves up. They'll look after you."

'Ashore again, we stumbled along a little track we'd found and bumped into the doctor again, on his rounds. He was taken aback but led us to a little lodge in the woods belonging to Nurse Emma, a little old lady who hid us for several days until the hunt died down, then arranged for a boat to take us up the coast. We were then handed on from person to person, crossed a fjord to Aalesund, and after four weeks' tracking caught up with the evacuation, and I recognized men and marines off the old *Barham*, dug in there to hold off the German Army. A coastal steamer took us back to Scapa, where we found out that the Squadron had been practically wiped out.'

The '*Ark*' was recalled urgently from Alexandria. She was loaded up with incendiary bombs in the Clyde, landed some Swordfish in exchange for more

Skuas and their turreted version, the Roc, and set off for the Arctic Circle to provide fighter cover for the Allied forces landed in Norway to resist the German invasion. There she was joined by *Glorious* from the Mediterranean.

LONG ODDS FOR *RENOWN*

Also patrolling Norwegian waters was *Renown*, watching for *Scharnhorst* and *Gneisenau*, which had been reported out. Ordered to lay the mess table one day, young Tom Bailey told his Leading Hand 'If you want the sodding table laid you're the best bastard to do it!' 'Bastard' was a mild word in the Andrew, but insubordination was not tolerated. Given 14 days' Number Elevens (doubling round the deck with a 6in shell), the Chief Quartermaster 'gave me a piece of advice which I have passed on to many a young sailor – "If ever you feel like saying things you will be sorry for to a senior, go forward to the heads and call him all the names under the sun, just make sure nobody hears you." Commander Terry added "Keep that sort of language for the Germans," so when, on the morning of 9 April when we engaged the *Scharnhorst* and *Gneisenau* off the Lofoten Islands, and I had been woken from a lovely sleep on the deck of the wheelhouse, with shells falling all round the ship, I used a few choice words and the Commander reminded me of my punishment I said, "I'm only doing what you told me, sir"!'

It was Captain (D) Warburton-Lee in HMS *Hardy* with the Second Destroyer Flotilla who first fell in with the German warships; then *Renown* engaged them at extreme range, in spite of poor visibility and high seas, and made several direct hits on *Gneisenau*. In the teeth of the appalling weather the destroyers struggled to keep up, and Petty Officer Neal in *Hardy* watched the whole dramatic battle.

'Suddenly, out of a blinding snowstorm, came *Scharnhorst* and *Gneisenau*. We cleared for action. Then we saw *Renown*. She was a splendid sight and in hot pursuit of the enemy. At 4.10a.m. we engaged *Scharnhorst*. We played our part alongside *Renown*. We blazed away at both enemy ships in a sea that tossed us about savagely. It was so rough that eventually we had to drop out of the action with all our accompanying destroyers – *Hunter*, *Hostile*, *Hotspur* and *Havock*.

'They were thrilling moments while they lasted. Every man was on his toes. The *Scharnhorst* straddled us with "bricks", and our part of the sea was hot for a time.

'*Renown* kept firing away. It was possible to see her shells hitting *Gneisenau*. Every hit brought a cheer. For a time it was like being in a ringside seat and seeing your fancy pummelling his opponent.

'One particular salvo from *Renown* will live forever in our memory. It put paid to one of *Gneisenau*'s after guns, which had been devastating. It tore it out as clean as if it was a surgical operation. There was a huge splash, a flash of colour, and a gun that had just fired four salvos in succession packed up.' Petty Officer Ted Baggley became *Hardy*'s unofficial commentator. 'Glasses to his eyes, he outdid Howard Marshall [a BBC commentator of the time]. We cheer his words: "A salvo from *Renown* within only a hundred yards of *Gneisenau* . . . An

Right: *Ivor Burston from Wiveliscombe, Somerset, as an Able Seaman aboard the battleship* Barham *in 1937.*

Below: *'Stand clear of the vent in rear!' – Royal Navy Boy Seamen training on a 6in gun pre-1939.*

Left: '*Manning the Mast*' *at HMS* Ganges, *a true test of courage for the boys of the* '*stone frigate*'.

Below: HMS Marlborough, *a battleship of the Training (and Third Battle) Squadron in the 1920s.*

Right: Christ Buist went from dole to drafting office, to the Royal Marines, to Chatham, to the heavy cruiser HMS York in the 'Hungry Thirties', and was with her in the West Indies when war broke out.

Below: The Parade Ground, HMS Pembroke, the Royal Naval Barracks at Chatham, Kent.

Above: *HMS* York *at St Lucia, West Indies, 1938, presents a typical picture of 'showing the flag' in times of peace – gangway down, snow-white awnings rigged in the sun.*

Left: *Harry Liddle from Yorkshire intended to go farming in Australia, but the Navy advertised for telegraphists and he went to HMS* Impregnable *to train. He humped coal and scrubbed icy decks in bare feet in the old* Marlborough, *then the new* Nelson, *and* Warspite *in the Med, before becoming a TAG.*

Above: The destroyer Wren *in calm seas, acting as 'crash boat' for the new aircraft carrier* Ark Royal.

Below: After Wren, *the 'Re-ven-gee' (HMS*

Revenge) *was like serving ashore. This class of battleship was originally designed to burn coal.* Revenge's *sister* Royal Oak *was torpedoed by* U47 *and sunk in Scapa Flow.*

Left: Watcher of the skies. Born in Potter's Bar – Zeppelin country – Freddie Longman was a gunner bitten by the flying bug while in the 'wing tip line' of HMS York's catapult Walrus. Here he has reached Petty Officer Airman rank.

Below: Many rating pilots flew Walrus amphibians from catapults. Here HMS Suffolk recovers her Walrus. Perched precariously on the top wing centre-section, the TAG is waiting to hook the aircraft on to the crane grab. One slip and he could fall into the scything propeller blades.

Above: Students of No 41 Course for Rating Pilots, Royal Navy, 1938, at 'Practice Camp', West Freugh. Left to right: Kimber, Morrelec, Richards, Rice, Lunberg, Clark.

Below: No 41 Rating Pilot Course graduates selected for fighters. Left to right: Clark, Monk, Sabey, Kimber, Hadley. Eric Monk won two DSMs, and commanded a Corsair fighter squadron as a Lieutenant-Commander aged 23. Sabey was also commissioned, having flown Fulmar intruder patrols from Malta over Sicilian airfields at night.

Left: Doug Cole and Bill Crowther. Crowther was later lost with HMS Fidelity, the only Q-ship in World War II to carry an aircraft.

Right: Mark Wells 'just loved ships'. Beached in the Depression, he got a job with the railway, on the footplate, and 'felt the exhilaration that I had at sea'. Here (near right) he is in the cab of LNER No 4797, a 'Green Arrow' V2-class mixed traffic loco ('Super engines they were too'). War took him back to sea, to the cruiser Arethusa and the sloop Bridgewater (far right).

Below: HMS Renown. This picture shows the beautiful lines of the battlecruiser after her final reconstruction.

HEROES ALL OF THEM. **R.I.P.** GONE BUT NOT FORGOTTEN.

Capt. W. T. Makeig-Jones.

IN SORROWFUL AND PROUD REMEMBRANCE OF THE GALLANT
518 OFFICERS AND MEN OF THE ROYAL NAVY, ROYAL MARINES,
ROYAL AIR FORCE, FLEET AIR ARM, ROYAL FLEET RESERVE,
AND PENSIONERS OF H.M.S. COURAGEOUS WHO WERE DROWNED
BY THE SINKING OF THEIR SHIP BY A GERMAN SUBMARINE ON
SUNDAY SEPTEMBER 17TH 1939.

Top left: HMS Courageous, *with sister 'light battlecruisers'* Furious *and* Glorious, *was converted into an aircraft-carrier in the 1920s, and her squadron pioneered flight deck procedures and dive-bombing. She was torpedoed and sunk by a U-boat in the first month of World War II.*

Left: HMS Kelly, *the late Earl Mountbatten's famous World War II destroyer command.* Kelly *was sunk by Stukas off Crete in the Mediterranean, having survived a torpedoing in the North Sea.*

Above: Workhorses of the Northern Patrol were the armed merchant cruisers, with their elderly 6in guns, some of Boer War vintage. Here a gun's crew closes up in Icelandic waters aboard Asturias. *The gun has no shield, and has therefore probably come from the secondary battery of a defunct old battleship.*

Left: New Zealand 'sparker' Jack Harker found Achilles 'unforgettable' in her spacious accommodation, big wireless operating room and new elecrical equipment.

Below: The new Achilles, a Leander-class light cruiser, seen in the Panama Canal in 1938.

Bottom: 'Crossing the Line' party aboard HMS Achilles .

The Battle of the River Plate. Boredom with endless drills was cured by hot action against Graf Spee. First Exeter, then Ajax, lost firepower after hits by Spee's 11in shells, and Achilles bore the brunt, losing men to a steel splinter storm.

Above: Achilles *men take a breather while her hot, blackened forward 6in guns cool down during a lull in the battle.*

Below: Graf Spee *burns after being scuttled on the Führer's orders in the River Plate. The sight broke Captain Langsdorff's heart, and he shot himself.*

Above: *The Flotilla Leader HMS* Keith *in which 'reluctant gunner' Iain Nethercott served.*

Left: *Group by 'A' gun, HMS* Keith, *March 1940. Most of these men (left to right: Wallis, Addington, Wadey, 'Scottie', Tongue and the ship's Chef) were killed at Dunkirk.*

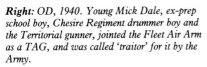

Right: OD, 1940. Young Mick Dale, ex-prep school boy, Chesire Regiment drummer boy and the Territorial gunner, jointed the Fleet Air Arm as a TAG, and was called 'traitor' for it by the Army.

Below: The German battlecruiser Gneisenau was, like her sister Scharnhorst, a battlecruiser, armed with only 11in guns, and designed mainly for convoy attack. The two ships were no match, even together, for the battleship Duke of York, which sank Scharnhorst in December 1943.

Bottom: The Blackburn Skua two-seat fighter/dive-bomber was the FAA's first all-metal and monoplane aircraft. It did good work in the hands of pilots like PO Eric Monk, DSM and Bar, and was the first Allied machine to shoot down an enemy aircraft in World War II. Skuas sank the German cruiser Königsberg. Behind the Skua is a Vought-Sikorsky Chesapeake.

Above: On 10 April 1940 Captain Warburton-Lee, RN, took five destroyers into Narvik harbour, northern Norway, where he discovered ten German destroyers of superior gun power. He lost his ship, HMS Hardy, and his own life, but sank or disabled three of the enemy. Here, men of HMS Havock stand in front of 'X' gun aft, with the hole made in the gunshield by flying debris in the battle visible. All wear huge grins of relief at being in one of the ships that got away.

Below: Light cruiser HMS Glasgow *was active in the Norwegian Campaign, landing troops, evacuating King Haakon, his country's gold reserves, and members of his government.*

Bottom: The aircraft-carrier HMS Furious flew her Swordfish to the limits of their performance, their crews' endurance and her own, in support of the Allied landings in Norway, until relieved by Ark Royal. Here the old carrier takes it green, in company with Renown.

ominous column of smoke rises amidships . . ."' The battlecruiser ran for the cover of the snowstorm, but 'details of the pasting given the *Gneisenau* were supplied to us in a manner that leaves no room for doubt. We saw a deal of wreckage come floating past us – kitbags, lifebelts and paravanes, all of German origin . . . Like a beaten dog she ran for cover. The snowstorm hid her in time'. *Scharnhorst* also screened her with smoke.

Tom Bailey, in his first action, was getting to know himself. 'I did not feel afraid, excited, yes, as telegraph operator in the upper conning tower, helping with tricks at the wheel in rotation, living on soup and corned-dog sandwiches, which the rough weather did not put me off. I was discovering that the rougher it was the happier I seemed to be. *Renown*'s 15 in were belching fire and smoke. Suddenly just ahead of us there was a flash and a puff of smoke, and shrapnel flew. We were hit several times, one 11 in "projjy" entering the half-deck, but fortunately not exploding. Either due to a near-miss or an extra-big wave I was thrown against the bulkhead, and the welded screws that held the channel plate for all the electrical cables pierced the back of my neck (I still have the scars to this day), but I still managed to shout encouragement to the guns' crews.

'While steaming at 30 knots the starboard anti-torpedo blister had been ripped open. Down on the messdeck they cheered every wave that hit the ship's side, hoping for more damage so that we could get more leave. Once again there was no fear, though if the ship's side had been stove in we would all have been drowned. In other actions, in the Med when attacked by low-flying bombers, I felt just the same, dodging behind a flimsy canvas screen, feeling confidently "If he can't see me he can't hurt me." It was all so distant, you were never face to face with the enemy.

'I have seen fear in the eyes of young U-boat survivors bobbing in the water with just their heads showing, and the absolute panic if we had to leave them until it was safe to pick them up.

'I must confess that I had one great fear, of losing my sight. Loss of arms or legs I think I could have coped with, but blindness – never.

'Then I might never have seen the beauty of the sea, both at its wildest and at its calmest, the beautiful hands of Siamese dancers, the facade of the rock temple in rose–red Petra – or the mutilation of the child beggars of India, all the squalor in the world.

'Today I saw the daffodils in bloom at the roadside, on my way to the Backworth Bowling Club, where I am Chairman.'

'WE ARE GOING INTO NARVIK'

With the German heavy forces driven off, Captain Warburton-Lee made his historic signal: 'We are going into Narvik.' There the Germans were digging in and throwing up defences, and he decided, in the belief that his five destroyers would be engaging six German destroyers (in fact there were ten), to sink as many of them as he could, shell the defences and destroy German transports there.

Neal recalls: 'Though the average age of our men was little more than twenty, all were keen as mustard.

'After traversing only a short distance we pick up a Norwegian pilot who speaks very good English . . . "What is the strength of the Germans in the fjord?" we ask. "I would not go up there unless I had three times your force."

'Nevertheless, at one o'clock the next morning, the 10th, we take up action stations as the flotilla creeps into the mouth of the fjord in pitch darkness.

'Again a blinding snowstorm. We miss an ice-floe. Tea is handed round to us. We gulp it down. There is rum in it! It keeps us warm.

'At 4.10 a.m. we are right up to Narvik. The first vessel we sight is registered at Hartlepool. We slew round to face the harbour and shore batteries which are tucked away to the north side of the fjord. We slew to port. On our starboard side is a German destroyer at the narrow neck, and we fire a torpedo.

'It hits! God, what a hit! Up she goes out of the water. She has no future but the scrap heap. Must have hit the magazine. Then a firework as her ammo goes off. Every gun we have is banging away. We send the nearest German merchantman to the bottom with another torpedo. We smash three destroyers and at least seven merchantmen. Men at the guns are slipping about in the thickening snow.

'We have just fired two torpedoes into the pier, timbers fly into the sky, when from an arm of the fjord come three more German destroyers. Two more appear on the horizon. We are straddled between them.

'An enemy salvo hits the TS. L/S Cockayne and Scouser Whearty fall, Whearty cries out "I can't reach the fire gong!" Our Captain has gone down, mortally wounded. I take over the for'ard guns. No 2's layer hails me. Crash! The gun is blown up, No 2 is dead; so are four of the crew: Hunt, gun captain; Lang, layer; Hay, tray worker; and Edwards – who has just asked me if he can take the place of a wounded man. At No 1, OD Watson is killed, my legs are splintered, I smack a bandage on. Most of the guns are mangled heaps, smashed by the enemy's big 13 cwt shells. The bridge is gone, the wheelhouse, the main steampipe. A scalding jet at 300 pounds per square inch is let loose.

'Lieutenant Stanning, apparently the only officer left alive, is going to ram one of the enemy. He gives the order. The coxswain is killed at the wheel. Young Smale takes over. But there's no steam, and the wheel is locked fast to port.

'CRUNCH! We are on the beach, and being machine-gunned. Now *Hunter* is hit. She turns right over at full speed and sinks.

'The shore proper is about 50 yards off. Out of the corner of my eye I see a movement where the bridge used to be. It is the Captain, barely alive. We put a lifebelt on him to float him ashore. "Swim, lads, swim!" he says faintly.

'It is 6.15 a.m. as we abandon ship, and I prepare to leave the wonderful little lady we all love so – love her even now, battered and broken. I am now pretty weak, but I shin down a rope over the side. The cold water revives me. I just make the beach.'

DAWN RAID ON BERGEN

That evening Nos 800, 801 and 803 Skua squadrons at Hatston were briefed for a dawn attack on a German cruiser in Bergen.

'None of us had ever flown with a 500-pound bomb and the trip was near our endurance limit,' says Eric Monk. 'Final note at briefing was, "If you have less than 60 gal of fuel after the attack, fly on to Sweden, destroy your Skua and try to get back." Not a very good sleeping draught. I went to bed shortly after briefing and my chum Ron Lunberg came along to wish me luck in the morning.

'The shake at 0300 was a relief but the thick corned-beef sandwiches we were offered at briefing remained untouched. Going out to the aircraft I had mixed feelings and wondered if my kite would fail to start. It was then I found out that once I was strapped into my familiar L2934 it was just another flight, no more worries. All was ready, bomb on, safety-pin for my bomb in my pocket in case it was not dropped, Colt .45 in my flying overall pocket alongside the compass, and L2934 started up first cartridge. Warm up the engine, check boost and revs, throttle back to check the magnetoes and check that the tanks are full. Lieutenant Finch-Noyes moved out, followed by Lieutenant Spurway, and I followed on behind. It was a fine morning as we climbed up to 16,000 ft, heater on, and doing 140 knots. Eventually the coast came into sight, the sun was up, the sky blue, the hills topped with snow, lower down the pine trees and then the water of the fjord. Wonderful, except that there was a war on.

'Naturally, I was tail-end Charlie of the sixteen Skuas and as I stall-turned to enter my dive the shell bursts covered Bergen like a black lace curtain. The *Königsberg* had been damaged by the Norwegian coast batteries but there were still quite a lot of shell bursts on the way down. Steady on the target, offset turret, no mistaking the *Köln*-class cruiser, 5,000 ft, check bomb is armed, 3,000 ft and release, down to sea-level, weaving away down the fjord, 80 gal indicated in the tanks, then out to sea into formation for the two-hour flog back to Hatston. We checked for signs of oil or fuel leaking on any of the aircraft in the sub-flight, and kept a constant check on my oil pressure. The leader's observer "zobbed" (Morse code by waving hand) "Report fuel remaining." Reply: "75".

"I was feeling rather hungry now. Two hours later we landed at Hatston with almost empty tanks and taxied in feeling tired but elated. On the way to the mess I passed the Captain who asked if I was ready to go again and I am pleased to remember that I replied "Not till I've had my breakfast."

'Two days later we did go again and Petty Officer Gardner failed to return, but he sailed into Kirkwall Bay two weeks later in a "borrowed" boat and still had a small bottle of Pusser's rum in his pocket. When the Captain sent to see him in the afternoon, the rum was in his tum and the Captain had to wait till next day. These raids continued for quite a time with Nos 800, 801 and 803 Squadrons taking part. I went on the first three but then *Ark* came back from training in the Mediterranean with *Glorious* and my squadron embarked.'

WARSPITE ENTERS THE FRAY

Warburton-Lee's five ships had sunk or disabled three German destroyers of superior gun power off Narvik but had lost *Hardy* and *Hunter*, and the enemy still dominated the Narvik fjords, with seven destroyers still operational there. Three days after this action, a much stronger British force was sent in to remedy the situation. Leading nine destroyers, including the new large Fleet destroyers *Bedouin*, *Punjabi*, *Eskimo* and *Cossack* of the Tribal class, and *Kimberley*, was Admiral Whitworth in the recently updated and reconstructed *Queen Elizabeth*-class battleship *Warspite*.

Petty Officer Pilot Rice and Observer Lieutenant-Commander W. L. M. Brown were briefed by Admiral Whitworth, the Captain of *Warspite*, Victor Crutchley, VC, and Commander Currie to:

(1) carry out a general reconnaissance for the squadron advancing on Ofotfjord, 'with particular reference to the presence of German warships inside the fjords, the movements of German forces, and the positions of shore batteries',

(2) bomb 'any suitable targets'.

Ben Rice, late of Colchester Technical College and a local Redwing Aircraft apprenticeship, which had ended when the firm went bust in 1932, leaving him jobless, had followed the trend and joined the RN at *Ganges*. He served in the destroyer *Brilliant* at Gibraltar until he was sent home to join No 41 Rating Pilot Course, on which he trained with Eric Monk. In his diary was the entry 'First solo! Wonderful!'

With Leading Naval Airman Maurice Pacey as TAG, they were launched in drizzly weather at 1152 hrs on Friday, 13 April 1940, in *Warspite*'s Swordfish floatplane L9767 ('Lorna'), carrying two 250lb high-explosive, two 100lb anti-submarine and eight 40lb anti-personnel bombs.

Kapitänleutnant Schulz's brand-new Type IXB 1,051/1,178-ton, U-boat *U-64* had had her trials curtailed to supplement the defending naval forces at Narvik. She was on the surface at the top of Herjansfjord near Bjerkrik when the Swordfish crew sighted her. Rice selected his two anti-submarine bombs, put the 'Stringbag' into a dive and released the bombs at 200 ft. 'I couldn't see the bombs fall as we pulled out, but Pacey saw the starboard bomb fall close alongside and the port one hit just abaft the conning tower; the U-boat was already sinking when I could see her again. She hit us in the tail with one shot. I think it was from her 37 mm gun.' There were 36 survivors from the U-boat.

At 1226 a German destroyer appeared out of the mist to port; she was immediately engaged by *Icarus*, *Bedouin*, *Punjabi* and *Cossack*, and turned back into the mist. Shortly afterwards a second enemy destroyer loomed up to starboard and opened fire, followed by another, to be met by rapid fire from the British destroyers and 15 in shells from *Warspite*.

Minutes before the British force came abreast of Ballanger Bay on the south side of Ofotfjord, Pacey in the Swordfish signalled that an enemy destroyer was lurking in the Bay. *Icarus* sighted and engaged her at 1307, joined by three Tribals. The German fought fiercely but in eight minutes was ablaze, her last gun silenced by *Warspite*. More enemy destroyers came up, fire was shifted to them, and a running fight developed. Rice in the Swordfish sighted a Heinkel, which kept well clear of them. At 1330 Fleet Air Arm aircraft from *Furious* bombed Narvik harbour, as *Warspite* prepared to bombard coastal fortifications. Four surviving enemy destroyers, one badly damaged, fled up Rombaksfjord, where they were attacked and destroyed.

Rice landed alongside *Warspite*, which had stopped off Narvik at 1600, and was hoisted in. Eight German destroyers were sunk during the action. Rice's

U-boat was the first German submarine to be sunk from the air in World War II. Rice was awarded the DSM, Brown the DSC, and Pacey a Mention in Despatches.

FIGHTER PATROLS

The Germans advanced on Trondheim in central Norway, and small Allied forces were landed at Namsos to the north-east and Aandalsnes to the south-west. The only protection they had from Luftwaffe planes – Messerschmitt Me 109s and Me 110s in great numbers – were two squadrons, Nos 816 and 818, of Swordfish from *Furious*. 'No fighters,' says Jack Skeats, the countryman from Aylesbury, ex '*Rev-en-gee*', who had turned down the chance of a commission to fly as a TAG, 'and only four 4.7s to fire ineffectively at the aircraft that flew just above their range of 10,000 ft and bombed at will'.

The Swordfish's first operation was a torpedo attack on shipping in Trondheim Fjord. '816 and 818 gaily left *Furious*, flying just above sea-level (flying at sea-level tends to rip off the undercarriage), passing over some skerries where the families came out to cheer and wave. We felt good although I for one had only a hazy idea what we were about. Air-gunners were not allowed to attend briefings – after all, we were only passengers. The approach to Trondheim was made at low height, with a short encounter with a flak ship and then a slow climb to top the mountains that surround the harbour and slide down the other side on our bottoms to the harbour itself and smite the Hun.

'Alas, the Hun was a damn sight smarter than we were and had left three days earlier, leaving lots of Swordfish sculling around without a target. Not dismayed, we proceeded to seek out a lone German destroyer making its way up a neighbouring, narrow fjord flanked by pines. The approach was made by side-slipping down over the pines, levelling out and then pressing the button after sighting. I am not quite sure of the pecking order but several kites preceded us in dropping their "tin-fish" and as we reached our drop position the bed of the sea came up to greet us in one big gout of sand and spume. And then another and yet another right underneath us flying as low as we dared. *Damn fine gunners, these Germans*, I thought before realization struck me. The depth of water was such that the torpedoes of the aircraft in front of us were blowing up on sandbanks in the fjord. Nevertheless, I saw at least two plumes of water rise up at the stern of the target and two hits were accredited.

'Back home to Mother who turned out to be Mother Hubbard. The mess-deck was empty when I reached it, lunch time was long gone and the cupboard was as bare as a baby's elbow. Cold and hungry I made my way to the Main Galley and did my Oliver Twist bit. The Chief Cook had obviously not read his Dickens, and said with deep emotion and great sympathy "Serves you bloody well right. You should have been here when the meal was served."'

The old *Furious* and her aircrews almost burned themselves out with the tremendous pressure of operations. Her machinery badly needed rest and repair. None too soon *Ark Royal* and *Glorious* relieved her, but even their four Skua/Roc squadrons and four Swordfish squadrons could not hope to keep the Luftwaffe at

bay. 'With our strictly limited number of aircraft,' says Eric Monk, now in the
'*Ark*', 'inferior in quality to the 109s and 110s we met, our only advantage was
that we had dive brakes and we came to the conclusion that our only real hope was
to wait until the enemy opened fire and was closing rapidly, dive down with dive
brakes out and full rudder to left or right to offset the line of sight. The enemy fire
should pass to one side and he should rapidly overshoot – immediately pull in
dive brakes and try to get a shot in as the enemy pulled up for a further attack.
Not much comfort, but the best we could think of.' In the Falklands War Sea
Harrier V/STOL fighters used similar tactics ('viffing') against faster Argentine
aircraft, with the vectored-thrust jets in place of dive brakes.

The Skuas battled with Ju 88s, Dornier Do 17s, Heinkel He 111s, Me 109s
and 110s, and shot down at least 20. For the flight deck rangers, Geoff Denny
recalls, 'the land of the midnight sun was one long greyness with persistent cloud
cover. As it never really got dark we were operating right round the clock and
being bombed intermittently, almost permanently at action stations, and at one
time we were almost ready to drop from having been without sleep for 52 hours'.

EVACUATION

At Namsos the cruiser *Glasgow* landed troops and her whole stock of depth-
charges for blowing up bridges. She then returned to Rosyth to embark 22,000
men, who were landed at Molde and Aandalsnes on 23 April. *Glasgow*'s Walrus
was seconded to Wing-Commander R. L. R. Atcherley of Schneider Trophy
fame, who had been detailed to find airfields for RAF fighters. Together they set
up three airfields, Skaanland, Bardufoss and Laksely; TAG Leading Naval
Airman Hunt from the Walrus crew was decorated in the field by the Navy
C-in-C, the Earl of Cork and Orrery, for services performed when setting up the
last-named field.

As the Germans pushed relentlessly north from Trondheim, the Allies tried
to keep a beachhead open round Narvik, and captured the iron ore port on 28
May, but Narvik and Harstad were bombed heavily, and there was no hope of
sending more aircraft to the area as the situation in France was desperate and had
priority. The 800-mile link between Narvik and Britain – longer if a detour was
made to avoid the Luftwaffe flying from Norwegian airfields – was too long and
difficult to hold, and it was decided to evacuate the whole of Norway.

Arethusa was sitting in Scapa between patrols when she was suddenly sent
to Molde to evacuate the British troops there, braving bombing attacks as she
threaded the fjord. 'It was better below in the boiler room or engine room,' Mark
Wells found. 'There were always things to do or keep an eye on, and there was
little time to ponder over what might be happening.' The soldiers climbed on
board. 'It was a sad sight to see the weary faces.'

Five 'Shagbats' (nickname for the Walrus) were embarked in *Glorious*,
which was in the offing. The surviving RAF Gladiator fighters also flew aboard
her, although they had no arrester hooks; but it was decided to abandon the
Hurricanes of No 46 Squadron, RAF, taking it for granted that these fast modern
fighters could not get down safely on a carrier's deck. Their pilots had other

ideas. They proposed at least trying a dart at the deck. They had no deck-landing experience, but enlisted the help of Lieutenant Johnny Ievers and his *Glasgow* Walrus crew. Ievers gave each pilot some elementary deck landing instruction before leading them out to the carrier, their tyres partially deflated to help them stick to the deck. The Walrus then flew round *Glorious*, monitoring each Hurricane as it came in to land. All fifteen fighters landed safely with plenty of deck to spare, but when Ievers himself made to put down he was waved off and told that the carrier was fully loaded, so he diverted to *Ark Royal*, some 30 miles away.

This probably saved his and his crew's lives. With two escorting destroyers *Glorious* was sent south independently of the other returning forces because of her comparatively low fuel endurance. She had five Swordfish embarked (the last of which, pilot Charles Lamb, TAG Doug Hemingway, both of whom survived *Glorious*, was also the last FAA aircraft ever to land aboard her) in addition to her mixed load of fighters; but they had been at full stretch for days and no reconnaissance patrols were ordered by Captain D'Oyly-Hughes. Thus *Scharnhorst* and *Gneisenau* caught *Glorious* unawares, disabled her before she could launch any aircraft, and sank her with ease. One of her brave escorting destroyers, *Acasta*, hit *Scharnhorst* with a torpedo and forced the enemy to return to Trondheim, thus removing what might have been a serious threat to a returning convoy 200 miles to the north-east which had had to sail without battleship escort. On 11 June 38 survivors from *Glorious* and one from *Acasta* were picked up by a Norwegian fishing boat.

Two days later in *Ark Royal* the Skua squadrons got ready to attack *Scharnhorst* and *Gneisenau* in Trondheim harbour, and any other shipping found there. As Eric Monk relates, 'Nine aircraft from 803 Squadron and six from 800 took part, briefed to act as fighter cover. About half way to the anchorage from the coast we were attacked by Me 110s and Al Spurway and I put our theory to the test. We neither of us claimed a victory although I know I hit my 110 still with the 500 lb bomb on the rack, and we were the only ones of 800 Squadron to get back to *Ark*.'

Hostilities Only

I tell you naught for your comfort,
Yea, naught for your desire,
Save that the sky grows darker yet
And the sea rises higher.

When the Luftwaffe failed to destroy RAF Fighter Command, as Goering had promised Hitler, and the Battle of Britain had been won, the war moved into the grim Atlantic and the wide-open coastal waters of the British Isles, with easy targets at sea for the Luftwaffe working from captured French airfields, and Befehlshaber der U-boote's submarines from Brittany and Biscay ports.

GLASGOW AND IMOGEN

When the balloon went up, TAG Norman 'Blondie' Hollis was instructing fledgling Air-Gunners and Air Observers in Morse at Pompey Barracks. 'But in June I went to Lee-on-Solent and before I had time to settle in I was on my way to join 700 Squadron, HMS *Glasgow* Flight, and about to form a relationship with a Walrus, with neither the pilot nor observers very exeeperienced. The cruiser was in dry dock, having suffered from a very near-miss off Norway.'

When *Glasgow* left to rejoin the Fleet she had aboard both her Walruses for the first time since 1939, with the second aircraft and PO Pilot Ron Lunberg and his crew joining shortly after leaving port.

On 19 July *Glasgow*, with three other cruisers and eight destroyers, was closing Scapa in thick fog after a search for enemy minesweepers off the Norwegian coast. She was making a fourth attempt to get into the Flow when, says Lunberg, 'a red light appeared close under her port bow, materializing into the destroyer *Inglefield*, which shot past, missing us by inches. As *Inglefield* disappeared into the fog, another destroyer, *Imogen*, appeared across our bows. Glasgow smashed into her at a combined speed of 34 knots, laying her hull open from bow to forward boiler room and spilling thousands of gallons of blazing oil fuel into the sea'.

As *Glasgow* lost way Captain Hickling ordered the forward magazine flooded to forestall an explosion from the burning oil, while Commander Cuthbert was down in the waist organizing his precious stock of Carley floats into a makeshift pontoon bridge between the ships. In this way 120 officers and men were saved, the casualties totalling some 20 men who had been in the for'ard messdeck. *Glasgow* managed to free herself from the clutching destroyer; violent helm alterations and full astern power finally brought her clear. As she limped away, the destroyer exploded in a column of searing flame as the fire reached the magazines. *Glasgow* limped back into Scapa with a 60 ft gash in her bows some 6 ft above the waterline.

Glasgow returned to dry dock, and her two Walruses were sent to Sullom Voe on the western Scottish coast to join more Walri belonging to damaged ships and a squadron of Short Sunderland flying-boats of RAF Coastal Command. The amphibious Walrus machines suffered the indignity of being moored to a buoy. 'The camp at Sullom Voe', recollects Norman Hollis, 'was a shocker, built on a bog, and though the RAF Squadronaires dance band visited us there, there was absolutely nothing to do. Even beer was in short supply, and when fresh supplies arrived we rarely had the money to buy it. The weather was usually atrocious, and to fly became a pleasure. Our time was spent on anti-submarine patrols on the east side of the Shetlands and these usually ended uncompleted because of the weather. We would usually take a basket of pigeons to be released at the furthest point of our patrol. When the weather was really bad most of the air-gunners would not release them and waited until we were nearly back at base.'

LEND LEASE *LINCOLN*

Iain Nethercott and other survivors of the destroyer *Keith* spent a short time in hospital after Dunkirk and their harrowing experiences there. After recovering, Iain qualified as a seaman torpedoman and returned to Chatham. Here, he complains that he 'slunk into the Barrack Guard and when on duty with my trusty musket guarded the entrance to an underground teleprinter tunnel in the grounds of the C-in-C, The Nore, at the end of his vegetable garden. I rather feel that my job was more ceremonial than functional. I was fully booted and spurred, with tin hat, 100 rounds of ball, 18 in bayonet, water bottle, gas mask, etc, with others to repel any hawkers or canvassers, and to give a butt salute to anyone but the C-in-C, who merited a Present Arms. Just what I was supposed to do if a battalion of German paratroopers were to drop on this complex I don't really know – fire off my 100, then, if still surviving, chuck the C-in-C's spuds at them!

'At this time the Luftwaffe was intermittently bombing Chatham, and a small bomb fell on the stone steps outside Nelson Block and knocked off the one outstretched arm from the giant figurehead of the renowned admiral and flung it across the terrace where it killed a Chief Cook – at least, that's how the buzz went, but there were so many Chief Cooks lurking in Chatham at that time that it would probably have gone unnoticed. Kipling wrote,

> 'And Ye take mine honour from me
> If Ye take away the sea.'

That could be the song of the Barrack Stanchion, only they're always too thick to think of it that way.

'On the Parade Ground at the Gunnery School stood an old World War I tank, "Old Bill", which had seen action, manned by a Naval Brigade crew, at

Arras in Flanders, many years before. In the prevailing panic, the Captain of the Gunnery School had the petrol engines of this relic restored to running order, the guns were overhauled, and eventually, to the cheers of the multitude and amidst clouds of black smoke, the old veteran clanked its way along the terrace and took up a strategic position behind the Main Gate, with its guns pointing up the Dockyard Road.

'Meanwhile, large numbers of matlows were marched down to the football field every day to practise grenade-throwing under the tuition of belted and gaitered GIs. No one had actually seen a real grenade. They were assumed to weigh about seven pounds, so baskets of round stones were provided to simulate live Mills bombs. Long lines of sailors spent many weary hours that summer stepping forward by numbers, removing imaginary safety pins, and flinging imaginary bombs at imaginary Germans. The senior officers in charge of the defence of the barracks always assumed that the Germans would assault from the Main Gate, and all trenches and defence lines were sited on that principle. The panzers would proceed down the Dockyard Road to the Main Gate, which would immediately be closed by the duty RPOs. Should the Gate be breached, our naval tank would then open fire and proceed toward the enemy armour, followed by serried ranks of matlows flinging salvoes of seven-pound bricks. The Master-at-Arms and Regulating Staff would also be in attendance to take the cards of anyone needing a haircut.

'Meanwhile the above-mentioned MAA requested my presence in the Drill Shed together with my bag and hammock, cap box and Ditty Box at 1600 one fine day in October. The draft was given only a Steaming Party number, though everybody knew that we were going across to Yankeeland to pick up some of those ancient destroyers that President Roosevelt was dumping on us in an attempt to get rid of Winston's ever-outstretched hand, and the smell of those terrible cigars.

'When we fell in, what a shock! *About 80 per cent of my crew were HOs*. Now, I had nothing against HOs but I was used to destroyers where everyone knew his job and had years of training behind them. This crowd of poor green little sods had done a few weeks in a holiday camp at Skegness, learned to salute an officer, do a bit of squad drill, wear a naval uniform, and were then sent off to war at sea. Some had never seen a warship in their lives.

'We were given a bag meal to last us 24 hours and marched down to special trains in the dockyard, completely surrounded by military police. The HOs scoffed their meal straight away. I didn't like the look of all this security. We travelled all night and eventually arrived at Liverpool, where the train ran right down to the pierhead. Shorewards stood row upon row of MPs.

'Alongside were a couple of troopers. Ours was *Duchess of Atholl*, a CPR liner of ancient vintage. We were fell in on the jetty, and eventually finished up down in the bowels of the ship.

'We sailed for Halifax that night in a fast convoy with no escort. I spent most of the week playing Crown and Anchor down in the saloon where a CPR steward was making his fortune cleaning out the young RAF sergeants going to Canada to qualify as pilots.

'When we tied up at Halifax and before we were allowed ashore, any English money we had must be changed into Canadian currency, as you could buy genuine English pound notes for about a dollar ashore on the black market. The Germans had captured the BEF bankroll in France, found they couldn't change it through the normal channels, so had to sell it off cheap in the USA and Canada. We were sternly warned that anyone caught with any British currency would be locked up for life.

'We were billeted underneath a grandstand at a racetrack renamed HMS *Stadacona II*. It was bloody cold with no proper heating. Halifax ashore was a dead loss. It was a dry city. However, I took some of the HOs up Barrington Street, where a city cop told us the way to a speakeasy. The whisky there was real rotgut, probably wood alcohol, at a dollar a shot.

'Eventually we were marched down to the harbour as separate crews and saw our future ships for the first time.

'They lay alongside in trots of three, our four-pipers, all with American steaming crews aboard. My first opinion was that they were top-heavy. The four pipe-like funnels (which gave them their US nicknames of "four-pipers" or "four-stackers") gave them an old-fashioned look rather like French destroyers of the First War. The fo'c'sle looked too low and the bow gun would obviously be submerged in heavy weather. The torpedo tubes were mounted in four sets of three at the ships' sides, not centrally as in British ships. As a torpedoman I could envisage the tubes trained outboard. The firing seat would be about twelve feet out beyond the ship's side, and in anything of a sea would be submerged. Still – "Never look a gift-horse in the mouth."'

Thanks to pre-war naval treaties the Royal Navy had begun World War II with 184 destroyers, far too few for its wartime commitments, and after a year of hostilities this total had sunk to 171, as the completion of new ships (21) had not kept pace with the heavy losses (34). Of the 171, many were under repair or in urgent need of it. Seventeen had been seriously damaged in the Norwegian Campaign, sixteen in the Dunkirk operations. The entry of Italy into the war in June 1940 drained off more destroyers into the reconstituted Mediterranean Fleet. Mr Churchill asked President Roosevelt for the speedy loan of warships to defend Allied convoys. On 3 September 1940, first anniversary of the outbreak of war, the first step was taken with an agreement to lend 50 old destroyers to Britain in exchange for 99-year leases on naval and air bases in Newfoundland, Bermuda, the Bahamas, Jamaica, St Lucia, Antigua, Trinidad and British Guiana. The first eight reached Halifax, Nova Scotia, on 6 September 1940 and on the 9th were formally handed over to the Royal Navy. All were renamed after towns, villages or districts in Britain.

These narrow boats, with their straight, flush-decked slope from stem to stern, were not without grace and character. Iain Nethercott's draft to HMS *Lincoln* (ex-USS *Yarnall*) spent about three days going aboard daily and working with the American ratings to get acquainted with all the unfamiliar gear: 'I think most of them were shocked at the quality of our seamen, most of whom were undersized, dirty, ill-equipped and completely ignorant of the working of a destroyer.

'The Americans had stocked up the ships' stores with the finest of tinned foods, things not normally seen on British destroyers with their good old diet of Pusser's peas, Straight Rush, Oosh and Potmess. Now we saw giant cans of tomato juice and grapefruit juice, tinned lobster and crawfish and a big fridge full of steaks. Not for the Yankee "gobs" the old beef screen on the Iron Deck, with Tanky hacking away at that long-dead camel. They never tasted the delights of herrings in Ally Sloper's Sauce, and the secrets of the Naval Sausage Mk1, the constitutents of which had been passed from one Chief Cook in Jago's Mansions to another down the centuries.'

The destroyers were old, but alleged to have been refitted. They had been scrupulously cleaned and, with typical American generosity, fully stored. There were full outfits of ammunition – shells, torpedoes, depth-charges; high-powered binoculars for officers and lookouts; sextants, chronometers, parallel rulers and dividers for navigation; ample stocks of paint and cordage; a typewriter, paper, envelopes, pencil sharpeners, pencils and ink in each ship's office; messtraps of silver and good new china. Store-rooms were fully stocked with provisions, including spiced tinned ham, tinned sausages and corn.

'However, all the wonderful scran was not for us matlows. As soon as the Yanks had lowered the Stars and Stripes and marched away, the special new food was removed, some to the wardroom, and normal RN rations stowed on board.

'We had a young Active Service First Lieutenant who was a good, sensible chap, but with the exception of the Engineer Lieutenant all the other officers were RNVR, who although dead-keen, were as green as grass, needing a good skipper to help and encourage them.

'I had been made a killick although I was only 19. As a torpedoman I was more interested in the depth-charges than the torpedoes, as we were unlikely ever to use them against the *Bismarck* – which God forbid. Whenever we dropped depth-charges set shallow, the contact breakers flew off, and the ship was plunged into darkness. In the end we jammed them on with wooden wedges.

'The Canadian Red Cross had sent crates of comforts to the ships, and we each became the proud owners of Canadian lumberjackets in various tartans, and flat leather caps with ear flaps. The Skipper came aboard one morning and found his ship manned by a multi-coloured apparently civilian crew. Poor old Jimmy! He took the rub for that. We were told that the jackets could only be worn at sea during the night watches. The caps were collected and sent back. Back to our thin No 3s for the Canadian Winter.'

The handful of regulars found the ship strange to get used to. The whole design, layout and internal arrangements were different from British. The Captain and officers had their wardroom and cabins in the fore part of the ship, beneath the bridge, instead of aft. The seamen lived on a large messdeck under the officers' quarters, and the stokers right aft. The messdecks were fitted with two- or three-tiered bunks.

Eventually *Lincoln*, with *Ludlow* and *Leamington*, sailed for St John's, Newfoundland.

'Once clear of the land we found that the ship would roll on damp grass. When I did my first trick on the wheel (there were initially only about six of us Active Service ratings who could take the wheel), I discovered she was a cow to steer with any sort of sea on the bow. She would drift off in a flash, and carried a permanent 5° of port wheel.

'Once she started to really roll, my poor little HO Jack-my-Hearties collapsed in heaps down below, most of them too seasick to go on watch. Jimmy tried to keep some sort of order, but as the weather got worse, so the ship's routine gradually fell apart.

'Our messdeck in the fo'c'sle was under the wardroom, we were practically at water level with two steep ladders leading to the welldeck abaft the bridge. The scuttles and deadlights were screwed down as far as possible, but during twenty years on reserve all the rubber rings on the portholes had perished, and they were some of the things that the Yanks had *not* refitted. As we were on the waterline, as she rolled and pitched, every scuttle squirted great jets of salt water, right alongside the bunks. And the screw-down covers in our messdecks which covered some fuel tanks started to leak, so the deck was swimming in fuel oil and about a foot of seawater raging around.

'As more and more of our lads crawled into their bunks and couldn't do any watches, we lashed them in so that they just rolled within their bunks and spewed into the raging torrent on the deck. For the rest of us there was no food, as the cook was prostrate and the galley was flooded, but some of the stokers managed to get the oiled-fired galley stove going, so we had some hot kye.

'I honestly thought the ship would turn over. One roll was 57° and she kept laying over and was very slow to come back.

'There were only a few of us steering, and the POs helped out. The bridge and wheelhouse were all in one, with glass windows. The steering wheel was about three feet in diameter and needed two men to hold it, as the wheel movements were transferred to the steering engine in the tiller flat by means of wires running the full length of the upper deck. On the wheel it was impossible to steer within 20° of our course, and time and time again the quartermasters were flung off the wheel, with the ship nearly broaching to.

'The Captain got the wind up as one crisis after another hit us. All sorts of minor things were going wrong. One wave took the motor boat away and wrecked the davits. One engine had to be stopped as the bearings overheated when the stern kept lifting out of the water. The engine room hatches were stoved in in places, and the ship was making water.

'None of these things was too critical, but as one calamity after the other was reported to the Captain he gradually fell apart. In the end he went to his cabin with serious stomach pains, and Jimmy took over. We kept plugging away and eventually crept into St John's. I was starving, having lived on corned beef and kye for days. Being killick of the mess, I booted my prostrate sailors out of their bunks, we bailed out, and I made them scrub the mess till it shone. They thought I was a right bastard but I was determined that they should become real sailors and start pulling their weight. From then on aboard that ship we gradually moulded those lads, *Ganges*-fashion, into real seamen.

'The Skipper, coming alongside at Guz, had a flaming row with the Engineer Officer on the bridge, and the next day disappeared from the ship, never to be seen again. We got a new two-ring Skipper appointed, and I knew him from the past as he had been Jimmy on the *Hasty*, and ran a very tight ship.

'These lads of ours were a real mixed bunch, mostly from the Midlands. I was the youngest in the mess and in charge of them. It didn't worry me as I was six feet tall and weighed fifteen stone, and in those days I could sort out any man. I had a solicitor and a schoolmaster in the mess, also a burglar from Darlington, but as the months went by they all learned how to put the dinner up to the galley and how to put Babies' Heads in the potmess; in fact they became real destroyer matlows. I and the other killicks used to teach them wire splicing and fancy ropework in the dog watches, and in harbour at Londonderry we used to take them away in the whalers and teach them to sail. Some of them became CW candidates and eventually officers.'

For the next three years ships of the 50 'four-pipers' of the RN saw service with some of the most heavily attacked convoys. For a time *Lincoln* saw nothing much but monotonous trudging to and fro across the North Atlantic. Iain Nethercott began to feel restless. 'I was getting more and more fed up with convoy work – jogging along as flank escort on a 7-knot convoy was bloody boring. My first destroyer in the war had been the old *Keith*, which had been in very hot action off Holland, in the battle of Boulogne, and finally carrying the Admiral at Dunkirk, when we were sunk. I wanted to get back into the action, so I went and volunteered for submarines. Christ, you'd think I was bloody all for it, wouldn't you?'

On 6 April 1941 HMS *Lincoln* made one of the most dramatic and brilliantly executed rescues of the war when she took off 121 men in heavy weather from the Armed Merchant Cruiser HMS *Cormorin*, which had caught fire.

FOUR-FUNNELLED *SHERWOOD*

Fred Lee from Bradford had what he saw as a narrow escape from the 'four-pipers'. When war began he was a junior in hospital administration, and a member of the Sea Cadet Corps, very well read on seamanship, and fascinated by his father Tancy Lee's stories of the Navy in the Great War. His other heroes were a big ex-Commissioned Gunner they had in the Sea Cadets 'with a voice like the sound of the guns, six-foot odd, with a black cane with a silver handle, and he was *God*', and there was Tosh Nichol, retired Chief Gunner's Mate, 'an all-rounder, a *real* sailor, sixty-seven or -eight, he'd put the gloves on and take anyone on, five-foot-seven, built like an ox', and veteran Spike Sullivan 'who could take a 3-inch manila and splice it without a marlin spike'.

Even with this background Lee was twice almost sent into the Army, but finally made it to HMS *Raleigh*, a training camp at Tor Point, Plymouth, so new that Fred's draft helped to build it, wheeling cartloads of bricks, window frames and doors about. But there was Scrumpy and doughnuts and tiddie oggies in the canteen. Someone pointed to one of the matlows, 'Know who that is? That's Robert Newton – the actor!' 'Never heard of him,' said Fred.

Then their training began. Their Petty Officer instructor was a typical old Guz rating. 'This is 'ow yer doos it,' was his favourite expression. Fred waited impatiently for the end of the course, and a draft to something glamorous at sea.

He endured the 'Wakey, wakey, rise and shine' ('even when it was pouring down with bloody rain'), Chiefie Fenton ('like a screaming harlot up and down the Parade Ground'), the preponderance of ex-policemen in the mess ('I think they were the bane of the Service, the coppers, they had an attitude, oh, I don't know, of . . . law enforcement, I don't know what you'd call it, like the screws in the prisons . . . If you don't trust a copper outside you won't trust him inside, will you?'), though there was 'a real variety of types, teachers, bus drivers, dockyard mateys, and one bloke played for Everton . . .

'There were no real problems where food was concerned. I hated porridge, all my life I hated porridge, till I went to *Raleigh*, and then when it came round every morning I suppose . . . the cold weather, and the time of day – 7 o'clock in the morning, in the nice steaming galley and the dining hall . . . everybody ate the porridge and there was the usual stiff sausage and the solid fried eggs and screwed-up bacon – like concrete, some of it, but it was all eaten! The only problem was the 2/6d a day, not worth a lot even in those days, 15/- a week pay from a job at £2 a week – and you were supposed to make an allotment out of that . . . and there was the shelters, you couldn't sleep in the shelters for the bloody Welsh, they were always singing, and always "She'll Be Coming Round the Mountain" or "Cwm Rhondda". And ashore, in the cinema it might be flashed up on the screen for blokes to return to their ship – in the middle of a film! And outside you'd see all the ships, well, not the ships themselves, but those blue masthead lights all going down the river, in the dark . . . The seamanship, that was either boring or fascinating. For me it was fascinating, I couldn't get enough of it to fill my appetite . . .'

After the course Fred chose HMS *Pembroke*, Chatham Barracks, as his depot. On his first night there he slept, or tried to sleep, in the infamous Tunnel, supposedly an air-raid shelter but actually holding an overflow of 35,000 men every night, 'stinking and snoring'. Then he was summoned to the Drafting Office:

'You've got a draft.'
'What to?'
'HMS *Sherwood*.'
'What is it?'
'It's a destroyer.'

(I thought *great, this is it, a couple of months in the Navy and I'm off to a destroyer already!*)
'Where is it?'
'It's at Portsmouth. You'll be there tomorrow.'

'And we went to Portsmouth, and the bombs were falling all round the Guildhall and everywhere else that night and we slept in the Barracks. The next morning we went round to HMS *Sherwood*, and to my horror it was one of those four-funnellers that Churchill had scrounged from the Yanks. And I was ready that day to give it back to the Yanks. I wandered about, and instead of having the binnacle and the wheel, and the telegraph, it was . . . it resembled one of our trams that used to run around Bradford. Levers – Half-Back 2, Back 2, Forward 3 . . . oh I thought *God, I don't want this*, and then I went up around the guns, *and they were painted solid*, they were *thick* in paint, absolutely useless, they had to be cleaned, I knew that as soon as I looked at 'em, and I felt, well, this is not Fred's cup of tea, it's time to be moving . . . And, miracles of miracles, the First Lieutenant of the *Sherwood* said, "We've had too big a draft. We only wanted 11, and they've sent us 22".

'So I stepped forward in the front rank ready to go back to Chatham. I'd rather have the bombs than go to sea in the *Sherwood*.

'Eventually I went to the *Glasgow* as a foretopman. The meals in the *Glasgow* were superb, no complaints about the food in the *Glasgow*. We had fresh bread, we had a bakehouse, there was a bakehouse in the waist. We had rolls, could never get enough rolls, and the eggs were fried a bit better than in Chatham Barracks. You could always go and get a glass of lime juice, it was free . . . Another thing about the *Glasgow* was the cinema, we had plenty of films, and the favourite films were Popeye or Donald Duck, and it's amazing to think that all those grown men, on the brink of death, could turn to things like Popeye and Donald Duck . . .'

Geoff Shaw was called up during the school holidays in December 1940, having already volunteered for the Navy.

'I had all the usual schoolboy interests as a child – cars, locos, aircraft, but mainly ships, and warships were my favourites. In 1939 we managed to fit in a day's visit to Portsmouth – it was wonderful to see all those grey ships.

'When it came to choosing a career I wanted to go in for architecture, but I couldn't face two more years at school for Higher School Certificate and University, and my parents were too hard up for an apprenticeship, and when the time came when I had to make a definite decision, with the country at war, I thought of those salty ships and a life in the open air, and I volunteered for the Andrew. I was 15.

'I was judged intelligent enough to be a signalman, a "bunting-tosser", and when I actually got a draft to a ship called *Adventure* I was excited. HMS *Adventure* turned out to be, not a dashing destroyer, but an old cruiser/minelayer, built in 1924. The accent was on the mines. Money had been saved on the armament (four 4.7 in AA guns) to carry 320 of them, and the main deck looked like a train ferry's, clear down each side save for the rails on which the mines ran to the two dropping ports aft.

'As a bunting I much preferred being outdoors to being cooped up down below as others were. Felt a damn sight safer, anyway – if that torpedo did hit us we always felt that we stood a better chance of survival. And it was so much more interesting to be there in the centre of things, to see everything that was going on, to be up to date as to what was going to happen and often to be amongst the first to know it. Being a small branch there was always more chumminess, and we mixed with the officers to a greater extent than did other ratings except perhaps stewards. We got to know them and they got to know us. Our Captain at one time was R. G. Bowes-Lyon, the Queen's cousin and a true gentleman. On the bridge he was just as likely to make some casual remark to me about nothing special – a lowly bunting – as to one of the officers.

'This business of being outdoors was lovely in fine weather – the thrill of being up there on the bridge or the flag deck of a ship at speed and to watch the bow waves slipping past, to see the first sight of that mast bobbing about miles away on the horizon (and hoping that it was friendly), to watch the other ships in company heaving all over the place.

'But in bad weather it wasn't quite so nice – a wild gale, rain belting down, spray blowing right back over the bridge, with you standing there soaking wet for four hours, ice floes in sight to port and bitterly cold (and the Chief Yeoman would never let us wear gloves on the flag deck on the grounds that it would impede our hoisting of flags). Always tired, aching with the effort to stand upright *and* keep a good lookout and no chance to sit down to rest weary bones – then off watch and below, only to find the messdeck with three inches of dirty seawater swilling about.

'And conditions could sometimes be unpleasant even in good weather. I once spent the whole afternoon watch on the bridge of a destroyer doing 20 knots with a wind coming from dead astern at a speed of about 20¼. The top of the funnel was exactly level with the bridge and we spent four hours breathing in the noxious fumes that came from the boilers and clung about us all the time, coughing and spluttering . . . and being up there on the bridge in thick fog, so thick that you couldn't see "A" gun or the water. You seemed to be floating along in nothingness.

'And doing cable flags – a difficult task, standing right there in the eyes of the ship as we weighed or anchored and indicating by hand flags the number of shackles of cable outboard, whether the anchor was up and down or aweigh – especially worrisome when anchoring, with the chain rushing out like a dangerous, demented snake . . .

'Always watchkeeping, unlike most others who (Quartermasters apart) could look forward to a full night's sleep when in harbour. Even when in dry dock we were on telephone watch.

'At sea – the need for eternal vigilance and smartness in order to see things before anyone else, and to answer or repeat the flagship's signals almost before she had hoisted them. In fact a bunting's life at sea was divided into two sharply different ways. When the ship was sailing independently there was little to do other than act as extra lookouts and report the occasional signals that came by W/T. But when sailing with the squadron it was a different thing entirely and things could be very hectic with flag-hoisting, and signalling by light, and the need to be always alert – always someone keeping an eye on the flagship and others watching the other ships. Buntings may have been a bit superfluous when sailing independently, but when in company with other ships there were often occasions when there didn't seem to be enough of us.

'In company with other ships and at night this non-stop vigilance became even more important. When in more dangerous waters we always used a "heather" light for signalling – a small cylindrical thing about four inches long and an inch in diameter which clipped on top of your binoculars and thus pointed in the same direction as did the binoculars. It gave a very faint blue light, and was operated by a little trigger which was pressed up and down. The trouble was that the light was too faint to be seen by the naked eye when another ship was transmitting, so there *always* had to be someone staring at the flagship through binoculars just in case she should send an urgent manoeuvring signal (this, by the way, being in pre-R/T days). It was a considerable strain, and whoever was keeping lookout had to be relieved quite frequently.

'We operated with the squadron (a minelaying squadron) for some months and became very efficient at flag signalling, getting to know almost when to expect signals and knowing all the routine flag signals and special communication instructions off by heart.

'We were then detached from the squadron and given different duties which entailed us always sailing independently for several more months with very little work for the buntings to do. Perhaps this resulted in a little rustiness developing with regards to flag signalling, perhaps it lulled us into a state of euphoria.

'Then one day, horror of horrors, we were ordered to sea with a fleet – Force H, no less, which at that time consisted of *Nelson*, *Rodney* and *Formidable*. And up on the bridge of the *Nelson* was a Very Important Admiral, and on its flagdeck was a Very Important Signal Bosun. Not only that but we had to sail as leading ship of the destroyer screen – though what use a rickety old minelayer who shook herself to pieces at 26 knots was as a destroyer I don't know.

'Great panic at once ensued. After all those independently routed trips with little for us to do we realized that we would suddenly have to justify those crossed flags on our arms, especially as one of our duties entailed repeating the flagship's signals for the benefit of the other eight destroyers in the screen. Everyone started frantically swotting up in the hours before sailing. Never had so many buntings been seen so assiduously studying so many signal books as then. And even then we had no knowledge of any of the local orders or peculiarities of signalling routine that ships which regularly operated together were apt to use. One slip-up and, great shame, the *Nelson* would have our pendants at the dip quicker than that. So we all sailed with crossed fingers. Luckily all went off all right and we eventually arrived at Gib without having made one silly mistake.

'Pendants at the dip – a reprimand, a mark of shame, a public telling-off. If a ship slipped up in its signalling procedure, then one of the other ships, usually the flagship, would display that ship's pendants hoisted at the dip and in conjunction with no other flags. Thus everyone on the bridge of every ship in the fleet knew at once that HMS So-and-so had made a bloomer. It was the ultimate in public degradation.

'One thing to be avoided was losing your halliards – usually caused by a combination of keenness and carelessness when the chappie whose job it was to hoist the flags did so rather too quickly and before the others had had time to clip on all the flags. The flag signal would then go up, perhaps incomplete, but always not clipped on to the halliard at its bottom end. There was thus no means of hauling it down again afterwards – and the hauling down of a flag signal was its executive signal. One day the flagship, *Southern Prince*, did this and was left with a long stream of flags, attached to the halliards at the head (the top) but not the tack (the bottom), blowing out horizontally astern. We all had a good laugh and considered hoisting her pendants at the dip but refrained from doing so in case the admiral was offended. On board the flagship they tried desperately to recover the flags, allowing them to blow out farther and farther astern by easing the halliards – but the wind was so strong that they would *not* drop to the deck and they just stayed up there, trailing horizontally, till they were way out over the funnel. How they managed to get them down in the end I can't remember. Perhaps some poor bloke had to go aloft.'

ROUGH-RIDING *ROXBOROUGH*

No incident in the grim Battle of the Atlantic surpassed what happened to HMS *Roxborough* (ex-USS *Foote*) during the night of 14/15 January 1943, when she was about 300 miles south of Cape Farewell, Greenland. There she met some of the worst Atlantic weather within living memory. A huge sea ripped open the bridge, crushing the Captain's cabin on the upper deck level under the bridge, and killing the Captain, Lieutenant-Commander A. C. Price. Ten others were also trapped in the upper bridge, all injured and caught in the mass of twisted steel, with seas still breaking over them; among them was the First Lieutenant, Lieutenant G. Osborne, RNVR.

Twenty-three-year-old Lieutenant G. M. Greenwood, RCNVR, the senior surviving able-bodied officer, stumbled from his bunk through ankle-deep water in the wardroom to the upper deck to find the ship completely out of control and smashing into the heavy seas. He took command, got her into secondary steering, turned her round away from the pounding seas to give the rescue party on the bridge a chance to work, and headed for Newfoundland.

The ship's doctor, Surgeon Lieutenant James Watt, RNVR, worked for seventeen hours under nightmare conditions in an emergency operating theatre in the stokers' mess, under lights rigged by torpedomen, and with his instruments in canned goods cartons screwed down to the table. Steadied by an assistant against the violent roll of the ship, he performed nine emergency operations, set compound fractures, and worked on shock cases. The First Lieutenant died on the operating table, but all the other injured men recovered.

'. . . BOILER GO BANG. . .'

It is a wonder that some of the smaller vessels could survive at all in those raging seas. The corvettes were the most roughly handled of the escorts. 'Have just seen down your funnel' signalled one of these little ships to another, 'Fire is burning brightly'. When another corvette, damaged in a gale, left the convoy to return to repairs, Senior Officer, Escort, signalled 'Hope you find necessary facilities in Belfast.' The battered corvette replied 'Hope I find Belfast.' When she finally made base she signalled 'Am tied up to No. 5 Berth,' to receive the stinging reply 'Shoe laces are tied up, HM ships are secured.' In another hard blow one old V-and-W destroyer made to another, lying dismasted, 'How come?' The hulk replied 'Scraping under very low cloud.' Minesweepers HMS *Prompt* and HMS *Jason*, which were completed, launched and commissioned on the same day, and attached to the same group, were always competitors. As *Prompt* settled in the water, decks awash, after hitting an acoustic mine, she signalled to her rival 'First again.'

As the war went on, Allied escorts joined the Battle of the Atlantic, to their cost. 'Can go no more,' signalled a Free French destroyer, 'Boiler go bang'. A fellow national in a Sea Hurricane radioed: 'Engine no good. I jump.' A US destroyer, unused to the British signal code, hoisted the Church pennant next to the Interrogative flag. When questioned as to the meaning, she signalled 'God, where am I?'

Convoy in 'E-boat Alley'

Oh I wonder, yes I wonder –
Did the Jaunty make a blunder
When he sent this draft chit round for me?

Song of the Barrack Stanchion

Battling against U-boats and the Luftwaffe were the forgotten small ships of the
East Coast convoys in 'E-boat Alley'. This was in one way a harder fight, as the
screaming Stukas could find them easily from their southern Norwegian, Danish
and home airfields.

ATTACK FROM ALL QUARTERS

Dennis Bond of Godalming, Surrey, had served an apprenticeship as a wireman
with the then Mid-Southern Utility Company (now the South-Eastern Electricity
Board), and played in the Godalming Borough Brass Band – until he was called
up in October 1940. He chose the Navy as most of his friends had gone into the
RN. One was a Royal Marine bandsman lost in *Hood*; another former sounding-
brass man was lost with the destroyer *Greyhound*.

He trained at a holiday camp on Hayling Island, Hampshire, and at *St
Vincent* at Gosport for electrical brushing-up before beginning a busman's holiday
as a wireman, RN – wishing he were blowing a bright brass horn in the Marine
Band which played every Sunday morning at Divisions. They were set a 'trade
test' which consisted of wiping a lead joint on two pieces of lead pipe – plumber's
work. But someone found a load of finished tests in a dump, and they all passed,
and before he knew it he was on draft to a ship called HMS *Whitshed* which,
initially, as no one seemed to know anything about her, he thought must be
another stone frigate. Then an elderly Chief told him that she was an old
V-and-W destroyer, but where she was and what she was doing he did not know.
He had not heard of the old ship's bravura dash into Boulogne harbour to support
Iain Nethercott's old and bold *Keith*, when she had exchanged salvoes with
panzers, point-blank.

The Drafting Office sent Dennis to Parkeston Quay, Harwich, where he
was told to report to HMS *Badger*, an old hulk used for accommodation
purposes. He reported to the regulating PO there, and was told that *Whitshed* was
out on E-boat patrol. He took shore leave in the town that evening and 'met some

of the other lads on the patrol who soon filled me in on the life, which looked anything but rosy, and the prospects of survival, which seemed poor!' About three o'clock the next afternoon he was told that the motor boat from *Whitshed* was alongside the quay waiting for him.

'After a rather choppy trip across the harbour we came alongside the *Whitshed*, and this didn't look at all like the recruiting posters of ships of the Royal Navy – dull grey, streaks of rust, dabs of red lead in places. As all electrical work in the RN came under the torpedo branch, I reported to the Chief Torpedo Gunner's Mate, a time-expired friendly man, who took me along to my messdeck, where I met a strange mixture of ratings – a PO cook, leading torpedo operator, PO Jack Dusty, leading supply assistant, leading seaman and two seaman torpedomen. There was a strange smell – damp clothes, food, fuel oil, hair cream. But they turned out to be a great bunch of lads who went out of their way to make me feel one of them. I had no trouble sleeping that night, although the hammocks were slung so close together that when the ship moved at her moorings we all swayed together.

'In the morning it was the familiar "Wakey, wakey, lash up and stow!" Washing was six basins for 150 men, a major operation, and some washed in a bucket on deck, but I was pleased to learn that for this kind of inconvenience we got 1/- a day "hard-lying money".

'After dinner the Tannoy blared: "The ship is under sailing orders. Last mail will go ashore at 1700 hours. Special sea dutymen to their stations 1830." The Chief came down and told me my duties – Depth Charge Party at Cruising Stations, which meant being on the stern and, if required, to set the depth-charges with the special key and do any electrical work necessary; meanwhile, action station on the bridge, telephone to all guns' crews and lookouts, and man the tubes if torpedo action was called for.

'Exactly at 1830 the call came: "Close all X and Y openings. Close all deadlights and scuttles. Special sea dutymen to your stations for leaving harbour." All other hands fell in in Navy blues lined up aft as we passed the other ships.

'The water got choppier. We were very near the boom defence and the open sea. (How will I react if we hit trouble? Will I do what I was trained to do, or will I just panic?) Then the guns' crews were testing the gun-firing circuits, firing blanks. I had to go and check all the navigation lights, which took my mind offf things. I rushed to the bridge. "Manning the phones, sir!" I checked on the position of the alarm rattler, which was also in my charge.

'Behind us, reassuringly, steamed two other escorts. When we sighted the convoy they were covered in a smokey haze, and looked funny with barrage balloons over them. The signalman took a message by Aldis lamp from the senior escort. He replied, the lamp clacked away, the vent fans roared, the ship creaked, the sea hissed. We were ordered to take up the rear position, which nobody likes. We ran down the side of the convoy, looking up at the tall sides of the ships. They seemed to want to crush us. We made a wide sweep into position, then began the monotony of holding our speed down to that of the slow merchant ships – up and down, up and down, just the clacking of the signal lamp now and again broke the monotony.

'One of the lads appeared, "Kye's up!" Hot Navy chocolate and corned dog sandwiches. A banquet!

'The sea was rising, we were doing the corkscrew antic so common to the old V-and-Ws.

'Suddenly the whole scene was lit up, like day.

'The port lookout shouted, "Escort firing starshell to port!"

'The OOW shouted at me, "Action stations!" I shouted it into the phone, pressed the alarm rattler and heard the distant ringing below. The whole ship erupted as men rushed to their action stations. Then came the calls in my phone. "A Gun closed up, cleared away . . . B Gun closed, cleared way, X Gun . . ." I heard the clang of shells being slammed into breeches . . . A Gun ready . . . B Gun ready . . . 12-pounder AA Guns ready . . . pom-pom ready . . .

'The Captain shouted to me "Escort leader has sighted E-boats! Tell all lookouts to be alert!" I thought – *This is not real . . . What am I doing here? I'm just an electrician, working for the Mid-Southern Utility . . .*

'Then the orders for me to pass to the guns' crews came thick and fast, I didn't have time to think about me . . .

'A lookout shouted "E-boats astern!"

'"Hard-a-port!" from the Skipper . . .

'The whole ship heeled over, I slithered across the bridge, the pencils and protractors fell off the chart table, from below came the sound of breaking. "There go our crocks," said the signalman.

'A new noise joined the rest – the ping, ping-pinging of the Asdics.

'"A and Y Guns load with starshell!" I repeated it.

'"A and Y Guns stand by!" "Guns" fingered the Gun Fire bell.

'"A and Y Guns FIRE!"

'Whoosh . . . It sounded like an express going through a station. The whole area lit up again.

'"All guns load with HE!"

'I repeated it and realized that I was not really frightened because everyone else seemed so cool and calm and some of it must have rubbed off on me.

'"E-boat bearing Red five-o!"

'"Independent fire when each gun bears!"

'The salvo rattled the bridge, the ship recoiled as if kicked. We could see the E-boat like a small white line. All the escorts were having a go. The noise was terrific. Tracers were everywhere, red, green, like fireworks.

'"Check, check, check" to the gun crews. The E-boat had turned away.

'Things returned to normal. I took stock of myself. I was keyed up, my heart was beating fast, yes, *but I hadn't panicked.* The main thing was how everyone worked together. Believe me, this does have a calming influence.

'It was 3.30 in the morning by then. I was not allowed below to my mess, because of the danger of mines, so I wandered into the seamen's mess and scrounged a cup of kye and a sandwich. Now – where to sleep? I found a small gap between the torpedo tubes and the engine room exhaust fan, pulled my duffle coat round me, my oilskin on top of me and tried to sleep. But I just lay there looking at the stars, watching the masthead going from side to side.

'The watch changed again. I climbed the ladders to the bridge again. It was peaceful, I looked at the lines of ships as we jogged along. The sky was empty save for a few clouds.

'But above was the Stuka's eerie cry. Like Tennyson's *Eagle* –

> Ring'd with the azure world, he stands.
> The wrinkled sea beneath him crawls;
> He watches from his mountain walls,
> And like a thunderbolt he falls.

'"Aircraft bearing dead ahead!". . . . The dull thumps of explosions . . . The pom-pom really does go *pom-pom-pom*. Planes were coming down either flank of the convoy. Now they were at masthead height and everyone was having a go at them. They were after the biggest merchantman and were too close for comfort. The E-boats were not too bad, but planes are the worst . . . they were coming straight for us! They were firing at us!

'"Heads down, lads", said the Skipper calmly. The plane zoomed over us, his bomb fell, and missed . . . We had put him off his aim!

'The action, short and sharp, was over. That was *really* frightening. One of the ships had been hit, but no casualties. "We got off lucky", said the signalman.

'We delivered the ships, stayed one night at Immingham and were to take another convoy back the next day.

'After a good night's sleep we were ready, but the Germans had dropped mines in the estuary so we had to wait till the sweepers had cleared a channel.

'Things looked a lot more peaceful. I was off-watch, and the weather was so lovely that I went to the quarterdeck and lay down in the sun. We were in the outer lane, going south, which meant even more vigilance was needed. I passed a pleasant afternoon on the phones. Everyone was dreading the night, but after dusk action stations, when most aircraft attacks occurred, all passed quietly. I took two hours off watch to get my tea. It was about eight o'clock and very difficult light when the sea and sky all looks one, and every gull looks like a plane. But all seemed quiet. At ten round came the kye and sandwiches. All was well with the world.

'"Ship on fire starboard side!"

'"Northbound convoy under attack!" They were passing inside us, and we didn't know where the attack was coming from.

'"Echo bearing starboard one hundred and closing . . ." The Asdic had a contact . . . U-boat?

'"Depth Charge Party close up!" *That was me!*

'My relief appeared and grabbed the phone. I scrambled aft, heart thumping, to the throwers, where the Chief TI was waiting. He gave me the key. "Shallow settings."

'The pin-ping-ping-ping was getting louder . . . The target was closing.

'*Whitshed* had formed the established pattern with the two other escorts – one ahead, one to port of us. Somewhere in between the U-boat.

'The Torpedo Officer fingered the DC firing button.

'"Fire charges!"

'I removed the pin and two charges rolled down the rails over the stern while two were shot from the throwers to either hand. The sea boiled and there came the most horrific explosion; the sea cascaded into the air, the ship shook, the funnel rattled, showers of soot fell, deck plates in the engine room were lifted by the blast. Then the sea subsided and the Asdic reported a lost contact. Whether we got the U-boat or not we never knew, but it did not bother us again that trip, and we did have a lovely fry-up that night with all the dead and stunned fish floating on the surface.'

TAKING ON *SCHARNHORST*

After his safe return to Harwich Dennis went ashore straight to the Salvation Army hostel and booked a bed for the night. There he had a nice hot bath, went to the pictures and then back to the 'Sally A' to sleep.

'I didn't get much sleep though as there was an air raid, and I missed the cool, calm faces of the gunners, the nonchalant but precise way the officers controlled the situation, and wished I was back aboard the old *Whitshed*. When I got back in the morning, the smell in the messdeck was cosy and familiar. I was home.'This pattern of life went on, five days out, three days in, unless the E-boats were pretty active and we had to leave in a hurry.

'One day came the order: "Change all torpedoes and re-ammunition with armour-piercing shells!"

'Something big was in the wind. We couldn't find out what, but were kept busy all through the night, taking out the old torpedoes, replacing them with new, filling them up with oil and water, like you'd service a car for a long journey . . .

'Then came the order: "Ships will prepare for sea immediately."

'All the preparations started for leaving harbour. Once through the boom the speakers came to life:

'"This is the Captain speaking. You will all no doubt be wondering why all the preparations over the last few hours have taken place. Well, now I will tell you. We have been informed that a large German surface force comprising *Scharnhorst*, *Gneisenau* and *Prinz Eugen*, plus a destroyer escort and also aircraft cover, has broken out from Brest and is making its way up the English Channel, so we and the other five destroyers you see with us will attempt to stop them. The task will be difficult, because of the large air escort, but I know that you will all do your best. Good luck to you all."

'"And good-bye," said someone. "It was nice knowing you." "Bloody sauce!" said the LTO. "Up the bloody Channel! What do they think we are – f★★★★★g stamps?" There was a lot of muttering from the lads. Everyone was thinking: Well, this is it, what we never thought would really happen – a torpedo attack . . . against the bloody *Scharnhorst* and *Gneisenau* . . . I couldn't take it in. Then I looked at all the lovely countryside we were passing on our way out of the estuary . . . Will I be seeing this again? I really never noticed it before. I was really nervous then. After all, we *were* a very old ship.

'"Man the torpedo tubes." We were told to strap ourselves to the tubes, with the lashings provided. I thought this was to stop us from deserting the tubes, but I found out the real reason later.

'We did several exercises to see how fast we could turn the tubes from port to starboard, and as they had to be turned by hand it was quite exhausting. We plodded on. Our radar picked up heavy vessels ahead plus aircraft.

'To cap it all, down came the fog, the sort you sometimes get at sea – one minute clear, the next in a fog bank, so we now relied on our radar a lot. We carried on. Suddenly the mist lifted and I saw them, and my heart stopped. They looked like the Houses of Parliament. Then they started firing their 11 in guns against our 4 in.

'"Prepare for torpedo attack. Train to starboard." It was hard labour trying to turn the tubes with the ship heeling right over and going at full speed. The racing water came up to my knees, and now I knew what the lashings were for. Without them we would have been washed away.

'"Stand by to fire tubes . . . *Fire one . . . Fire two . . . Fire three.*"

'"All torpedoes running, sir."

'All this time shells were falling round us. We saw the poor old Swordfish planes getting shot out of the sky. They were no match for Messerschmitts, but still they carried on.

'After firing all our fish the inclination was to turn away, but that was an open invitation to get blasted to pieces. Then fortune smiled on us. Down came the mist again. We turned away. I thought, with a bit of luck they'll be busy with the other destroyers.

'Then as if in rebuke of my unworthy thoughts, down came the Stukas through the thinning mist. They really were something, screaming down with that awful siren they had, wailing . . . It made my hair stand on end.

'The Skipper was laying right back on the bridge with his binoculars to his eyes and as a plane came screaming down and the bomb left its belly he ordered sharply "Hard-a-port!" or "Hard-a-starboard!" and the bomb near-missed us alongside. This happened several times, until at long last we were clear, though *Worcester* did get hit, and there were casualties, and one of the other old warriors broke down. None of us hit the Germans, which we blamed on the mist, and they got clear away.

'After this the convoy plod went on much as before, until one day in March 1942. We were escorting a convoy and as usual were the tail-end Charlie. I had just come off watch and was sitting supping a cup of tea when there was an almighty Bang, the ship went right over on her side and out went all the lights. I came out of the upper messdeck and found that I was going uphill. I saw the Torpedo Officer. He said, "We've hit a mine. Go into the engine room and try to put on the electrical circuit-breakers – they've jumped off – and we must have them to keep the guns firing."

'The prospect of going down below in a listing ship didn't appeal to me at all. When I got below it was chaos. One generator was useless. The Chief Stoker said he could keep one running, but as this meant that the switchboard couldn't handle the load, we had to turn off all electrical circuits except the gun-firing circuits. This we did, and I wedged up the circuit-breaker to make sure it didn't drop off when we needed to fire the guns, as we were now a sitting target for aircraft. The mine had gone off under the stern, which meant that the depth-charges had to be made safe and all the primers removed. The compartment where the spare charges were stored was now under a lot of fuel oil where one of the fuel tanks had ruptured.

'We were then informed that a tug with an escort was coming to tow us to the dockyard at Chatham, and so began a long wait. We were attacked several times from the air, but these were not pressed home too hard as we could give a good account of ourselves with the guns still working. It was pretty awful lying stopped where we could just see the beach at Great Yarmouth, with very little to eat as fuel oil had got everywhere, even into the lockers where our clothes were. One thing we were pleased about was that we had fighter cover. Every now and then the Spitties would fly over us.

'The tug arrived and took us in tow, and it seemed ages until we got to Chatham dockyard. We were then given seven days' leave, and while at home I received a telegram to say that the ship would pay off at the termination of my leave. We went back to Chatham and put her into dry dock, and then we could see that the poor old *Whitshed* had broken her back.'

After the struggle to reach Montevideo the decrepit old tramp *Stangrant* went up-river and loaded a full cargo of grain for Hull – Third Mate and former bus conductor Alan Mathison's home town, but fate did not intend him to see the lights of home just yet. At Pernambuco, Brazil, Alan was put ashore with typhoid; he spent three months in hospital there and was shipped home as a Distressed British Seaman in the Booth Line's *Crispin*, of Liverpool, which was later converted into a Q-ship. While recuperating at home he was able to study for his Second Mate's certificate. The Dunkirk débâcle occurred, and his brother joined him, his ship, the *Leo*, having been sunk off the beaches by German bombers. He passed for Second Mate in October, and was passed fit for sea service, although some misguided drafting officer obviously thought that he still needed further non-operational time – and sent him to the Fleet Ammunition Supply Vessel *Aire* at Scapa Flow, as Third Officer.

Aire had been commandeered from the Associated Humber Lines (Ellermans, Wilson and London Midland Railway Company), and was permanently moored at a buoy in Scapa, only leaving the buoy when a warship needed ammunition.

'We had on board every type of shell from the 15 in armour-piercing variety down to 0.303 in bullets. We also had on board several technicians who used to examine any faulty ammunition returned to us. Their job was to render the dodgy ammo safe for transportation back to the munitions factory at Fort William, and as far as I was concerned they could keep it. I didn't see much action while I was there, except when there was an air attack; then the air was so full of shrapnel that it was dangerous even to go out on the open deck, the air being full of exploding shells.

'After about nine months I was transferred to the *Rother*, another of the Company's ships, and spent a year on her running up and down from Leith to London with frozen meat, passing through E-boat Alley twice a week. As we had passenger accommodation we were always the Commodore's ship, and in consequence were never attacked, the Germans being wise enough never to attack the leading ships of the convoy, but always picking on the rear ships first. In misty weather we could hear the E-boats rev up their engines as we approached the swept channel – the cunning buggers used to tie up to the channel buoys waiting for a convoy to pass through. Woe betide any ship which went outside the swept channel! It was well and truly mined. I saw several ships come to grief that way. On one voyage up to Iceland with stores for the British forces stationed there, in the 24-hour daylight of their mid-summer, submarines were the things to fear, and we had to dodge a whole field of floating mines sown by a U-boat. By that time I had passed for First Mate, and was transferred to the SS *Fort Livingstone*, a ship loading in Hull with Army supplies for Monty's troops in North Africa – munitions, food, tanks, Bren-carriers and other hardware, and a new theatre of war opened its doors to me.'

DEMS IN ACTION

Eric James Craske came from a seafaring family par excellence of Sheringham, Norfolk. His father was a fisherman and lifeboatman, his uncle a Lieutenant RN, and his three brothers served in RN and MN ships. In 1940 there was a great and growing call for gunners to serve on merchant vessels – the DEMS (Defensively Equipped Merchant Ships) unit – and Eric James chose this unique type of sea service. He joined in Hull and was rushed down to Guz.

'The confusion had to be seen to be believed. The barracks was packed, and no one seemed to know just what we were supposed to be. Well, we were packed off again back to Hull for training on 12-pounder and 4 in guns by a Royal Marine sergeant whose voice could be heard all over the city. After a hurried course we cut our teeth on coasters down E-boat Alley.

'The MN needed us badly, and I was dumped at Dundee aboard the SS *Kyle Castle*, 845 tons, general cargo (lost off Granville, 8 March 1945), one of the small coasters offloading from large freighters to carry goods down the "Alley", and lived in the luxury of a small caboose or hut built on the boat deck specially for us next to the spud locker! Do you know how we did our dhobi-ing in those cockleshells? Hammocks we tied to the guardrail, let 'em trail in the ship's wash (excuse the pun) and they would come up snowy-white. Smalls we put in a bucket of cold water, bribed a stoker with a roll-me-own and he'd put it under a steam pipe tap and, Hey Presto! you've got a bucket of hot laundry! Then rig a clothes line up on the boatdeck and dry it – you couldn't do that on the *KG V*! And going ashore – we'd put a ten-bob note in our sock for emergencies (came in useful in Alex). Not much trouble from Jerry, except a scare off Middlesbrough from a Ju 88, but he flew straight by us, didn't want to know, not worth bothering about.

'We were discharging in Woolwich Docks when two of us were given the usual DEMS pierhead jump down to Falmouth for the MV *Oud Beyerland*, a small Dutch oil-carrier, very neat and tidy like all Dutch ships, to proceed in convoy west and round into the Western Approaches for Milford Haven oil terminal for crude oil. Well, the convoy rounded North Foreland and went through the channel in the clear, round Land's End and north-east for the Bristol Channel, hugging the coast before darting across the Channel to the Haven. So far, so good, we thought. But oh, no, out of the sun, as usual, they came, I don't know how many. I was below, my mate had already opened fire with the Lewis before I got there, the Dutch cook handing him fresh magazines. I had to run from our quarters right aft to them on the fo'c'sle. Before I could reach them the plane dropped a 250-pounder, a near miss, but the blast flung me against a bollard, and killed my mate at the gun. It was an international affair, the Dutch cook swearing in his horrible language at a Jerry plane, and a Free French tug coming up to tow us in. And my mate lying dead on the deck. I should have been with him, that's all I could think of. To make things worse, I knew his wife and parents back in Hull – What do I say to them? They had welcomed me into their homes when I couldn't get home. I had to go to the funeral – Will they look at me and think "Why not you? Why our boy?" Well, if they felt it they didn't show it. I have one consolation. After the war I traced his brother, still in Hull, and we write to each other. But, it's against all reason, I still feel that guilt. I should have been there, by his side, not that brave Dutch cocoa bosun.

'It was a quick-change scene, in DEMS. From the Dutch oiler I went to the *Cetus*, a Norwegian freighter, 4,500 tons, escaped from Bergen on the fall of Norway. I joined her at Hull, one of four gunners, with two Lewis guns – and I'd have taken on the bloody *Bismarck*, any day, the way I felt, after the funeral. Only the Master could speak English, and we had a real ding-dong over where to site the Lewises, settled by the DEM PO who put us aboard, pointing out the fouled anchors on his sleeve – "The Lewises go *there*, and *there* – right?" There was no further argument, and we sailed empty to Oban to join a convoy for the New World. Then those in high places realized that we had no gun on the poop deck, so it was back to Hull, and there we were split up, with me and one other going to an unknown ship in the Tyne. There we loaded our bags and hammocks into a truck. "Ah, yes," said the driver, "*Birker Force*, you two." I said "What's that?" He grinned. "A ship."

'He dropped us at the coal hoist. Who was it said "Dirty British coaster with a salt-caked smokestack"? He must have seen the SS *Birker Force*, about 1,100 tons of coal-dust-caked collier. A coal-dusted mate showed us to our readymade coal-dusted "cabin" next to the chain locker. It was going to be a nice, quiet place, and was already tastefully coal-decorated inside, with the black diamonds still thundering down into the holds. A coaster then wasn't victualled like a deepsea vessel. We were issued with ration books, just like civvies, only ours had more coupons. If the cook was so inclined we could use a small place on the small cooker in the small galley. We closed the portholes, but the dust still got in. We wondered if bangers and mash and coal dust would do our insides a heap of good. A coaster is built for maximum cargo, minimum crew space. After loading, the crew went to work with hoses, and we saw the true colour of our ship – black.

'We formed convoy at the mouth of the Tyne ("The Tyne, the Tyne, the *coaly* Tyne, the Queen of *al* the rivers" the Geordies say. How right they are – about the coal, anyway.) We were bound, not for the Rio Grande or the Isles 'Neath the Wind, but for Beckton Gas Works, London. It was my first taste of

E-boat Alley. Off the Humber we saw the results of the work of the Luftwaffe, E-boats, U-boats, mines – masts poking up out of the water, marked by a mass of wreck buoys. More masts off my home town (I wonder what Dad's doing? I'm glad he can't see me).

'It was four hours on, four hours off – but not for long. Off Yarmouth they came out of the sun again. The armed trawler escort let fly with her 12-pounder, everybody firing every which way. Then they were gone. Then the Thames Estuary, more masts, funnels, bell buoys. We tied up at the gasworks, and the DEMS contingent got ashore as quickly as possible and vanished towards the Big Smoke before the great coal dust shower could hit us.

'I did four trips in the *Birker Force* up and down to the Tyne, and, do you know, you can actually get to like a little coal carrier, if you love ships. It wasn't always the Jerries that bothered us. Our first run back to Geordieland looked like being quiet, no Luftwaffe, no E-boats, but when we got abeam of my old coast the nor'easter hit us, and being a light ship we (and the others) rolled something awful. When you're in a swept channel and have to keep station, the Old Man can't put her nose into it.'

However, if Eric thought that local weather was bad, he found the North Atlantic something else again. Two days out from New York for Liverpool he recorded in his diary:

'We can feel the change in the weather now (Father used to say "Watch the white tops, boy, they'll tell you"). The little corvettes roll and the wind is getting up. Duffle coats and wool jumpers now, boys. The bosun and his mate are checking the deck cargoes. Then the first one comes over the bows. The old *Clan Ronald* has deep well decks, the water rushes down and through the scuppers.

'Now it really hits us. It's quite dark now, and when you see the bosun's crew rigging life lines you really begin to get the shakes . . . Can barely see the *Irene Dupont* now . . . Gunlayer has traversed the gun so the shield will give a bit of cover . . . God, I've never seen the size of these breakers! The gunlayer tightens the wing nuts on the ready-use ammo locker – Won't need them!

'The hand crank phone to the bridge is near the lockers. It rings. It's the Old Man . . . "Abandon the poop and get to your quarters . . . The convoy is to scatter . . . Get to your quarters . . ." That's a laugh – our quarters are on the boat deck. If you leave the poop you have to go along that well deck, already awash, and up a ladder to the main deck, then up to the boat deck. There's no catwalk like on a tanker . . . (Well, Dad, you had some rough seas in that old Sheringham lifeboat . . . Were you scared?)

'The Third Mate has somehow got to the poop . . . "You'll have to go back by the shaft tunnel. Follow me." We go down the small hatchway under the poop along the tunnel into the engine room . . . Someone says, "*This*'ll keep the U-boats down!" The comedian says, "Yes, and we'll soon be joining 'em!"

'Two days of this weather. All the rafts lost. The bosun says, "Skipper's taken over the wheel, put her nose into it." We just about have sea-way. When things calm down a bit we return to the poop. The Third Mate comes along. "What a blow!" he says. Twenty-nine Clan Line ships were lost in the war. 3,935 DEMS gunners died. But I'd rather face a sub attack than that terrible North Atlantic storm. There was such *fury* in those *huge* seas . . . They still haunt my dreams.'

'One battleship in sight'

Suddenly around me
The Gunnery Jacks all spoke
Their terrible words of gunpowder
And sentences of smoke

SALOPIAN TORPEDOED

The Armed Merchant Cruiser HMS *Salopian* served for a time on the Freetown run, and was then transferred to the Halifax Escort Force. Losses among these substitute cruisers, with their slow speed, lack of armour, ancient guns and conspicuous bulk, had been high. Apart from the loss of *Rawalpindi*, sunk by *Scharnhorst* and *Gneisenau*, and *Jervis Bay*, sunk by *Scheer* in a brave and successful defence of her convoy, nine AMCs had been destroyed by U-boat torpedo – *Carinthia*, *Scotstoun*, *Andania*, *Transylvania*, *Dunvegan Castle*; and *Laurentic* and *Patroclus* within hours of each other by U-boat ace Otto 'The Silent' Kretschmer in his *U99*, with its famous Golden Horseshoe badge; and *Forfar*; with *Voltaire* sunk by the guns of the German armed merchant raider *Thor*, which had been twice beaten off, by AMCs *Alcantara* and *Carnarvon Castle*, but got away.

On 12 May 1941 *Salopian* handed over her slow convoy from Halifax on the western edge of the submarine danger zone to a destroyer escort. She then turned west and headed back for Halifax at 15 knots.

Just before first light on the following morning, at about 3.30a.m., the officer of the watch sighted a submarine on the surface, sounded Action Stations, increased to full speed and put the helm hard over to turn away. Almost immediately the ship was struck by two torpedoes on the starboard side, one near the bow, and one at the position of the bulkhead between Nos 3 and 4 holds, which fractured many engine room pipes and stopped the main engines, brought down all the wireless aerials and shattered the starboard lifeboat. A third 'tinfish' was too much for the bilge pumps, and an Advance Party left the ship in the remaining boats, leaving the Retard Party, which included the Captain, gun crews and damage control parties.

The U-boat surfaced and *Salopian*'s guns opened fire, which only triggered off another torpedo hit. The Captain ordered Abandon Ship.

Engineer Sub-Lieutenant Bert Poolman – whom we last saw being seen off by wife and son to join *Salopian*, at the darkened Midland Railway Station in peaceful Bath; who had served on the Western Front and in submarines in World War I, and was not one to panic easily – 'Saw no signs of fear or urgency among the ship's company. A lot of men were going back down to their cabins to grab rabbits and personal nick-nacks, and I thought I'd go down as well and retrieve a few things.' Nervous at the thought of keeping a watch in the engine room again, he had quickly found, like Kennedy of *Rawalpindi*, that 'it has all come back'.

He was a popular man on board, and had struck up a friendship with the Captain, Sir John Alleyne – 'Two old retreads together', as he put it. On his silver wedding anniversary the members of the wardroom had presented him with an elegant silver inscribed salver, and it was this that he especially wanted to save. He picked this up, all his pipes, tobacco and watches, a carton of cigarettes, and his gas mask bag, which had long since ceased to contain a gas mask, and was usually full of chocolate for his wife and son – in fact he was known as 'The Chocolate Sailor'.

'Once down there, I thought "Blowed if I'm going to let the fishes have my best uniform!" and changed into it.' His absence on deck had been noted, and a young fellow engineer hurried below to find him. 'For Christ's sake Bert', he shouted, 'the bloody ship's going down!' The older man said casually, 'Oh, she won't go just yet.' Up top, he climbed into the boat, clutching his precious salver.

With the wireless aerials down, no message had been sent out, but at 0830 a signal 'AMC torpedoed', giving their position, was transmitted on the old Board of Trade emergency set, which had a range of only 50–100 miles, in the motor boat.

George Monk was Second Radio Officer of the Ocean Transport and Trading Group's MN *Empire Confidence*, which was returning to the UK from Vancouver; she had been held back at Halifax from joining the next convoy because the ship had passenger accommodation and was considered suitable for the Commodore of the following one. On 4 May the Convoy Commodore, a retired Commodore RN, arrived aboard with his staff, and on 6 May *Empire Confidence* left for her anchorage in Bedford Basin. The convoy formed up and sailed in the afternoon.

On 13 May George 'came off morning watch at 0800, and returned at 0830 to relieve my Chief for breakfast. At about 0835 I heard signals on 500 kcs, but they were unreadable, due to interference. When this cleared I received this message: "AMC *Salopian* Torpedoed. In lifeboats. Position 59.04N 38.15W. PSE. QSP."

'I waited for a repeat but heard nothing more. However, the vital part of the message was the position. It was dead ahead of the convoy and under 100 miles away.

'As soon as the Commodore had examined the message, signals were exchanged between him and the Senior Officer, Escorts. None of them had received the message, so SOE requested details for immediate transmission to C-in-C Western Approaches. Obviously, it was vital that other ships in the vicinity were warned of U-boat activity, and rescue of *Salopian*'s crew had to be organized. *Empire Confidence* had no HF gear to make this signal.

'By 0900 the Commodore had alerted the convoy to the emergency course it would have to make. Turning a convoy of 50-plus ships in nine columns through

Eastleigh November 23. 39

My dear Todd,

I was extremely pleased to hear today that you have not broken anything after all. I very much hope that this is true, and that you are, and are feeling all right.

We were very lucky and very unlucky too. If we had had a few feet more height we would have made the brown ploughed field on top of the hill, and might have got nothing worse than very muddy feet.

I congratulate you very much indeed in keeping your head so well under rather difficult conditions, and I hope you will be back with us before long.

Yours very sincerely

Ralph Richardson

Previous page: The apologetic letter which Lieutenant (A) Ralph Richardson sent to Alan Todd following their crash-landing in a Shark outside the village of Hursky near Winchester.

Left: L/S Nethercott mans a Hotchkiss AA gun aboard HMS Lincoln. (ex-USS *Yarnall)*

Right: Some of Lincoln's *HOs share a food parcel – the original stocks of American food were mostly appropriated for the wardroom galley.*

Left: AB Walt Hardman on HMS Lincoln's *port torpedo tubes.*

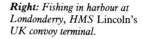

Right: Fishing in harbour at Londonderry, HMS Lincoln's *UK convoy terminal.*

Left: Lincoln's *Active Service veterans taught their green HOs splicing in the dog watches.*

Left: Dennis Bond (ex-apprentice wireman, Godalming Borough Brass Bandsman) asked of the screaming Stukas 'How will I react?' – and was answered.

To Dennis Bond HM destroyer Whitshed, Admiralty Modified W class, built 1918, 'didn't look at all like the recruiting posters' – but she had been to Dunkirk, and she took on Scharnhorst and Gneisenau, *as a change from dodging dive-bombers in* 'E-boat Alley'.

Left: Wiremen making fishing nets. (M. Collins, D. Bond)

Top right: Hauling up the whaler.

Right: Torpedo party, with Stuka suntans. (D. Bond bottom right)

Left: The author's father, Sub-Lieutenant (E) B. Poolman, RNR, who served aboard HMS Salopian.

Right: Ride-a-cock-gun aboard Suffolk.

Left: Bill Earp joined the Navy to escape 'a world of poverty'. Here he is quite an old salt, a gunner with a three-year Good Conduct stripe and the white tape of a Naval marriage to a 'Dorothy', who replaced HMS Suffolk in his affections – almost.

Right: A sea wolf if never very far from Bill Earp's Suffolk 'Red Riding Hood' as she goes to get the rations for Granny and is sent on her way rejoicing after meeting Aladdin, in the ship's unorthodox pantomime, written by Bill, who took off Cole Porter in a duet with the Commander.

Left: The elegant battlecruiser HMS Hood, *which between the wars had symbolized the whole Royal Navy in ports all round the world.*

Below: HMS Alcantara, *armed merchant cruiser.*

Below right: Alcantara's *FAA contingent, Durban, 1942. Aircrew are (middle row, left to right): PO Stan Brown (observer); Sub-Lieutenant (A) Hosegood, RNVR (pilot); Sub-Lieutenant (A) Wilson, RNVR (observer); PO Freddie Longman, RN (pilot). The two rating pilots were not allowed to fly together and were never briefed before a patrol.*

Left: Ken Illingworth from Bradford wanted a sleek destroyer, and not a tramp in E-boat Alley; but in the MAC-ship Acavus 'the aircraft made a difference in my life'.

Below: Escort carriers, merchantmen wholly converted to warships, were spacious below decks, especially those built in the USA. Forty-two of these ships were loaned to the Royal Navy.

Right: Manning the AA guns on the escort-carrier HMS Battler. Note the narrow bridge 'island' and the three Swordfish ranged on the flight deck.

Left: *Mick Dale, now a Chief PO, commanded the TAGs of* Vindex's *famous No 825 Squadron. Mick was Tag in Squadron Co Freddie Sheffield's aircraft when it sank U765 in the Atlantic, but in his excitement forgot to photograph the event.*

Right: *The Air Headquarters team in* Vindex, *supplemented by three Air Artificers from No 825 Squadron, invented many effective pieces of hardware, under the command of Lieutenant Molineaux, RNVR. Here among others are Chief PO Charlie Waldram (third from left, back row), armourer Norman Pickup (second from left, back row) and Bill McCall (extreme right, second row).*

Below right: *Young aircrew are debriefed after a sortie by Commander (Operations).*

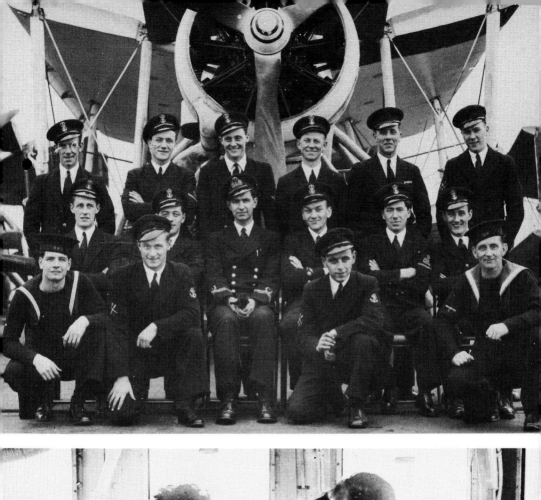

Left: *Armourers at work on a Fulmar.*

Below and top right: *Carrier flight decks allowed far better recreation than other warships. Deck hockey on a US-built escort carrier (note the wooden planked deck). Snowball fighting on Vindex's flight deck in northern waters.*

Below right: *Russian sailors are entertained by Vindex Air Headquarters staff at the Murmansk terminal of one of her Russian convoy runs.*

Left: Combined Operator. Isle of Wighter David Satherley wanted 'a sleek destroyer' – and got Combined Operations, but found that 'It was still Navy,' and was proud to wear the badge.

Below: The new crew of HM LCI 127 were delighted that she 'looked like a real ship', and behaved like one in a hairy crossing from Burmuda to Gibraltar. Note the 'eye-shooting' cap tally bows of real Jack-my-Hearties and the lowered gangway ramp (one of a pair port and starboard from which the troops went ashore).

60° is not an easy task, but when the manoeuvres were completed we proceeded at maximum speed, away from the boats.

'I was the only operator to receive the lifeboat's SOS on my Marconi receiver, which had a crystal control on 500 kcs, because the lifeboat's transmitter (with a maximum range of 100 miles) was luckily spot-on our listening frequency. None of our officers knew of the *Salopian* by name (not realizing that it was a comparatively recent made-up one). In fact the "SOS" was suspect, the "PSE" (Please) "QSP" not being the normal format for a distress transmission. It was thought that a U-boat, knowing of the approach of a large convoy, had transmitted it on a lifeboat-type transmitter, hoping that radio silence would be broken and give him a D/F bearing. However, our convoy proceeded eastwards without further incident.'

Meanwhile, in *Salopian*'s boats they saw the U-boat's periscope cutting through the water close by them, then there was an explosion in *Salopian* where another torpedo struck her. 'The old ship rocked but still sat there like a duck', Bert Poolman thought. Then yet another tinfish hit her, and she broke in half, both halves stood on end and disappeared together in less than a minute.

The boats and Carley floats drifted for two days. They were all rationed to half a biscuit, an inch-sized cube of corned beef and two half-measures of a small white-enamelled water dipper per day.

'There was nothing to cut up the bully beef on properly,' Bert Poolman remembered after the war, 'only my blessed tray and they used that'. The tray is now in my possession, as is the dipper, and still bears the knife scratches on the back – it is not polished as often as it should be.

On the morning of 15 May Captain Alleyne despatched the motor boat to steer as far south as fuel would permit in the hope of sighting a convoy which he believed was on its way from Halifax. Just as he was losing sight of the boats astern, Lieutenant-Commander Peate in the motor boat sighted a destroyer right ahead. She had also seen them, and soon picked up the survivors. The boat's feeble SOS, picked up so luckily by George Monk in *Empire Confidence*, had been relayed to C-in-C Western Approaches in Liverpool via the Cypher Officer on duty, Second Officer Sheila Isherwood – Bert Poolman's niece. Anxiously she waited for news of survivors, unable to tell the family anything. Destroyers were sent to make an anti-submarine sweep in the area of the attack and look for *Salopian*'s boats. HMS *Icarus*, her fuel running low, was on the last leg of her final broad sweep when she sighted them. She took the survivors to Iceland, and by the time she got there she was down to 12 knots to conserve fuel. Captain Alleyne told his men that he wanted them to march off the ship smartly, and not 'shuffle off like a flock of sheep', as survivors usually did. *Salopian*'s barber gave them all a haircut, and they did their best to look like conquering heroes. Peake spoke to them before they disembarked: 'Men, although we're all very sorry to have lost our ship, don't forget – it will only take 18 months to build another, but it has taken 18 years to build the youngest man here.'

THE *BISMARCK* BATTLE

By this time a far more dangerous predator had been let loose in the North Atlantic.

'The reason I joined the Royal Navy was quite simple and clear-cut,' says Bill Earp. 'I wanted to get out of the environment that kept me and my kind in a world of poverty and low-paid factory work. I had heard many tales about the Navy from my father who served in it from 1917 to 1922, and I resolved to follow in his footsteps as soon as I was old enough to join, which I did, via the Recruitment Office in Birmingham. I found myself in that first cold winter of the war at HMS *St George*, the former Cunningham's Holiday Camp, just outside Douglas, Isle of Man. Training was tough but no tougher than civvy life for me, and, after all, I now had things of my own that had previously been denied to me . . . clothes that fitted, ample food and a chance to be part of something better than factory life, underwear, pyjamas, toothbrush and toothpaste.'

It was not until February 1941 that Bill was fully trained and then, with the other boys, he was drafted to HMS *Suffolk*, a County-class cruiser docked at Glasgow. 'In just over twelve months I had changed my life from a scruffy little factory boy to Boy Seaman on a cruiser – not much you could say, but to me it was. I had discovered a world I never knew existed.

'*Suffolk* towered above us like a huge steel fortress when we boys joined her lying alongside at Glasgow. Our messdeck was right above "A" turret magazine, and the barbette of the turret was in the centre of the mess. On the port side of the messdeck was a small partitioned caboose which was the domain of our betters, the Petty Officers in charge of us, two men completely opposite in appearance and personality. One was a three-badge veteran, like matlow poet Charles Causley's Chief. . . .

. . . older than the naval side of British history . . .
His narrow forehead ruffled by the Jutland wind . . .

. . . always with a melancholy look on his face, tall and lean and a worrier, looking for trouble round every corner, known (behind his back) as "The Dripper", his pet hatred being dripping taps. The other PO was quite a different kind of Pusser's Prefect, a fully fledged Physical Training Instructor, and I *mean* fully fledged, all muscle and some 15 stone, face bearing the marks and scars of a long pugilistic career . . . "If any of yew boys fink yew can come the old sailor wiv me then yew can fink agin, cawse if yew do I'll unship your f★★★★n' 'ead!"

'None of us boys realized just how privileged we were. We had joined just in time to meet the *Bismarck*.

'Even though it was 47 years ago I can still remember most of the things that happened in that caper. From fear I passed to relief (that we were alive) to disbelief (that it had happened at all). My memories are of being extremely cold, tired, hungry and apprehensive, of men trying to make jokes to hide their fear, nervously fingering one's inflatable lifebelt (Mae West), casually inspecting nearby Carley floats, and above all the waiting for something to happen. My Action Station was at Port 1 twin 4in AA gun as a loading number, and I consequently had time to observe the action, as this was very definitely a case for Main Armament, aided, for the first time in a sea battle, by radar, then known as RDF.'

Suffolk, patrolling the Denmark Strait within RAF distance of the ice edge on a line running north-east and south-west, was the first ship of the Home Fleet to sight *Bismarck*, but neither of her radars was responsible. 'One of our Port 1 4in AA gun's crew, Alf "Ginger" Newell, was the duty lookout who first spotted and reported the *Bismarck* and *Prinz Eugen*, and for this received a well-deserved DSM, as did AB Tinkler, our senior radar operator.'

Newell sighted the great battleship at 1922 hrs on 23 May at a range of seven miles, which was dangerously close to her eight new 15 in guns for *Suffolk*; but the British cruiser was able to turn back into the mist unseen, and Tinkler then picked up *Bismarck* on the 284 gunnery-ranging RDF.

Norfolk, patrolling about 15 miles abeam of *Suffolk*, inshore, with her fixed-beam RDF, hurried to get into contact with the enemy, and also sighted her (at 2032) before obtaining an echo. When she did she was closer still, and *Bismarck* fired on her but she too managed to disengage. For the next 10 hours the two Counties shadowed the German, reporting her position to Admiral Holland, who was steaming up with *Hood*, *Prince of Wales* and six destroyers to engage the enemy. The C-in-C hoped that this force 'may head them off and force them to turn back to the southward'. In spite of the bad visibility prevailing during that anxious night, Holland in *Hood* imposed a rigid radio and radar silence on his group, but at 2 o'clock on the morning of the 24th the cruisers lost touch with the enemy, and he asked *Prince of Wales* to use her 284 set to search an arc for *Bismarck*. When told that this radar would not bear, he refused permission to use the 281, which could pick up an aircraft at 20,000 ft from 100 miles, a battleship at 11 miles, and find a range within about 30 yards. Perhaps the Admiral had not made himself acquainted with these potentialities of his new weapon. Tinkler knew, but he was only an Able Seaman, and he was never asked.

At 0535 on 24 May Holland sighted *Bismarck* at 17 miles' range, much further away than his radar, 284 or 281, could have reported her. *Hood* opened fire first, at 26,500 yards, followed almost at once by *Prince of Wales* – and both German ships.

Contrary to popular misconception, of the four nations which developed radar before the Second World War, Britain was the last. Experiments in Germany to develop a radar rangefinder began in 1933, and in 1936 'Seetakt' sets were at sea in *Graf Spee*, the cruiser *Königsberg* and the torpedo boat *G10*, and ranges of 17 km were recorded on a large ship, 8 km on a cruiser. *Bismarck*'s Seetakt, mounted in front of the main armament director, was principally a rangefinder but had good directional properties as well; it could also be used for warning of the approach of ships. Although it could not spot the fall of shot, *Bismarck* used it to make already superb gunnery even more accurate. *Prince of Wales* got no results from her 284 or 281, her first salvo fell 1,000 yards short, and she took six salvoes to cross the target. But *Bismarck*'s first salvo, perfect for range, fell just ahead of *Hood*; her third salvo hit the great battlecruiser and penetrated a magazine. At 0615 *Norfolk* signalled: 'Hood blown up.'

With little to do, AA gunner Bill Earp 'had a grandstand view of the first action, and I, who was doing a spell as lookout, saw the pall of smoke that rose as the *Hood* was sunk. At the time I did not know who had been hit but learned later when it was broadcast over the ship's Tannoy.

'How our hearts sank and how the news made us more edgy, but even so more determined to avenge *Hood*.' *Prince of Wales* was also badly damaged and forced to turn away under smoke, signalling: 'Bridge out of action. "Y" turret out of action.'

But she had hit *Bismarck*, which was trailing oil. By now British radar had picked up the enemy again, and *Suffolk*, *Norfolk* and *Prince of Wales* continued to shadow her, with Tinkler on *Suffolk*'s 284 mainly responsible for keeping contact, 'until *Bismarck* turned and fired on us. We fired back and took evasive action under a smoke screen. I saw their first salvo straddle us and thought like many others that the next one would have our name on it, but mercifully we were safe in the smoke screen while *Prince of Wales* and *Norfolk* fired back. All this enabled *Prince Eugen* to make her escape.' (The latter was following orders from *Bismarck* to oil from a supply ship and 'engage in cruiser warfare independently'.)

At 2056 *Bismarck* signalled Group West: 'Impossible shake off enemy owing to radar. Proceeding directly to Brest owing to fuel situation.'

Meanwhile, the C-in-C aboard *King George V* with the rest of the Home Fleet was steaming to intercept, and detached *Victorious*, a brand-new carrier, to launch her aircraft, although they were not properly worked-up with her, to try to slow *Bismarck* down.

Just after midnight on 25 May one Swordfish fitted with ASV Mk II found her and scored one hit but failed to reduce her speed. Three hours later *Bismarck* altered course south-east, just at the moment when *Suffolk* was turning on to the outward leg of her zigzag, with her radar at that point temporarily out of touch with the enemy. When *Suffolk* swung back on course *Bismarck* was gone from Tinkler's A-scope. *Suffolk* was sent to search to the westward, unaware of the German's change of course, and of course could not find her, nor could any of the hunting ships.

Five fruitless hours later Group West signalled *Bismarck*: 'Last enemy contact report 0213. We have impression contact has been lost.'

An hour later Admiral Raeder, C-in-C of the German Navy, signalled to Admiral Lutjens: 'Heartiest congratulations on your birthday. May you continue to be equally successful in this coming year.'

Five hours later Hitler himself added his best wishes, and *Ark Royal* and *Sheffield* were heading for *Bismarck* to give her a birthday present.

British Direction Finding stations had picked up the *Bismarck* – Group West exchange of signals, and although British cryptographers could not break the code, the position indicated that she was making for France. At 1015 on the 26th *Suffolk* left the scene of the main action under orders to search for the enemy supply ships *Belchen* and *Lothringen*. At 1030 a Coastal Command Catalina flying-boat with ASV Mk II signalled: 'One battleship in sight.'

Sheffield was sent on ahead to supplement the shadowing aircraft. At 1115 an *Ark Royal* search Swordfish with ASV signalled: 'One battleship in sight.'

At 1746 the chagrined CO of the Swordfish squadron reported: '11 torpedoes fired at Sheffield.' Thankfully he was able to qualify this with: 'No hits.' However, one aircraft did hit *Sheffield*, but the torpedo was a dud. She signalled to the cruiser: 'Sorry for the kipper.'

At 1954 *Bismarck* was attacked by a second striking force from *Ark Royal*, and at 2015 the German ship reported: 'Ship no longer manoeuvrable. Torpedo hit aft.'

A damaged rudder was sending her round in circles. Destroyers *Zulu*, *Maori* and *Cossack* attacked her with torpedoes, claiming two hits. At 0351 the Führer signalled *Bismarck*'s Gunnery Officer the award of the Knight's Cross 'for the sinking of the battlecruiser *Hood*', but it was a last breakfast for him, and for *Bismarck*. Her destruction was completed by *Rodney*, *King George VI*, and finally by torpedoes from the cruiser *Dorsetshire*. *Suffolk* had no luck hunting the German supply ships, and headed for Newfoundland, low on fuel.

LIFEBOAT TO ST VINCENT

Bert Poolman, survivor from *Salopian*, travelled down to London in the train with the young midshipman, one of only three survivors, from the tragic *Hood*, and realized his own good luck in being alive. *Bismarck* had been sunk, but he thought what might have happened if she had got among the ships of a convoy – 'my blood ran cold'. In fact, at Liverpool they had thought for a time that *Salopian* had run across the path of *Bismarck*, which would have meant another, and swifter *Rawalpindi* or *Jervis Bay*. Bert arrived home, and the first thing he noticed when he walked into the sitting room was the new model I had made of *Hood*, and set on brackets on the wall. 'She's down, son,' he said, 'along with the old *Salopian*.' I stared at the model. I couldn't believe it. My safe little world of models had just crumbled, and a gust of cold Atlantic wind blew across my face.

George Monk was on leave when he saw in his *Daily Mail* the announcement: 'The Admiralty regrets that AMC *Salopian* (Captain Sir John Alleyne) has been sunk by enemy action.'

He was 'gratified to see this report, as it confirmed that the distress signal I had received was genuine. I think that *U98* (Kapitänleutnant Gysae), the submarine that had sunk the *Salopian*, was positioned (with possibly one or two other boats) to intercept the convoy. The unfortunate *Salopian* was seen first and torpedoed. Through her SOS she enabled our convoy to take appropriate action and escape. It could have been a different story if *Salopian* had not been ordered back to Halifax.'

What George could not foresee was that he himself would soon be involved in an adventure more fraught than that of *Salopian*'s crew . . .

'On 13 June 1941 I joined the SS *Auditor* (T & J Harrison, 5,444 tons, Captain E. Bennett). We sailed from the Royal Albert Docks London on 15 June for Capetown, Durban and Indian ports, fully loaded with general cargo and Army stores.

'At Southend we joined a northbound convoy, calling first at Methil before passing round the north of Scotland to Oban. Sailing northward our convoy had just passed Flamborough Head when the ship ahead – a motor ship of Ellerman's – set off an acoustic mine which exploded just under our bows. Fortunately for us the mine was lying in deep water, and although it gave us a severe hammering, it did not damage the hull or the engines. At that time, merchant ships in East Coast convoys were provided with an anti-aircraft balloon; one was delivered to us at Southend and we would fly it to Methil. It was flown just above the top of the foremast, and let out several hundred feet when an air attack was imminent from a large drum attached to a cargo winch, but when the mine exploded, the shaking was so severe it loosened the winch controls, and the balloon rose, literally, to the end of its tether. The Commodore signalled "Stop playing with your balloon."'

The coastal convoy arrived at Oban on 20 June, and the ocean convoy – of some 40 ships – sailed the next day. A week later it dispersed, and the merchantmen then sailed independently to their destinations. Naval Control at Oban had given the Master a route which was to take *Auditor* due south to the Brazilian coast, then across the South Atlantic to Capetown, to steer us away from the U-boat danger area.

'On 4 July – just as the moon was setting, about 2 a.m. – she was torpedoed by *U123* (Kapitän Leutnant Hardegen). A violent explosion near No 4 hold on the port side destroyed No 4 lifeboat. I was asleep at the time the torpedo hit. I quickly put on my clothes and grabbed my "hammer bag" and lifejacket. Making my way to the radio office, which was on the boat deck aft of the funnel, I found my Chief was already there and had started sending our distress message: "SSSS SSSS SSSS *Auditor*. 25.47N 28.23W. Torpedoed."

'The emergency spark transmitter was being used, as the ship's power supply had been lost. The radio office had emergency lighting, but I could see that it was a shambles. Fortunately the emergency transmitter was in working order and the aerial intact. My Chief called out, "Get the lifeboat transmitter into No 1 boat – I'll carry on here." I left and made my way to No 1 boat station under the bridge.

'When I got to the boat deck I saw Captain Bennett who had dressed in his shore clothes (he was worried about being taken prisoner by the U-boat). He called, "Go and get your Chief – she's going fast." I lowered the emergency transmitter into No 1 boat. By this time – about 7 minutes after the explosion – my eyes had become accustomed to the darkness, and it was a clear night with stars shining brightly, I was able to move around the ship easily. When I got to the radio office I found that my Chief was still transmitting our distress signal. He asked me to get his coat from his room which was on a lower deck. This I did, and when I got there I could hear the sea pouring into the engine room below, just like the sound of a large waterfall. On returning to the radio office, we checked that the code books had been thrown overboard, and then made our way to the bridge deck.

'The only lifeboat still alongside was No 1 – the Captain's. I went down the rope ladder, followed by my Chief and the Captain. The boat rope was cut, and we pulled away. When about 80 yards off, and about 15 minutes after the torpedo hit, the *Auditor*'s bow rose up until vertical, then she sank slowly into the Cape

Verde Basin – some 3,000 fathoms below. Besides wreckage floating around, all that was left of a fine ship were a number of large crates (deck cargo), and the three boats.

'A little later the sound of diesels was heard. It was the *U123* cruising around. Obviously, Hardegen wanted to make sure that *Auditor* had sunk; he did not contact us.

'There were 23 survivors in the Captain's boat, including the Chief Engineer, Chief Steward, Third Officer, Chief Radio Officer (my Chief), myself, one AB, one Gunner and fifteen Lascars. Nothing could be done until daylight, except to keep in touch with the other two boats. As our boat was leaking it was necessary to bail continuously.

'At sunrise on Friday, stocks were taken of our provisions and these were found to be: 1½ kegs of water (about 9 gallons), 1 case of small tins of condensed milk, and a large quantity of hard ship's biscuits. The daily ration was: ½ dipper of water (3 fluid ounces), 1 spoonful of condensed milk, 1 biscuit. Later the three boats closed. As we were in the zone of the north-east trade winds, there was a stiff breeze blowing, with a choppy sea. It was difficult for the boats to keep together, and they were riding to sea anchors.

'A decision had to be made – what lands or islands should we make for, bearing in mind the prevailing winds and currents. We had no Atlantic charts, the only navigational aid in each boat being a compass. For many years prior to the war, I used to buy a pocket Shipping Diary; when in London in December 1940 I got one for 1941, and had it in my coat. Many times in the past I had seen a couple of pages giving the latitude and longitude of ports, and when I looked at this section it gave the co-ordinates for St Vincent – the port of the Cape Verde Islands. As I had my pay book as well, I was able to draw a chart and lay off a course to St Vincent which was 580 miles SSE of our present position. With this information, these islands were the obvious choice for a landfall, and so the officers worked out a course for each boat to steer. The estimated time for the voyage was 11 to 12 days. However, a factor which greatly influenced the decision was – the islands were mountainous. Captain Bennett had visited St Vincent many years ago, and remembered that these mountains were very high, around 6,000 ft to 9,000 ft, and therefore could be seen from a great distance, perhaps 40 miles or more. If they had been low-lying the decision would have been, no doubt, to set course for the NE coast of South America – some 1,700 miles distant with a voyage of around 21+ days. At the Ocean Convoy Conference in Oban, the Naval Control Officer had advised all Masters, "If you are sunk and your distress message and position has been sent and acknowledged, then do not attempt any long distance lifeboat voyage. There is always a naval vessel within 2 days' sailing distance from your position – so just WAIT – and you will be rescued." My Chief, who was with Captain Bennett at the conference, confirmed that this was the instruction given.

'So we waited, through Friday and Saturday, drifting westwards. Captain Bennett was adamant that we must wait, as it was a Naval Control instruction. By Saturday evening the officers "rebelled" and said that as our provisions were limited "Let's get sailing." So it was agreed that if no ship had been sighted by Sunday morning, the boats would set sail independently for St Vincent. During these two days the lifeboat transmitter was used to send distress messages at regular times.

'Early Sunday morning the sea anchors were hauled in and each boat set sail. By sunset the Chief Officer's boat was well ahead, and the Second Officer's boat was hull-down astern of us. The NE trade winds were blowing steadily, and our speed was estimated at 2½ to 3 knots. The boat was sailing well, but a good lookout could only be maintained when we rode the crest of the swell.

'By Monday morning the other boats were out of sight. It was fine weather, and during the day it became very warm; some of the crew were already suffering from sun-burn. At night it was very cold. As the boat was still taking in water it was essential to bail frequently, but during the day we would sit with our feet in water in the hope that our bodies might absorb some moisture this way. Steering the boat was the main task of Captain Bennett and the Third Officer; occasionally the other officers would relieve them. Steering at night was difficult as there was no light in the compass. Lifejacket lights were used to check the course, but mainly we steered by the moon and stars.

'During the next three days the weather was fine with fleecy clouds and a strong breeze. At times the sea became choppy, which reduced our speed. When in the valley of a swell, one could look up at the sides of it and see many varieties of fish swimming above the level of the boat. In this area the sea was a marvellous colour and so clear but, of course, undrinkable.

'On Friday – the 8th day – the Master estimated that at dawn we had made some 300 miles since setting sail. It was cloudy, and during the morning there was a light rain shower. The inside cover of the transmitter was used to collect some of the spots of rain, and was licked dry. Thirst was a great problem and Captain Bennett increased our water ration to two half-dippers a day. On this basis our stocks should last for another seven days. If our present speed could be maintained, one of the islands should be sighted before the water was exhausted. Ship's biscuits provided for lifeboat use were a disaster, being so dry and hard that no one could eat them. The only food that could be eaten was condensed milk, and the ration of this was increased to two spoonfuls a day. Unfortunately, the Third Officer, who was unwell when we took to the boats, became delirious.

'Monday – 11th day. During the previous three days the weather had been good, and fortunately we had remained in the zone of the NE trades, which enabled us to maintain a steady speed in spite of the heavy swell. Captain Bennett estimated that by dawn we had sailed about 550 miles, an average speed of 2½ knots. As we were obviously getting near the islands, we again transmitted distress signals at regular times. In the late afternoon a bird was sighted. Land must be near.

'Tuesday – 12th day. It was cloudy, and the men who were on lookout at dawn thought that there was a grey smudge on the horizon on our port beam. Could it be land? If so, then we were 40 or more miles off course. The effects of wind and current must have been greater than was estimated. This smudge was watched by all of us for at least half an hour to see if there was any movement – like a cloud. It did not move – so it must be one of the islands. The course was now altered to east-north-east, and we met headwinds, which meant frequent tacking. This gave us problems straight away; the sea was choppy with quite a swell running. The heel of the mast broke shortly after the course had been altered. It was repaired but broke again in the forenoon and afternoon. On all occasions it was repaired to the best of our ability, but with no tools available – except a knife – it was difficult to make a good job. Due to the stiff breeze the boat was getting a severe pounding, but luckily the mast stays held. When tacking we shipped a lot of water, and so it was all hands to bailing. Headway was made, and as the day wore on the island became larger, but at sunset we were still some 20 miles from it.

'Wednesday – 13th day. I was at the tiller for the first watch; the light of a lighthouse was seen and this helped in maintaining a course, but the wind was dropping as we came into the lee of the island. Later, when about 8 miles from the shore, the Master said "Hold her there." It was not wise to get too close to the shore until we could see what it was like. When dawn broke we could make out the layout of the island. It looked very menacing. The steep rocky cliffs came down to the sea, with no place to land. As the sun rose behind the mountains it began to get very warm, and the wind dropped completely. It was now time to get out the oars and row, and as the cliffs looked less steep to the south, that was the way we headed. Every man took turn at the oars, but it was hot and very tiring, particularly as we had not eaten anything substantial for almost thirteen days. After rowing for three hours there appeared some colours on the mountain side, and these turned out to be small houses. A little later we saw two boats making for us; they had brought out two carafes of fresh water. How good it tasted! The boats – manned by fishermen – took our ropes and towed us for the last two miles to the village of Tarrafal on the island of Santo Antao!'

SING FOR YOUR SUPPER

There was little respite for the overworked cruisers and destroyers of the Home Fleet, but in the summer of 1942 *Suffolk*, whose Able Seaman Tinkler had been solely responsible for holding *Bismarck* in the hunters' net, was sent to the Tyne for repairs, which meant leave.

'This was great for morale,' says gunner Bill Earp, 'but had one drawback – one needed money to enjoy the run ashore, and Naval pay for junior ratings was hardly adequate to ensure liquidity both financially and alcoholically. However, the Lord provides and helps them that help themselves. One of my oppos was the Padre's Comforts Fund Stores Sweeper and had access to its contents – an Aladdin's Cave of Navy blue knitted garments supplied by the good women of Britain. There was no shortage of customers, the dockyard mateys took all we could supply, socks, gloves, scarves, at one and sixpence a pair, each sale equal to at least three halves of best bitter. When we were back at sea the Padre was at a loss to understand why we had so few socks, gloves and scarves but so many balaclavas.

'Another method of raising funds was my natural ability for mimicry. As a member of the ship's concert party, I had the chance to improve my repertoire and put it to good use in the talent competitions in the pubs round the dock area. My impressions of Churchill, Roosevelt and Hitler always went down well. One of my oppos was my manager, who organized my turns in the pubs which did this sort of thing, and also led the applause, which almost every time ensured that I got a money prize. He also organized the share-out of the prize money, and the beer it could buy for our little band of mates.

'Not all enterprises were successful however. One unfortunate rating was caught red-handed sneaking through the dockyard with a large side of bacon slung over his shoulder en route to making a sale. He was sentenced to 90 days' detention for his pains, and as well as I can remember the side of bacon was charged with breaking out of ship and was sentenced to provide wardroom breakfast for a week.

'Spare blankets were also a good commodity for sale, and many of them found their way on to dockyard mateys' beds. Tinned food was a popular item. Removing it from the stores was a work of art. If dockyard workmen were required to work in these stores, then it was customary to provide a sentry to supervise this, and he would tip off his oppo who would go down to the stores with a half-full bucket of dirty water and place a few tins of food in the bucket, which raised the level of the water and at the same time concealed the tins in question. If asked what he had been doing he would say that he had been sent down to mop up some water that was on the stores deck.'

In the ship's pantomime Bill and the Commander performed a version of Cole Porter's 'You're the Top', rewritten by Bill:

> You're the Top, you're a real old Caulker,
> You're the Top, you're a Matthew Walker,
> You're a Forward Guy, a Thimble Eye, in rope,
> You're a Chain Check Stopper, a Wash Deck Locker,
> You're Pusser's Soap,
> You're the Top, you're the Hook-a-Cockbill,
> You're the trial of the whole damn Watch Bill,
> You're a Leatherneck on the Quarter Deck with Band,
> You're a Jaunty's Runner, a Dagger Gunner,
> You're Duty Hand. etc . . .
> But if, Baby, I'm the Fo'c'sle, you're the Top!

THE MEDITERRANEAN SHUTTLE

The old *Adventure* kept up a shuttle between Mediterranean ports. Bunting-tosser Geoff Shaw made occasional entries in his diary:

'Jan 1943. A Beaufighter, flying past us, crashed into the sea. The whaler was sent away to see if we could recover any bodies with me, as duty signalman, in it. There were plenty of bits of wreckage floating about including a complete wheel and we did find one body which the subby and I pulled inboard. It was in quite a state. Upper body still wearing tunic (he was a sergeant pilot), lower body from waist down completely skinned so that all his muscles and ligaments were showing, and head cut off. The subby covered it with his duffle coat and told me to send to the ship, "Have recovered one decapitated body. Am continuing search." Somehow I managed, though standing in a heaving boat, one foot on each side of the body, trying to keep my balance and trying to keep out of the way of the cox'n and stroke oar; wasn't at all like sending semaphore in the relative comfort of the drill shed at the training ship. Eventually we went back to the ship where I found to my consternation that instead of being hoisted back on to the ship with the whaler, I had to climb a flaming rope, trying to clutch my hand flags in one hand because the Chief Yeoman would have played up hell if I had dropped them in the 'oggin.'

'April 10th 1943. On our way back from Gib, shadowed by a Focke-Wulf all forenoon which left us at lunch time, having reported our position to U-boats ahead. To avoid the U-boats the skipper decided to alter course but in towards the Bay of Biscay rather than the obvious move of out into the Atlantic. As a result, later that afternoon, we sighted a ship at about seventeen miles which, when we closed it, turned out to be a blockade-breaker. She eventually scuttled herself and we captured the crew. The irony was that we only managed to get that ship through trying to avoid trouble, while had we sailed at our proper time – twelve hours earlier – we would have missed her completely. (The skipper had asked, and received, permission for us to spend the night in Gib so that one watch of the lads could have a run ashore.) The blockade-breaker had come all the way from Japan, across the Pacific and Atlantic Oceans without being seen. They must then have been just a few hours' sailing time from the German naval bases in western France. How galling it must have been to them that after all that long trip they were captured by a rickety old ship that was only trying to dodge U-boats and that the next morning, instead of packing their suitcases to go home on leave, they should find themselves en route to a PoW camp.'

Wings at Sea

Young Joseph Soap to the war has gone,
In a Stringbag you will find him,
A big propeller clonking round in front,
— And his O and his TAG behind him,
Chorus: R/Ps, D/Cs, RATOG too,
Were all made to confuse us,
We're only waiting for our demob suit,
Which no one can refuse us!

A WALRUS AND THE *ALBATROSS*

In December 1941 Mick Dale, who had struggled through a TAG's course and, with Alan Todd, flown in the hands of Lieutenants (A) L. Olivier and R. Richardson, RNVR, joined No 710 Squadron to fly in 'Walri' from the seaplane-carrier *Albatross*, based at Freetown, West Africa . . .

The land of the violet lightning and the
thunderstorms of sheet iron,
The hills, rich and bursting with the
brown and orange of Gauguin . . .

with periods at RNAS Hastings nearby, then just a few huts and a dirt track, and spent 'half our time there flying, the other half laid out with malaria . . .'

'We flew daily anti-submarine patrols from the harbour, with an occasional sortie in a Swordfish up the coast to Conakry to see if any subs were alongside.' *Albatross* had been built in Australia for the Royal Australian Navy in which she served from 1928 until transferred to the RN in September 1938. Although originally fitted with a catapult she now operated her Walrus by lowering them over the side on a crane for take-off from the water. As a TAG, Mick Dale's job was 'to sit on the top wing and unshackle the Walrus when we were in the water, then climb down inside, ready for take-off. Once airborne we maintained radio contact with the ship and looked out for U-boats, etc. On our return we taxied up to the ship, and the TAG climbed back on to the top wing and hooked on again to the ship's crane. If we missed we had to go round and try again. With the prop spinning round a few inches from our heads, this could be a slightly dodgy operation!

'We were once beaten up by one of our own subs. I never found out what exactly happened, but there was an almighty bang, our prop disintegrated, and we had to ditch. The sub had taken a pot-shot at us, but nothing was said officially.

'On another occasion we flew into a tropical squall and had to come down and beach the aircraft on a tropical island. It was two rain-lashed days – without Dorothy Lamour – before we could take off again. A couple more times we came down, out of fuel or gremlin-struck, and had to be ignominiously towed back to Freetown by corvettes or merchant ships – I got rather a reputation as a Jonah after a while.'

In January 1941 a 'Sub Attack' signal was picked up by *Albatross*. The routine dawn patrol aircraft was contacted but was unable to divert to the position, 110 miles west of Freetown, for lack of fuel, so Lieutenant Cheeseman, with PO Knowles as Observer and Dale as TAG, was 'rousted out in a hurry', observes the latter, 'and we took off to see if we could find out what was going on.

'We searched the area and eventually spotted men in the water, some swimming, some hanging on to rafts or floating debris – all that remained of the SS *Eummaeus*, which had been torpedoed. We chucked our inflatable dinghy out of the after hatch, radioed our position and circled around for a while. Then we spotted an empty lifeboat a mile or so away from the men in the water. We landed, in a heavy swell, secured the lifeboat, and towed it back to the main group of survivors.

'The Walrus by now was a bit battered, and there was no chance of taking off, so we did what we could to help the survivors until two trawlers arrived to pick them up. One of them took us in tow, and we had quite a rough ride back! We'd been "adrift" for about 22 hours. Lieutenant Cheeseman was awarded an MBE, and, for some reason, I got a BEM, though I really hadn't done anything to deserve it.'

A rating pilot in *Albatross*, ex-Writer Jack Francis Smith, was afterwards commissioned, and landed an unusual job, especially for a new sub-lieutenant, of vetting pilots who had been grounded for various reasons, some of them for 'Lack of Moral Fibre' (the dreaded LMF, which was stamped all over the sufferer's papers, and of which the FAA sometimes made very free). He flew with them, 'discussed at length what had gone wrong, and was required to recommend their future employment,' in liaison with the Air Medical School.

AMC FLIGHTS

Some AMCs were refitted and armed with catapults to operate aircraft. HMSs *Canton* and *Pretoria Castle* were each equipped in the summer of 1941 with two Fairey Seafox seaplanes – the type which had served so well at the Battle of the River Plate, flying from *Ajax*. Each ship's Flight included two pilots, two observers and some eight maintenance ratings under an air artificer, all from the Fleet Air Arm.

PO Pilot Doug Elliott in *Pretoria Castle* had been educated at the City of Bath School, passed his Higher School Certificate and tried to get into banking or insurance, but it was 1932, and eventually he joined the Navy. In China with the gunboat *Cockchafer* he read the Rating Pilot AFO, and after training at Short's and at Netheravon won his RAF wings in April 1939.

This was followed by purely Naval Aviation training, during which any rating pilot who failed any of the qualifications was sent right back to General Service, while an officer was allowed a re-scrub. This was potentially a stupid and scandalous waste of an expensive flying course; the father of one 'dipped' rating pilot contacted his MP, who complained at high level, with the result that shortly afterwards a dipped candidate was given the option of joining the RAF, where several of them achieved Squadron-Leader status and above.

In *Pretoria Castle*, says Doug, 'not once was I ever called aft for a briefing, which was held in the officers' quarters somewhere. I never had a clear picture of any operation I was on, the time of the attack, the Mean Line of Advance of the ship, or anything. The best I could hope for was to scribble any information I could squeeze out of the observer on my knee pad'. His accommodation, however, was above his station. 'For a petty officer to have a large ship-side cabin (with a scuttle), hot and cold running water, and capacious wardrobe, was unheard of, and many destroyer captains would gladly have swapped cabins with me.'

Other AMCs were equipped with aircraft during refit, including the South American Station stalwarts *Alcantara*, *Asturias*, *Carnarvon Castle* and *Queen of Bermuda*.

Freddie Longman from Potter's Bar, who had got his rating pilot's wings just before war broke out, was drafted to the *Alcantara*.

'I shared a cabin with my oppo, the PO observer, and we had our own bathroom attached. But AMCs were divided ships. The engine room staff, stewards and one or two others were MN, serving under the T124X scheme, which basically gave them twice as much pay as similar RN rates. The wardroom steward received danger money for being at sea in a war zone. We didn't. This anomaly did not make for a happy ship.

'We also had, as I think most other AMCs did, a CO brought back from retirement to captain the ship. During the whole time I was on board *Alcantara* I never met him.

'The ship's company were never told *anything*, like where we were going or why we suddenly went to Action Stations and then stood down. We only heard buzzes.

'Many senior naval aviators were very much against the rating pilot scheme ever starting, and many rules and regulations were drawn up to make sure that the rating pilot was kept in his place. Wings, for instance, were at first worn on the right arm as a non-substantive badge by Leading Air and Petty Officer Air Pilots. When made Chief their wings were moved to the right cuff. PO pilots were not allowed in TBR squadrons as it was considered that they were not qualified to make tactical decisions.' (Petty Officer Pilot Charles Wines, the only rating pilot to drop a torpedo in action, on an anti-shipping strike from Malta, saw a memorandum stating that the Lower Deck aviators lacked 'the moral fibre' to make a close torpedo attack.)

'In the RN,' Longman continues, 'the senior officer in an aircrew was always the Captain of the Aircraft. Therefore in AMCs, where two RNVR sub-lieutenants and two POs were the aircrew for the two aircraft, the subby pilot always flew with the PO observer. I was treated by my observer in the same way as the coxswain of the motor boat. My job, when the aircraft was required for A/S patrol or anything else, was to go on deck, carry out a pre-flight inspection of the aircraft, make sure the bomb load was correct, make sure the Catapult Officer knew the all-up weight, discuss with the senior maintenance rating any snags, sign the 700 and we were ready.

'In the meantime my observer had been up to the bridge for a briefing and met report, and then came down to the aircraft to take charge. I had no idea where we were going or what we had to do until I got the first course to steer, and my "O" gave me no further information.' On all flights, like Doug Elliott, Longman 'took the precaution of jotting down on my knee-pad courses steered, time on each course and my own estimate of wind-speed and direction, plus the last course I had seen the ship on, and estimated speed. If my "O" were killed on a flight, my only hope of survival was a quick look at my jottings and a guess at a course back to the ship. Our only communication was by W/T, and of course all the radio gear was in the back cockpit out of my reach. I was never invited to the bridge for a briefing or after a flight for a de-briefing. Only in fighter squadrons with Skuas did a PO pilot and a PO or LA TAG fly as a crew.'

Alcantara had returned to Britain after her refit at Newport News, Virginia, when her catapult was installed, and resumed her old South Atlantic patrol work.

The 7,160-ton Liberty Ship *George Clymer* was a few hundred miles from Ascension Island on 30 May 1942, when her main shaft broke down. She sent out an SOS. Ascension had no aircraft available, and C-in-C South Atlantic sent *Alcantara*.

George Clymer drifted. At 2000 hrs she was hit by a torpedo from the disguised raider *Michel*'s special motor boat *Esau*. *Alcantara* arrived at 4 o'clock that afternoon and got her towing hawser out, but *Clymer*'s deckload of wooden railway sleepers and tractors for Iran made her an almost impossible tow. The AMC struggled on for a week, awaiting instructions from the Admiralty, and eventually orders came to sink *Clymer*.

The Seafox had first crack, on 11 June. 'I scored two direct hits,' reported Freddie Longman, 'but my little 100 lb bombs made no impression, just exploded on her deck cargo of thick wooden sleepers. We next carried out a shoot with our main armament of very ancient 6 in guns, but I don't think the shells even scarred her. The next bright idea was to depth-charge her, so we steamed at our best speed of about 15 knots as close as we dared and fired two DCs from our port throwers over towards her. I wouldn't like to guess whether they dropped nearer us or her, but she did shudder and turn upside down, so now we had about three inches of black keel sticking above the water, kept afloat very efficiently by wooden railway sleepers, and this is how we left her, while aboard *Alcantara* the engine room staff were going mad, as we had blown the port stern gland.'

LOST FROM *INDOMITABLE*

The ocean was a wide and lonely place. In October 1942 TAG Ben Kennedy was working up with No 800 Squadron in the Fleet carrier *Indomitable* in mid-Atlantic when the Fulmar he was in ran out of fuel.

'Sub-Lieutenant Lucas brought her down beautifully in the trough of a 20-foot breaking Atlantic swell. As she tipped I grabbed the Very pistol and compass, and together we struck out for the dinghy which had successfully inflated automatically. As we settled in, the other aircraft flew very low overhead and made off. They were not seen again.

'The first impression was of absolute silence except for the breaking waves. To give myself something to do I set up a lookout routine – an all-round sweep from the crests of waves followed by a rest period. I was very wet, of course, and tired, but I do not remember being particularly cold. After dark I dozed, and dreamed of home, girls, rescue by U-boat – but never that the ship was looking for us. I was not afraid – I don't know why – just very lonely and hungry. Mike was very still and quiet. A fish flapped into the dinghy. Very stupidly I threw it back over the side.

'The following day the sea moderated a little and the sun came out – I became desperately hungry and opened the ration pack to find it empty except for a tin of condensed milk, which was academic as we had nothing to open it with. During the afternoon I heard an aircraft but didn't see it. Later it came back – an Albacore – I fired my Verys and very nearly shot myself. The aircraft seemed to pass over but in fact had seen us and, maintaining radio silence, had flown back to the ship to tell them. On its return it flew so low over us its trailing aerial nearly hit us. We were picked up two hours later by the ship's seaboat.

'This incident changed my attitude to flying. Not at first, but gradually I became fearful of losing sight of the ship, and then of flying itself. It took more courage to own up to this than I possessed, so I suffered for the duration of my flying career. Still do, for that matter.'

MAC SHIPS

Ken Illingworth started as a clerk in the Electricity Department at the Town Hall in Bradford, Yorkshire, and worked there for three years before he joined the Andrew. He was a keen sportsman, a well-known figure on the soccer and cricket fields, the track and at swimming galas. He always spent most of the family holidays wandering around the port area, and went on pleasure cruises and fishing trips in small vessels. He loved a choppy sea, often to be met off Flamborough Head. He was a natural for a seagoing life, and it was not long after war broke out that he found himself a Convoy Signalman. This was a disappointment at the time – sailor Ken had always seen himself on the signal deck of a sleek and rugged convoy destroyer. But winter at Butlin's, Skegness, 1941–2, was bitter, producing chilblains on hands and feet, and he was glad to get to sea (vowing never to go to a holiday camp when he returned to civilian life, a promise he has kept faithfully – no Hi-di-Hi! for the Illingworths).

He was drafted to East Coast convoys based at Southend, where he managed to get in some cricket, made possible by bat-and-ball fanatic Lieutenant-Commander Gurney Braithwaite (later an MP), 'who did a U turn when the buzz came to his ears that RN cricketers could count on being permanent at breezy Southend – and promptly got the whole cricket team drafted to Liverpool for disposal'.

Hoping wistfully for a change from merchant ships, Ken was drafted to the MV *Acavus*. Learning that she was a tanker of the Anglo-Saxon Petroleum Company, he became confused when told that she was also something called a Merchant Aircraft Carrier. This was a type of ship, tanker or grainer, quite distinct from the Escort or 'Woolworth' carrier (which was wholly converted to a carrier); the MAC ship carried its original cargo, plus a flight deck and three or four Swordish.

'We still flew the Red Duster, but we could be a fighting ship if needed. I joined her at Falmouth, where she was still being converted, and we sailed with our first convoy in October 1943.

'The aircraft made a difference to my life, with all the excitement of take-offs and landings, which were a bit like the old Hendon air shows to us. We cheered the old "Stringbags" as they lumbered into the air, always perilously close to the bows, and our hearts were with them as they disappeared into the cloudy sky on their weary, lonely patrols over the endless ocean. Other MAC ships saw some action, or their planes did, in duels with U-boats, with the slow old Swordfish usually getting the worst of it, as at this time the German subs bristled with guns to fight it out on the surface.

'We never sank a U-boat, never even saw one, but we kept a lot of heads down. No convoy with a MAC in it ever lost a ship. When *Acavus* was converted, sword into ploughshare, back into her old form she gave good service as the *Iacra*, running to the Persian Gulf, and was actually the last of the old Anglo-Saxon (by then the Shell Company) tankers to go to the knacker's yard, being scrapped in 1963.'

The ex-merchant escort carriers, which flew the White Ensign, saw service all over the world, from Murmansk to Okinawa.

INVENTIVE *VINDEX*

Bill McCall remembers clearly how the sirens sounding over Edinburgh on Sunday, 3 September 1939, 'threw everyone into a bit of a panic'.

'The war, of course, had been expected, and my friends and I had discussed it in great detail, and I had decided that the Navy appealed to me as being about the furthest from what I was doing as an apprentice sheet metal worker in a factory. After a long wait I was accepted and told that as a sheet metal worker I could be an Air Fitter (Airframe) in the Fleet Air Arm. I hadn't a clue what that meant, but I was eager to do my bit and off I went to Guz Barracks, much to the surprise and alarm of my parents, as I had not told them about joining the Andrew. After they had recovered I think they were very proud of me. My employer was none too pleased but he couldn't say anything without looking unpatriotic, and I became FX77206.

'After the shock of square-bashing I started to enjoy the life. At that stage I remember a small man in some sort of uniform with a somewhat short neck coming to inspect us, as we were a novelty, the first of the volunteers. Somebody said, "That's Winston", which it was, in his Trinity House costume. I came to like the life so much that I transferred from HO to Active Service, and signed on for twelve. Everyone thought I was mad, but it turned out to be the best decision I ever made. I was promoted to Aircraft Artificer, and after five months with No 836 Squadron, Maydown, Northern Ireland, which supplied all the Swordfish to the MACs, I got my first sea draft, to the escort carrier *Vindex*.

'Most of the RN escort carriers were on loan from the Yanks, but *Vindex* was one of the five converted in the UK. The British conversions were very different from the American. The Yankee boats had short, wide flight decks of Oregon pine, *Vindex*'s was long and narrow and made of steel. They (the American ships) had a lot of openings in the sides of the hangar, whereas ours was a closed box forming a strength girder. They might have been all right for the Pacific, but we were built for the rough Atlantic and the Norwegian and Barents Sea, where we worked until VE-Day.

'I looked after the Stringbags and the Sea Hurricane fighters of the famous 825 Squadron, which had attacked the *Bismarck* – in which our Commander (F), Percy "Press-on" Gick had flown.

'*Vindex* became famous in the FAA for her technical inventions. The flight deck had to be lit, but not too brightly. I was detailed to produce about 40 shades to allow a slit of light to penetrate on to the flight deck. One of the T124X Engineering Officers laid a cable with lamp bulb sockets down each side of the deck. I then made a series of shades approximately one foot wide which were hinged to allow bulbs to be changed but also allowed about one to two inches of light on the deck, which, with the deck coaming, it was reckoned could not be seen by the enemy even when the deck rolled. The system was successful and gave the pilots a little assistance.'

Chief PO Charlie Waldram, in charge of the electrical staff, put together a pair of illuminated 'bats' to aid night landing, based on some electrical conduit, reflectors from the lighting in the 'heads', and an aircraft dimmer switch; and he and armourer Norman Pickup fitted an illuminated target disc on the windscreen of each Swordfish to help the pilot aim the aircraft in the dark. Another useful mod they made was a repositioning of all the switches in the Swordfish cockpits from the starboard side to the front, to avoid finger trouble.

Serving in No 825 Squadron aboard *Vindex* was a familiar character, Mick Dale, now a Chief PO and in charge of all the squadron's TAGs, his face still yellow from the malaria he had contracted in *Albatross* at Freetown. He had joined No 825 at Thorney Island in January 1943 as a newly made-up Temporary Acting Petty Officer, and it was quite an ordeal for him. 'Not only was I in charge of other TAGs for the first time, but this particular outfit was already famous for the Channel affair, and, to make my ride even rougher, my TAGs made no secret of the fact that they missed my predecessor, the famous Les "Ginger" Sayer, who had flown with Percy Gick against the *Bismarck*.'

Had he but known it, Les Sayer had himself had a tricky time to begin with. A diary entry of his reads: 'So now I am PO I/C TAGS 825 Sqdn HMS *Ark Royal* . . . most of the TAGs are wartime conscripts or volunteers – I find I have a chemist, an insurance agent, a gas meter collector, a window cleaner, a gentleman

Scottish farmer. Lt-Cdr Esmonde is the CO. He doesn't talk a lot, even less to the TAGs. But he supports me to the hilt in whatever I decide to be right for TAGs, and I have already made up my mind that the old naval disciplines are not going to get the best out of these raw recruits who have come from all walks of life . . .' Later he was able to write, 'We have quickly become a team, with a degree of trust in each other which I found very rewarding.'

'Odious comparisons soon faded,' Mick Dale later reported. He 'struck up a close friendship with Dave Todd,' Ginger Sayer's 'gentleman Scottish farmer', 'whose big, clumsy-looking hands could tie the most intricate trout flies,' and with Londoner Joe Palmer, 'a breezy character who was wont to give officers a friendly hug and a "Wotcher, mate!"'

At 2048 on 24 April 1944 *Vindex* weighed from Moville, Northern Ireland, for operations in the Atlantic against U-boats.

At 0518 on the 28th the Asdic operator in the sloop *Bickerton* reported 'Contact firm, classified submarine', and the sloops began an attack with a 26-charge pattern. As the last charge was exploding, the 750-ton *U765* broke surface half a mile away and wallowed, engines stopped. The hunters could see 'the twisted, buckled plating of the U-boat's conning tower', and the three sloops opened up on the enemy.

Sheffield, Vallely and Dale saw the U-boat about a mile on their port beam. Sheffield opened up to full throttle and turned his Swordfish towards her. At 100 yards he dived to attack through mingled fire from the escorts and a weak defensive fire from the U-boat's ack-ack, which nevertheless damaged his centre-section and starboard mainplane.

Coming down at 120 knots on the submarine's port bow, he released his DCs at 75 feet. Dale 'saw them straddle the conning tower, 40 feet apart, one exploding under the conning tower, one close to the U-boat's starboard quarter, just abaft the conning tower. Some 30–45 seconds later the sub broke in two, bow and stern each rising to 45 degrees, and the two halves sank, leaving a dozen survivors in the sea. Two of them waved at us as we flew low over them.'

Swordfish 'V' landed aboard *Vindex* at 6.43. 'As the flight deck man released the deck hook from the arrester wire, Commander (O) Stovin-Bradford rushed across to the aircraft and asked me for my camera, and a man from the photographic section stood by to rush the film down below for developing. I had to tell him that in the excitement of the action I had completely forgotten all about taking pictures for evidence . . .'

'A Hunting We Will Go'

In the Atlantic the U-boats were getting a hammering. 'The Brits were getting cheeky these days. You couldn't feel safe anywhere, not even inside our own approach buoys,' says Lothar-Günther Buchheim in *Das Boot* (The Boat). Anyone who served in the corvettes, taut sloops, sweepers or CVEs (escort carriers), 'the little ships that Churchill clean forgot', in the steep Atlantic stream, the freezing runs to Russia or the angry North Sea, when a ship would stand on her screws and roll her decks under, can call himself a sailor. But even smaller vessels were now braving the rough northern seas.

COMBINED OPERATION

David Satherley was an Isle of Wighter, 'so ships of the pre-war fleet coming and going round Spithead and the Solent were well known to me, plus my sister married a Chief Shipwright, and I spent my holidays in Pompey and knew the dockyard and Pompey-based warships as well as teenagers today know pop stars. My favourite reading was the lives of Drake and Nelson, so you can say I was a hopeless case. I wanted to be a boy seaman at HMS *St Vincent* but my parents insisted on a trade. I was indentured to a printer's and publisher's at Cowes, and sat at a desk overlooking the Solent miserably watching destroyers and subs sailing by and "Stringbag" Swordfish from Lee-on-Solent dropping dummy torpedoes. War is a terrible thing but I actually did cartwheels when it began as I saw now nothing could stop my joining the Navy.

'I was informed that as we did work for flying-boat makers Saunders-Roe and J. S. White, shipbuilders, I was in a Reserved Occupation. J. S. White had built a long string of destroyers for the Navy . . . *Vampire, Vortigern, Westcott, Winchelsea, Forester* and *Fury, Keith* and *Kempenfelt, Impulsive, Intrepid, Jersey* and *Kingston* . . . the names still roll off my mind . . . and I wanted to *sail* in one of them . . .

'So like many a boy before me I ran away to sea, volunteering as a seaman and being accepted. Once I had sent a postcard telling them where I was, and the police had been informed I was no longer missing, my parents were delighted for me. My father had served four years in the Sussex Regiment, First World War, two older brothers were regular RAF and Wellington bomber sergeant pilots, and two other brothers were Territorials in the splendidly named Princess Beatrice's Isle of Wight Rifles. If I hadn't tried to join up I think my father would have disowned me!

'I was trained at the new HMS *Collingwood* stone frigate, and felt at home when the instructor pensioners yarned about Jutland and HMS *Lion* and the *Warrior* and Jack Cornwell. I still dreamed of a draft to one of White's sleek destroyers, and nearly heartbroken I was when I drew something called Combined Operations, then in its infancy, and went to Troon, Ayrshire, to serve on barge-like Tank Landing Craft. I thought the only time we'd go to sea whould be to land tanks when the invasion of Europe took place, which, from the state we were in, wouldn't be for years.

'I need not have worried. The Combined Ops life was great. It was still Navy, and the TLCs (later LCTs) were fun to serve in with small crews. While our Fleet counterparts were convoying to Malta, etc, we put in at ports around Scotland and the North of England, and even, when the Combined Ops fleet was extended to Landing Craft, Flak, and Landing Craft, Guns, escorted East Coast convoys and saw action between invasion exercises. Meantime we sloped off ashore in our tiddley suits, a new Combined Ops badge on the cuff of our left sleeves, and wowed the girls in dance halls from Aberdeen to Middlesbrough.

'All this came to a stop when we sailed south and loaded with tanks for a rather testing morning at Dieppe. The Germans knew we were coming. The Second LCT Flotilla beached and was annihilated, as were the tanks they carried. Others waiting to go into the cauldron were ordered to the "Waiting Pool", to see if further landings were at all possible in the appalling circumstances. My LCT had been rigged as a hospital-plus-rescue craft, and there were smaller craft coming off the beaches with wounded, under heavy fire from the batteries ashore and plenty of air activity. Towards noon we were ordered home in a mixed convoy, well protected overhead by our fighters, though some of them got shot down by trigger-happy gunners who had spent a morning not calculated to improve the nerves. I resigned myself to not surviving the war if all landings were going to be like this. But tremendous lessons were learned. Apart from more and better landing craft, with gunns, rockets, etc, at Normandy every Allied aircraft had three wide white stripes painted on their wings and fuselages (as an afterthought, overnight) to stop happy gunners blasting them.

'So I had gone "overseas", and was to go further. The new sleek LCIs (Landing Craft, Infantry) were being built in the States, and there I went on the *Queen Elizabeth* – bit of a change from an LCT, and joined *LCI(L) 127*, building at Quincy, Massachusetts, near Boston. It was great fun for us, autumn 1942, seeing lights again and being invited to High School dances, where the pupils were about our own age and there we were in Royal Navy uniforms, old salts, with a Croix de Guerre and Mentions, chatting up girls right out of a Mickey Rooney "Andy Hardy" film. When we sailed it was to join the North African landings, via New York, Norfolk, Bermuda and Gib, all good landfalls – but with an awful lot of deep sea in between!

'Skipper of one of these was actor Peter Bull, crossing the Atlantic in company with another LCI captained by Alec Guinness. He called his autobiographical record of this little adventure *To Sea in a Sieve*. I can think of no better title.

'Of the eighteen crew of *LCI 127*, three of us had been to sea before (not counting the outward pleasure cruise in the *Queen*). We had a subby RNVR skipper of the ancient age of 24. The average age of our crew was 19, three of the ODs being 16. We were delighted with our LCI, which looked like a "real" ship, with four Oerlikon guns and bunks for 200 troops.

'On leaving Bermuda with our flotilla, plus a rescue tug for the Atlantic voyage, heavy seas stayed with us the whole three weeks of the trip. Every night after dusk the convoy would scatter – unintentionally, and at dawn there we'd be in an empty ocean. A rendezvous point had been agreed, however, and then we'd either sail like crazy to catch up, or circle about until other LCIs showed up. One night in a storm we ran into a huge convoy of massive ships heading the other way and had a terrifying time dodging being run down and rammed, Skipper very calm, though only a subby then. I strained my eyes like never before. One monster missed us by inches. My diary reads "Of course no cooking on our galley stove, so sandwiches our lot. Very proud we all made it to Gib, hairy and filthy, but there. Got spotted by a circling Focke-Wulf and went to action stations for first time for *127*, but too far away to fire at."

'The Skipper, then Sub-Lieutenant H. John, RNVR (later awarded the MBE), showed at this early stage in command that he was a calm man in all situations, and a very good skipper who interfered with the lives of his crew as little as was necessary. We would do anything for him, and he, as proved on many occasions, would do anything for us. First Lieutenants came and went (we carried just two officers) as they qualified to be Landing Craft captains. Even I was offered CW candidate training but was quite happy as I was.'

HUNTERS AND HUNTED

Hunting in the North Atlantic was Captain Walker's crack 2nd Escort (Support) Group, HMS *Starling* (Captain D), *Woodpecker*, *Wild Goose*, *Woodcock* and *Magpie*. In *Woodpecker* as a brand-new Asdic Submarine Detector III was Tom Bailey, man of *Renown*. He had joined the Bird-class sloop when she was still only a job number at Denny's, Dumbarton, Scotland, and since then she had played an important part in Walker's outstanding success. They operated from Gladstone Dock at Liverpool. When entering or leaving harbour *Starling* would play 'A Hunting We Will Go' over the Tannoy, and *Woodpecker* 'The Woody Woodpecker's Song', made famous by the Andrews Sisters.

'We woke up to that tune, turned in at night to it. Sometimes the Sisters even called us to Action Stations, "And certain stars shot madly from their spheres to hear the seamaids' music." We were a famous, crack team, but a lot of the spirit went out of us when Captain Walker died of a heart attack, brought on by the strain of his ceaseless drive to scourge the U-boats.'

Perhaps their most unforgettable fight was the 15-hour running hunt and gun battle ending in the ramming and destruction of *U473* on 5 May 1944, after which *Starling* signalled: 'Cease firing. Gosh, what a lovely battle.'

Another small ship which did her bit in the Atlantic was the sloop *Chanticleer*. The name baffled Ernie North when he was given the draft. He was another ex-*Rev-en-gee* – 'A happy ship', he remembers. He had also served in *Hood* ('Even in peacetime hopelessly overcrowded'), and felt that 'a new modern ship for me was overdue'. '*Chanticleer*?' said one messmate, 'Free French carrier, isn't she?' 'No,' said another, 'Frog submarine'. He didn't find out until he arrived at William Denny's at Dumbarton with the remainder of the draft, and there she was, 'A neat little sloop, *U05*. Not exactly a fleet greyhound, but well armed, and capable of handing out a terrific wallop down aft in the sub-hunting season. I liked her from the start. The officers were a great lot, and my particular messmates a grand bunch. The seaman POs knew their job, and soon trained up their branch, 40 per cent of whom had never been to sea before.'

'In the spring of 1943 a section of our hunting group waited at Oban for the weather to clear to escort a huge capital floating dock to replace one sunk in Grand Harbour, Malta. The go-ahead was given and we were told that fine weather could be expected. Out in the Atlantic we were hit by a hurricane with really mountainous seas. The dock broke free from its tugs and was spinning round like a matchbox. We thought it would sink at any moment.

'The seas were so bad no one could turn for fear of broaching. The upper deck got smashed up, and depth-charges broke loose on the quarterdeck. In securing them, two men went over the side and were lost. No rescue or search was possible, not being able to turn, and it lowered our spirits for the rest of the trip.

'After about twenty months in commission we took a convoy from Argentia in Newfoundland back to the UK, during which we were detached to join a convoy coming up from Gib. It was mid-November, and we all thought that a bit of sun would be just the job, and what nice people they were back in the Liver Buildings!

'We joined the convoy in the forenoon watch, somewhere near the Azores. It was a glorious morning but we were told that German aircraft and subs were around. About 1220 I went down to the mess, had my tot and my dinner, when there was the sound of DCs in the distance. The ship altered course and increased speed, and the submarine alarm went almost at once.

'As we had done literally hundreds of times before, everyone rushed to their action stations, hatches were closed, fans and ventilators shut, and within one minute *Chanticleer* was ready to defend her convoy.

'My action station was as Officer of the Quarters on the two foremost twin 4 in mountings. The guns' crews told me that a sub had been sighted astern of the convoy by those already closed up . . . A quick check around the mountings to make sure they had the right ammo, range and deflection dials at zero, everything ready to open fire . . . We could hear the HSD searching for the U-boat, and the voice of the Skipper ordering the sectors to be swept by the Asdics.

'Orders came a bit quicker now. "Follow Director. Load, Load, Load!" All guns were loaded, and the gunlayers and trainers followed their dial pointers. We started our run in on the submerged U-boat, and we could plainly hear the echoes right down to the HSD's "Instantaneous echo!" A shallow pattern had been ordered, and the Gunner, normally on "X" gun, had already moved on down the quarterdeck to take charge of the Depth-Charge Party, and as I neared "X" gun the first charges were exploding astern.

'At this point, with a tremendous roar, the whole quarterdeck seemed to disintegrate upwards in a jumbled mass, and a wave of pressure and heat hit me. The ship shuddered horribly and rolled to port, then slowly came upright, moving most unnaturally. We had been well and truly fished. I thought – A helluva lot of people have just died.

'The young depth-charge telephone number was sitting on the deck by the starboard screen, his phones still on his head, looking in a bad way – the only man left alive on the quarterdeck. The ship's rudder, which weighed between 30 and 50 tons, had flown up into the air, and had come down like a great butcher's cleaver and was knifed into the upper deck a few feet from the lad on the phones. Both after Oerlikon power mountings and all the upper deck had gone and the cabins and offices below were open to the sky and sea. The prop shafts were hanging out of the wreckage, and loose depth-charges were hanging in various positions.

'I returned to the guns up for'ard. The upper deck was littered with debris from aft, and there were huge ridges and rents athwartships round the funnel. In various places there were also the more horrible remains of our late messmates. A young officer was found alive, just, in the wreckage of the cabin flat aft, but he died within minutes.

'The ship was fairly steady but was well down aft, and we were lucky in that the weather was kind. All the boats were holed and some of the Carley rafts damaged but the Damage Control Party amidships and the engine room staff were shoring up the bulkhead between the engine room and the boiler room. At the guns we remained closed up. The remains of one of the Oerlikons was on the fo'c'sle, and we ditched that and a lot of other wreckage over the side. Soon after I returned to the mounting we picked up another U-boat bearing on our starboard bow. A Sunderland then flew overhead and circled the ship, and asked if they could take pictures. They were brusquely told to go and look for the U-boats that were going to slap another fish into us.

'One of our chummy ships in the Group, HMS *Crane*, then came up to assist us, and we prepared to abandon ship, *Crane* being asked to sink us by gunfire. The men were advised not to go between decks as she might decide to leave us at any moment, but someone decided that we needed some fags, and cartons of Churchman's No 1s appeared on the upper deck from the canteen. Our canteen manager, also a dear messmate, was dead, and if the ship was to be sunk, who was there to complain?

'While the *Crane* was waiting for us another torpedo was fired, and she attacked an echo at least once. She was obviously in danger and moved off again.

'The Skipper told us that a tug was on its way to see if it could help. A frenzy of lightening ship was taking place. Everything that was ditchable was ditched. Everything that was unscrewable was unscrewed and thrown overboard. I, God knows why, decided to cut down a stubby little mast with a saw. We had only about three or four bodies available to bury, and a short service was held and we committed our very dear shipmates to the deep. There were over 30 killed in all, and on a small ship with a very close-knit set of officers and men it was a crushing blow. Not all small ships reached the happy state of understanding we had. For them it was

> Farewell, Aggie Weston's, the barracks at Guz,
> Hang my tiddley suit on the door,
> I'm sewn up neat in a canvas sheet
> And I won't be home no more.'

Hooligans' Navy

Each man waiting was two men,
The man with Paybook and number,
A rank and duty, Sick Berth

Tiffy, Torpedoman, Tanky
And Stoker, and another man inside
With a healthy fear for his own skin.

Alan Ross, Sub-Lieutenant RNVR

MINES IN THE MUD

Dennis 'Vic' Oliver from Basingstoke, Hampshire, worked for John I. Thorny-croft, and in his teens joined the Air Training Corps to train as a Ground Staff Motor Mechanic, but when registering for call-up on impulse he chose the Navy. His technical ability became clear and, after initial training at HMS *Collingwood*, Fareham, and short spells at HMS *Excellent* and in the cruiser *Jamaica*, he was drafted to HMS *Vernon* to work on magnetic and acoustic mines, partly in counter-measures against enemy mines, but with a special job involving a new sonic underwater buoy for marking a passage through a minefield on D-Day. This work was carried out mostly in the mining trials area off Stokes Bay, west of Portsmouth. From there Dennis was moved to the Old Pier, Weston-super-Mare, Somerset, chosen 'because it was tucked away from town and out of sight of inquisitive locals, with the second highest tide in the world – ideal for trials'.

Here, under Admiral Casement, a team of 'engineers, inventors, physicists and various ranks and ratings down to the common OD' worked enthusiastically together, for the most part regardless of rank. Mines, acoustic or magnetic, for investigation and trials would arrive from Gosport, 'be checked over and set, then loaded at Weston Airport on to a Lancaster bomber which would fly to the target area at Langford Grounds, a large sandbank uncovered at low tide but at high tide with some 40–45 ft of water over it, to drop on the target already indicated by direction and wind direction arrows, with a Naval photographer filming it.'

'Meanwhile another party had set out with a skiff, pennants and marker buoys. After walking a mile across fields to the shore nearest the target, as the tide ebbed four ratings rowed across to the sandbank, now being uncovered, and three men set off across it with a strop, pennant and buoy on each shoulder, looking for the mines. When you came across one you sat across it, placed the strop round the centre, shackled the pennant to the strop, stretched it out and fastened the marker buoy to the end; then trudged off to look for the next one. It was like quicksand there, and you had to keep moving. If you were lucky you located all the mines dropped before the tide turned. Next morning you sailed at high tide in our wooden-hulled MFV (Motor Fishing Vessel) and an old car ferry to find the marker buoys and recover the mine for examination.

'One important job was the development of a small mine which could be dropped by aircraft in the canals of Germany. For this we had the use of a Boston night-fighter/bomber, which would come tearing along the coast spewing out these mines, some of which hit the water and flew up again, like playing "ducks and drakes" with pebbles on a pond. Then we would go down in a lorry at low tide and race the flow, trying to dig them out.

'Owing to the unsociable hours we had to work, we were glad of some rest at the end of the day, or a run ashore, and there was no barracks routine, it was all work, and everybody mucked in, ratings and officers alike. We once turned up for a mine recovery job well sloshed on farmhouse-brewed cider from a generous farmer, obviously not fit for wandering about on the mud flats, and the officers simply turned to and did it themselves, with nothing said, then took us all into the Royal Pier Hotel to celebrate one officer's birthday.' This treatment was far removed from the divisive snobbery separating wardroom from fo'c'sle in many situations.

THE BIG ONE: NORMANDY

In contrast to the victims of the Depression who had joined the Navy for 'three square meals a day', HO Fred Hall had been part of a totally different strand of English social history. Fred came from a comfortable middle-class home in Balham, South London, his father a hard-working jobber in the Stock Exchange in the City of London. In 1932, when Fred was eight, they bought their first motor car, a 1928 Singer 8 four-door saloon costing £15, which was the start of an annual fortnight's seaside holiday at Littlehampton, Sussex, 'common now but not then', where they always stayed at 65 Arundel Road, a private boarding house owned by Mrs Barnes, an elderly widow. 'We would see about four or five other cars. Once past Purley you were on safari into the unknown.'

Mrs Barnes had three sons, the eldest a Petty Officer in HMS *Hood*. At Navy Week in August 1933 Fred and his father spent a day at Portsmouth aboard the great battlecruiser as guests of PO Barnes, with dinner and tea and a complete guided tour of the whole ship. It needed another whole day to visit the battleships *Nelson* and *Warspite*, and the carrier *Courageous*. 'What a contrast to today's Navy Days! In those days you could spend the whole week there and still only see about a quarter of the ships. There were usually one or two battlecruisers, four battleships, a dozen cruisers, about 30 destroyers, and perhaps 30 or 40 lesser craft, plus one or two aircraft-carriers.'

Hall Senior enjoyed these annual Naval visits as much as young Fred. He had served in the Harwich Patrol in the Great War, in the destroyers *Ullswater*,

Lennox, Sharpshooter and *Swallow*; his eldest brother Fred, a gunlayer in Q-ships, had been killed three weeks before the Armistice; an uncle had served in the engine room in battleships; and Fred's great-great-grandfather was Admiral Sir Charles Popham of the famous Royal Naval family. In 1936 Mr Hall moved the family out to a new house at Morden in Surrey, which had been a small village until the Underground reached it in 1926; the house was one of two just completed on an unmade road in a semi-built estate, and they were the first occupants, pioneers in new suburbia. Fred joined the 12th Morden Boy Scouts.

In September 1938, time of the Munich crisis, all members of the 12th Morden Scouts aged 14 and above were enrolled as auxiliary members of the ARP (Air Raid Precautions) service. In August 1939 they became permanent part-time members as cyclist messengers, and were given training in first aid, anti-gas precautions and simple fire-fighting.

With the eruption of the Blitz in September duties rose to four or five evenings a week and all-night during air-raids. 'This continued for 57 consecutive nights. I had left school in March and was working as an office boy at 6/- a week for stockbrokers A. Miller & Company in Pinners Hall in the City. With the fires raging along the river, an average day began with an uncertain journey by bus and tube to the office, varied by raids, working hours interrupted by at least two hours in the shelters underneath the old Stock Exchange building, home by 7 p.m., duty till about 4.30 a.m., home, an hour's kip, then off to the City again. Then Balham Station was bombed and it took three hours to the office, by devious routes through bomb damage.

'One morning I was crossing London Bridge when out of the murk from Tower Bridge roared a Heinkel 111 and dropped three bombs in the river. The packed bridge cleared in record time, the four-minute mile being broken, I'm sure, many times over. Another time I was on the top of a bus passing Clapham Common when the whole AA battery there (eight 4.7 in guns) opened up and blew out all the windows on the bus. On another bus I found myself directing a new driver from the top deck by banging my feet on the floor (one for left, two for right).

'This form of civvy Active Service gradually eased up as the Blitz fizzled out, and in early 1943 I realized that most of my colleagues and friends had joined HM Forces, and I volunteered, so that I could enter the Service of my choice – the Navy, of course.

'I did my basic training at HMS *Glendower*, Pwhelli, North Wales, by courtesy of Billy Butlin, at the end of which I was offered a choice of: Steward, Writer, Coder, Supply and Stores or Sick Berth Attendant. As I had enjoyed my first-aid training in both the Scouts and ARP, I opted for the latter, and became a PSBA (Probationary Sick Berth Attendant). I was passed fit and able and sent to HMS *Pembroke*, RNB Chatham, and slung my hammock in the sweaty, foetid underground tunnel, shortly afterwards going thankfully to the RN Hospital, Gillingham, Kent, for my medical training – eight pleasant months of lectures, demonstrations and practical work.

'After a fortnight my class was marched into the mortuary to witness two post-mortems. One man fainted and others went a bit green, and a dinner of fat pork finished off a few more. This apparently was a calculated way of weeding out the unsuitables, and several men were reallocated to the Stoker Branch. Shortly after qualifying, I was drafted to HMS *Westcliff* for transfer to the Combined Operations branch, that they used to call the "Hooligans' Navy", then to HMS *Mylodon*, Oulton Broad, Lowestoft, a Combined Ops base. D-Day was near, and it was unarmed combat, small arms firing (Tommy guns, Stens included), and a crash Commando course, with me, as a medico, humping a 56 lb first-aid valise on my back the whole time. I was never so fit again.

'And I went to sea for the first time in the Service, as a new member of the 8th LCT Flotilla in the Flotilla Leader *LCT 7040*, for intensive sea manoeuvres and practice beachings.

'On the Glorious First of June the 8th Flotilla left Lowestoft and sailed south, reaching Southampton Water two days later and tying up amongst hundreds of other landing craft.

'Late on the night of the 5th, having earlier loaded Sherman tanks and a contingent of Pongoes, we headed out into the Channel, arriving off the coast of France the next morning. We beached and discharged the tanks, which took some time owing to beach obstacles. I was told to report to the Beachmaster ashore, and there I found some other SBAs. The craft carrying the Royal Army Medical Corps party had not arrived, and we were to fill in for them – temporarily. The "temporarily" became seven days . . .

'Noise, smoke, dust and death . . . Salvoes from *Warspite* and *Ramillies* tearing overhead like hurtling express trains . . . a strong smell of burning . . .'

Anchored off the beach-head was Alan Mathison's SS *Romney*. 'After nine months swinging round the buoy in Scapa Flow in the ammunition ship *Aire*, waiting for a carelessly thrown fag-end to send her sky-high at any moment, followed by a year on the meat run through E-boat Alley, I had been glad to go deepsea again.

'I sailed from Hull in the SS *Fort Livingstone* for North Africa in October 1943. We went to Loch Ewe for convoy and on sailing from there were joined by ships from Liverpool and Glasgow also bound for the Med. The night all the ships joined up was in early November and it was a dirty night, blowing more than half a gale with a big sea running.

'About 7 p.m. I turned-in, more or less fully dressed except for boots. I had the "graveyard" watch – midnight to 4 a.m. I'd only been asleep about an hour when I heard the alarm bells chattering, I jumped off my bunk and was putting my seaboots on when there was the most unholy crash and the ship suddenly started to heel over to starboard. I grabbed my lifejacket and dashed out on deck and up on to the bridge. I thought – this is it, we have been torpedoed. When I got into the wheelhouse a most amazing sight met my eyes. There on our port side was a fully loaded inward-bound tanker (high octane spirit) stuck in our No 1 hold, and we had gone down by the head until our foredeck was awash. The tanker extricated himself by going astern. By this time it looked as though we might founder, and the Master signalled for assistance to stand by in case we had to abandon ship. They sent us an armed trawler to stand by and escort us back to Londonderry. Several ships were badly damaged that night, all because some fool in the routing office of the Admiralty had routed an inward-bound fully loaded convoy on the exact same route as the outward-bound convoy. The result was that about 140 ships got mixed up in that affair. I know one of them was towed into Londonderry with a broken back, a write-off.

'We spent two weeks in Londonderry while Naval divers put temporary repair plates over the hole in our side to enable us to get across to Glasgow to discharge our cargo. The damage to the *Fort Livingstone* was so bad that they had to completely rebuild the forward section of the ship. I left her when she went into drydock in Cardiff for repairs.

'The next ship I joined was the *Romney*, after she had docked in Hull from a 27-month voyage, which had earned her a "Mention in Dispatches" from Field Marshal Montgomery for her service in the North African campaign. She had loaded a cargo in New York for North Africa, a cargo of such importance that she was routed not across the Atlantic, but down through the Panama Canal, down the west coast of South America, through the Magellan Straits, across the South Atlantic to Capetown, up the East African coast into the Red Sea, and finally into the Med, that passage having taken 127 days, which I can vouch for, having read the scrap logbook for that passage after I had joined her. There was a rather poignant entry at the end of that logbook, entered by whom I do not know. It simply said, "End of voyage, thank God". After being away for that length of time at sea during the war, I can fully appreciate the feelings of the person who wrote it. I sailed in the *Romney* to the beachhead at Normandy during the landings there. Our position at anchorage was in the "Sword" sector, nearest to the guns at Cherbourg. We were frequently fired on by those guns, especially if the MTBs on the "Trout line", as it was called, let up on the smoke they were supposed to keep going to stop the German gunners getting our range.

'One day they did just that, for some reason or other, and in seconds the Germans had our range and dropped shells right abeam of our ship only yards from us. We had to up-anchor and get out as fast as we could before one of them landed on us. We made it safely away, but the *Iddesleigh*, one of Tatums' ships, was not so lucky; they got her and killed several of her crew and she became a total loss. We did two runs to the beachhead from Hull with supplies. The second time Jerry nearly had us. Their one-man subs had placed an acoustic mine under our stern during the night. In the morning when the LCT alongside us switched on his generator, the mine exploded and virtually lifted our stern out of the water. We survived and so did the LCT, but I saw the *Fort Lac La Rounge* get a torpedo from a one-man sub. It killed about 150 soldiers sleeping in her 'tween decks when it exploded, and badly damaged the ship, putting her out of commission for a long time.'

Fred Lee, now a Leading Hand, paid off *Glasgow* when she berthed at Hartlepool for a refit, and returned to 'HM Hellhole' at Chatham. He was not pleased to be given a draft to Combined Operations.

'I'm not going to Combined Ops, I'm a *seaman*!'

'Well now you're a *seaman* in Combined Ops!'

LST 364 was just back from Anzio. 'If I said they were bomb-happy that's the least I could say . . . I asked them what they were doing now. "We're getting kitted out and ready for the next invasion . . ." The Skipper was an RNR two-and-half ringer, a Merchant Navy officer but one of those ambitious types, and the more damage he could do on the other side the better.

'We started loading and unloading and getting ready to go to Normandy, well, we didn't *know* where we were going actually but we had a good idea. We went down to Portsmouth and loaded up with Canadians, and lorries, and we had a few tanks, and we went and lay out in the Solent, and on the eve of 6 June everything started moving, all those concrete piers and dock walls that they landed on; it all moved down the Solent towards the sea. They were there ahead of us, we left that night, and this RNR Skipper of ours was shouting and bawling at everyone to get out of the way, he wanted to get on the beach. We sailed up and down Piccadilly Circus, as they called it, and when we got there it was four o'clock. There were some LCPs running around putting ropes round bodies that were in the sea and towing them ashore. We had to wait until the tide next day, so we emptied and made off, to make many trips to the beach.

'The first thing to aggravate us were the destroyers and MLs, they were nipping up and down with smoke cans, making smoke everywhere, protecting us and suffocating us. The most horrific of all were the German bombers coming over in the dark, and underneath them came the Dakotas going the other way, and people were firing at the bombers and bringing down Dakotas, and that was a terrible thing to endure, to watch the Dakotas crashing in the sea. What bloody fools gave that order? They even used their Aldis lamps signalling to us and they still got shot down, and were still using their Aldis lamps when they crashed into the sea. There was just a big flash and everything disappeared. So that was D-Day.

'Then we ran on the beach, and we had a walk round ashore, helping the troops to get ashore. We couldn't get off. We got all the stuff out of the tank space, scrubbed it out, and laid tables out. We carried about five surgeons, and the wounded were already coming back into the LST, so as the tide came in we hauled off and the surgeons were operating. As we were having our tea these bods kept coming up from the tank space bringing cloths. What the hell had they got in the cloths? Then it dawned on us. While we were eating they were coming through with bits of legs, bits of arms . . . By Christ, it put everybody off their tea! Then we got to see some of the blokes and went round giving them fags. Most of the casualties were burns, they'd been trapped in tanks, by flame-throwers . . . They were covered in picric gauze or whatever they were treating them for burns with.

'It was certainly a nasty affair and we came back to Portsmouth and unloaded that lot as fast as the Old Man could get the thing going; he wanted to get back again and wait for another load. He travelled so fast and did so many trips that he came back one day as a commander and within the next few months he came back as Captain of LSTs at Tilbury . . . all between June and December. He was a magnificent man, though a bloody nuisance. He had a French wife that he shut up in a tower in Ryde. I went across to tell him he was wanted about half-past three one morning and I caught the flak. He said "You haven't scrubbed this bloody boat out!" At four o'clock in the bloody morning!'

The cruiser/minelayer *Adventure* lay off the French coast, acting as a repair ship for landing craft and coastal forces. Bunting-tosser Geoff Shaw recorded the high drama of the invasion in his diary:

'Early June 1944. – Off the French coast. Day and, mostly, night attacks by FW 190s and Ju 88s, sometimes bombing, sometimes minelaying. Gunfire, noise, explosions, smoke screens, constant Action Stations. Bombardments of shore by battleships, cruisers, rocket craft. Return fire from ashore. Parachutes seen descending from Flying Fortress, Spitfires and Mustangs. Mines exploding. All very hectic.

'Monday, 19 June. – Weather deteriorating. Visibility bad. Gale warning. Set anchor watch and raised steam. Weather worsening rapidly. Several ships dragging anchor during forenoon including *Bulolo* (trooper, ex-AMC), *Thysville*. Numerous small craft in trouble. Trawler *Colsay* and coaster *Eldridge* driven aground. We were flooded with requests for help but could do nothing – all we could do to save ourselves. Several ships drifting out of control.

1830 – warning of attack by glider bombs.

2030 – tug went to help *Colsay*, towed her clear.

2140 – landing craft out of control passed down our starboard side.

'Tuesday, 20 June. – Mine exploded nearby. *LCT 947* reported being mined, having casualties, engine out of order, anchor lost, in trouble. Unable to help.

0215 – explosions nearby. Shellfire?

0235 – *LCT 947* reported breaking up fast.

0330 – Air-raid warning red.

0550 – Abandoned coaster flying distress signals drifted past.

0650 – Coaster ran aground.

0655 – Air-raid warning red.

'Wednesday, 21 June.

1100 – Moved berth. LSTs ordered to land cargoes and accept all risks. Weather still wild. *Eldridge* reloaded, anchored in deep water.

1700 – *Eldridge* drifting on to US merchant vessel. US MV got under way. Tug managed to hold *Eldridge*. US MV drifting on to *Adventure*. *Adventure* berth again. Destroyer *Fury* mined, taken in tow and brought alongside *Despatch*.

'Thursday, 22 June. – *Fury* broken adrift, drifted past us, driven aground on rocks west of Cap Manvieux. Countless craft of all kinds high and dry along beach stretching out of sight in both directions – some damaged, some upside-down, some on one side, some on or against each other, some completely wrecked.

p.m. Weather beginning to improve. Counted 355 Fortresses flying overhead with Mustangs and Lightnings.

2000 – Fortresses on return journey. Wing broke off one at root, some crew members baled out. *Adventure*, *Frobisher* (cruiser) and *Thysville* returned to berths held before gale.'

This was a record of the 'Great Gale'. After that the scene off the Normandy beaches returned to normal . . .

'Friday, 23 June. – Air-raids last night. Plane shot down nearby. Large number of mines dropped during dark hours. Heavy gunfire to SE. Spitfires overhead. Mine exploded off starboard bow.

1900 – Destroyer *Glisdale* mined, towed to "Mulberry".

2115 – Landing craft mined, sunk.

2230 – Cruiser *Scylla* mined E23 berth.

   'Saturday, 24 June. – More air-raids. More mines and bombs. Another plane shot down.

0655 – Trawler *Lord Austin* mined C17 berth, sunk.

0730 – Destroyer *Swift* mined, sinking.

0735 – *MT41* (US MV) K14 berth, mined, sunk.

0930 – *Fort Norfolk* mined.

1700 – LCVP blew up on mine, close to starboard, nothing left.

Evening – can still see bows of *MT41* showing above water.

2320 – *Nith* hit by bomb, casualties, towed to UK.

2340 – Near miss by bombs or mines.

   'Sunday, 25 June.

0045 – Cruiser *Arethusa* mined, slight damage.

Over 40 Landing Craft inshore, discharging. Over 140 craft of all types wrecked on beach. Coaster upside-down to starboard. *MT41* bows still visible to seaward. *Fury* still aground on rocks. Several mines exploded during day. *Rodney* and a cruiser bombarding to eastward.

0914 – *Empire Roseberry* close by to port, approaching anchorage.

0915 – *Empire Roseberry* exploded mine.

0916 – *Empire Roseberry* split in two.

0919 – both parts sank, just a few heads left bobbing about in the water between the two parts. Went down in four minutes.

Orion bombarding

ML sunk by mine. MMS damaged by mine. MT mined and sunk

Heavy artillery heard.

   'Wednesday, 28 June. – Sinking MT ship towed in, down by stern, decks awash aft.

Adventure shifted berth to a point near artificial harbour

2300 – *Maid of Orleans* mined, badly damaged.

   'Thursday, 29 June. –

0050 – *Maid of Orleans* sank. Three more MTs mined and sunk.

No more potatoes left.

   'Friday, 30 June. – Entered artificial harbour 1000 and made fast, stern to sunken blockship *Alynbank*, bows to buoy.

   'Thursday, 6 July. – Fifty midget submarines reported to be in or near area, all ships in first degree of readiness. Frigate *Trollope* torpedoed a.m., towed stern-first into artificial harbour during afternoon and beached, whole ship forward of funnel blown away. Operation 'Alert Three' at 0716, 1121, 1347, 1455.

   'Friday, 7 July. – *Rodney* bombarding. Two more mines went off nearby. Midget sub scares 0410 to 0800, 0930 to 1400. LCVTs dropping charges round harbour. Lancaster crashed, two casualties brought on board.

   'Saturday, 8 July. – More air-raids last night. Ju 88 and night fighter shot down. Three more midget sub scares during day.

   'Sunday, 9 July. – *Dragon*, cruiser, hit by torpedo or mined, towed inshore. Four midget sub scares. Usual air-raids.'

Above: Sick Berth Attendant Fred Hall went from the London Stock Exchange to LCTs and the Dunkirk beaches on D-Day, and on to the bouncing 40-knot Fairmile D MTB/MGBs in the North Sea seen here.

Below left: In Ceylon (Sri Lanka) Fred Hall also drove ambulances.

Below right: A maturing SBA Fred Hall before Dunkirk.

Left: Catapult Swordfish did good work in the Mediterranean flying from battleships of Admiral Cunningham's Fleet. This one belonged to Barham Flight.

Renown's war:

Right: *PT on a sunny day.*

Below left: *Under fire.*

Below right: *PO Shaw was Renown's cartoonist.*

"POOR OLE BERT'S TAKIN' IT 'ARD."
"YEAH! 'E LEFT 'IS TOT ON THE MESS TABLE"

Left: The Ark *in rough weather.*

Below left: Swordfish dropping a torpedo.

Right: TAG Alan Todd among the dry stone walls of Malta.

Above: Fleet Air Arm prisoners of war, Laghouat Camp, Algeria, December 1941.

Left: Bored with destroyer life in the Atlantic, L/S Ian Nethercott transferred to the Submarine Service. Here he is (exreme right) with three other Tactician ratings in Algiers.

Top right: HMS Tactician and ship's company. LTO Nethercott (extreme left, back row) looks, as he was, very young to be a Leading Seaman and LTO (Leading Torpedo Operator). The boat's Jolly Roger shows her to have made two sinkings at this stage, conducted two successful gun actions, and mounted five 'cloak and dagger' operations.

Right: There's no end to it! Cleaning out HMS Suffolk's 8in guns.

Left: HMS Antares, *Fleet Minesweeper, in Grand Harbour, Valletta, Malta. The author spent some amusing months in her as an OD (Radar), working for hostile Yugoslav partisans, paying off with a bang in Tunis.*

Men of Antares:

Below: Killicks – Charlie Jones (Leading Wireman), L/S Liversedge (back, middle), Jock Campbell (L/Tel).

Right: Chris the Asdic.

Below right: Oppos ashore – AB Gear (left), AB K. Poolman.

Above: HMS Kimberley *receives the surrender of all German troops on Rhodes. General Wagner came alongside while the General's aide saluted the Führer.*

Below: HMS Nelson, *in which 'Scribe' Cliff Smith found himself at Action Stations deep down in the 6in shell room.*

38B·5   H.M

NELSON.

COPYRIGHT PHO

Above: Ghost ship, or a new Marie Celeste. HMS Kimberley returned home, too tired for the Japanese war, and moored at Dartmouth. The entire ship's company was ordered below for the photograph.

Below: The 'fore-ends' (crew's quarters) of a British submarine.

Right: HMS Illustrious. From her decks was launched the Swordfish torpedo attack which crippled half the Italian Fleet in Taranto Harbour, 11 November 1940.

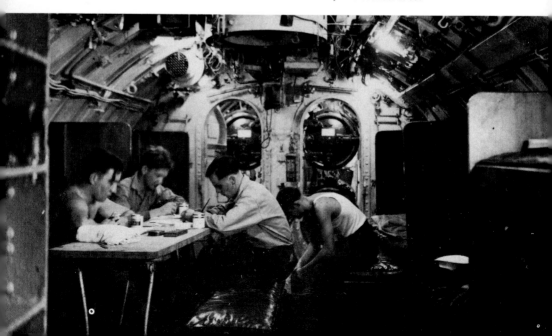

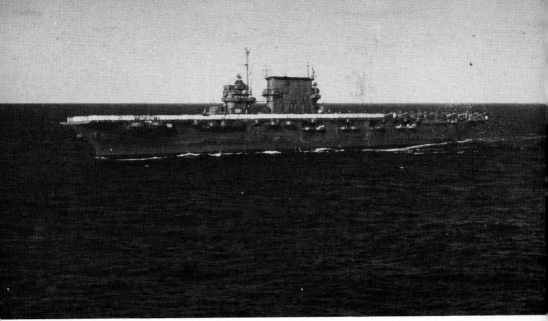

Left: *White Flight of No 1833 Corsair Squadron in* Illustrious. *Left to right: Londoner Reggie Shaw, Colonial Gordon Aitken, New Zealand Neil Brynildsen, and Flight leader, later Squadron CO, Norman Hanson.*

Below left: *'Hurrah for the next man that dies!'* Illustrious *entertains USS* Saratoga's *air group, China Bay, Ceylon (Sri Lanka), 31 March 1944. Norman Hanson, a Gilbert and Sullivan buff, is at the piano.*

Above: *USS* Saratoga *joins the British Eastern Fleet. The huge smokestack made her and her sister* Lexington *unmistakable.*

Right: *Eric Rickman, pre-war Art School graduate, and his Avenger crew aboard* Illustrious, *March 1945. Left to right: L/A Barfoot, TAG; Sub-Lt John Rendle, RNVR, Observer; Sub-Lt Rickman, RNVR, Pilot (N).*

Above: 'Kamikaze' – A
Japanese 'suicide' plane dives
on a carrier in the Pacific.

Left: Royal Navy Chief
Petty Officer Tom Bailey
joined the RN for 'three
square meals a day and a pair
of boots' – and found much
more.

Also on the beaches of Normandy for 'The Big One' was David Satherley's by now rusty *LCI 127*. 'On landing our troops, airborne soldiers they didn't have enough gliders for, we struck an underwater obstacle some forty yards from the beach, which was being washed by quite big waves after the previous few days' poor weather. Fortified with a large gin from the skipper, I swam towards shore with a heaving line, resting about halfway there on the turret of a sunken tank (the pennant stuck above water). On the beach (with the help of some beach party and RM Commandos), I hauled in a 4 in manila hawser and made it fast to the wrecked railings on the prom, coming under fire from a church steeple. I and another sailor who had swum ashore to join me then pulled together several dead men to cower down behind as the bullets were hitting the pebbly beach around us. However, our soldiers, laden with bicycles, mortars, ammo, rifles, were finding it hard to get ashore by the rope. Several floundered in the sea, so I could not but help go in and drag them out, though warned the beach could be mined. For this deed, done on the spur of the moment, I was recommended for the DSM but had to settle for a Mention.

'Even with a hole, hastily patched, we made some dozen trips to the beachhead before (in July) we were in danger of slowly sinking. We were towed to, of all places, Fishbourne Creek, Isle of Wight, for repair, a fourpenny bus ride from my parents' house. The skipper told me to disappear, and for the next six weeks I lived at home. My brother Ed (away in North Africa in the Long-Range Desert Group) had a splendid civvy suit which I wore for the whole of that time; once desperate to get into bell-bottoms, now chuffed to be a "civvy". At the local dances I was often told by squaddies to "join up", which I didn't mind at all in a superior sort of way and didn't even mention I was a serving sailor, enjoying the private joke. Every Friday night a good dance was held at the local Albany Barracks (now part of Parkhurst Prison), where rookie soldiers were in training, 18-year-old conscripts. Here I received the worst insults.

'A trestle table had been set up to serve drinks, etc, and while waiting to be served I was studiously ignored by the ATS girls at the makeshift counter. The local Newport girls knew who I was, of course, so such treatment didn't affect my standing with them and I enjoyed the dances. The only person present in a suit, I did stand out like a sore thumb, however. Waiting to be served one evening, I was faced by a woman in her thirties with laurel leaves and crown on her sleeves, a company sergeant-major of ATS, no less. She asked me how old I was (I was twenty) and why I wasn't in uniform, a healthy young man. I mentioned war work and asked how old was she, and would she care to dance? All pretty sneaky of me, I agree, and later that evening she (having refused the offer of a dance) actually came up to me and took my hand, pressing a white feather into it, the sort of little fluffy one that comes out of a pillow. I thought such things had gone out with the First World War! Still I suppose I'd asked for it.

'The following Friday I went to the dance in uniform, with half-a-dozen mates from *LCI 127*, having informed them what a good evening it provided (as it did), with good 40s music, plenty of girls, both service and civilian, to chat up. We breezed in like a blue cloud, all with ridiculously wide bell-bottoms; tiddly "eye-shooting" bows on our cap ribbons that covered our eyes; wide "U" fronts; scrubbed, almost white jean collars: gold badges and a good variety of medal ribbons (the then 1939–43 Star with the North Africa rosette had recently been issued to us, plus, pretty good for the size of ship and small crew, we had a DSM, BEM, and two oak leaves for Mentions, and thought ourselves no end of tarry Jacks). This invasion was not welcomed by the Army recruits in their stiff new battledress and big boots.

'Remarks flew, one of ours being that "the only *crack* troops in the barracks were the ATS" and soon a little squaring-up took place with the threat of a punch-up. The ATS sergeant-major, recognizing me and telling me what she thought of me, asked us to leave. This we did on my suggestion, and my mates went off to the pubs of Cowes. I stayed, had drinks with the sergeant-major over the situation being resolved, continuing the session in her private cubicle in a Nissen hut. During the night she plucked a white feather from the pillow and gave it to me to hand back to her for services rendered. I had to sneak out before Reveille, the back way across football fields and into Parkhurst Forest, pondering the fact that I had slept with a sergeant-major.'

AIR-SEA RESCUE

Back in Lowestoft, as there were no more landings contemplated in the immediate future, SBA Fred Hall was sent on loan to Coastal and Patrol Forces, and a hectic eight months began, working from HMS *Mantis* at Lowestoft, HMS *Midge* at Great Yarmouth, and RNSQ (RN Sick Quarters) there.

'From *Mantis* I did night operations with MTB/MGB flotillas operating off the Dutch coast, hunting enemy coastal convoys and E-boats. These flotillas did not normally carry SBAs. I was always aboard the flotilla leader at sea, and got into various actions, carried out at 40 knots plus, mostly in the *Fairmile* D-class "Dogboats", and anyone hurt in one of these boats was my responsibility. I would transfer from one boat to another in pitch darkness with both of them heaving up and down about twelve feet. Once I ended up in the hoggin in a night fight.

'With 90 per cent of crew RNR or RNVR and HO, discipline in the boats was very relaxed. Once ashore, all of us, officers and ratings together, marched to the nearest pub in our white sea jerseys, sea boots and white seaboot stockings. The boss was always "Skipper", never "Sir". At sea, when not required as a doc, I was extra lookout on the bridge. The Captain, usually a peacetime trawler skipper and a superb seaman, gave orders by hand signals and "Left a bit" or "Steer that way", "Slow down a little", etc. At 40 knots there was no time for RN formalities. Conditions were cramped, luxuries unknown, though we were only at sea for 12 hours each patrol. You sailed with your knees bent to cushion the continuous *thump, thump, thump,* as you bounced from wave to wave, and for a couple of days back ashore I couldn't carry a pint a few feet without spilling some.

'Other ops I was often involved in were the rescues of ditched airmen, carried out by *Fairmile* B-type RMLs (Rescue Motor Launches). Again I was only aboard for operations, and was involved in many, my clients exclusively men of the "Mighty Eighth", the US 8th Air Force, stationed widely over East Anglia. Every day the Fortresses and Liberators of the 8th were over NW Germany, returning over the North Sea and crossing the coast between Cromer to the north and Harwich to the south.

'During the forenoon we could see hundreds of aircraft crossing the coast and heading out over the North Sea, which would prepare us for the afternoon's operations, though nothing was said. Shortly after noon I would be ordered to report to RMLX, lying at the quayside in the River Yare, where I would make a careful check of my medical equipment, kept in a special deckhouse aft large enough to accommodate four stretchers on racks.

'About six boats would leave, and once clear of the river mouth proceed at cruising speed (12 knots) to a given position some 25 to 30 miles offshore. There were also three or four RAF air/sea-rescue launches out as well, though I never saw any of them as they covered the area south of us. There would be about eighteen vessels out in all, radiating from Great Yarmouth like the spokes of a wheel. Once at the designated spot it was heave to and just wait, engine ticking over. Every man available was on the upper deck on lookout – the Luftwaffe loved sitting ducks, and most boats had only a 2-pounder for'ard and a couple of light MGs aft.

'Sometimes we hung about idly until about 5 p.m., then went home. Mostly, the first sign of a job would be Sparks rushing to the bridge with a signal that an aircraft had ditched, with the position given. Engines went to Full Ahead (20 knots), everyone keen-eyed for survivors, sometimes in small life rafts, sometimes just heads bobbing in the water, on one occasion the plane itself, still afloat. Overhead Forts and Liberators struggled home, props feathered, great jagged holes in fuselages, trailing smoke.

'As soon as a sighting was made, nets were flung over the side, and the seamen got ready to lift the survivors on board. This was delicate, as we could not know if a man was injured or not. Once we picked up nine men, the other three having died in the aircraft. Once they were aboard I found that two were badly injured, three suffering from partial drowning and immersion, the other four relatively unscathed. I told my three seaman assistants to look after the three half-drowned airmen, while I tended the badly injured men, whom we put on stretchers right away. While the boat went flat-out for base I dressed their wounds and burns, stitching where required and putting splints on broken limbs, with the Skipper radioing base with details of their condition and our ETA so that the injured could be transferred straight away by naval ambulances to our sick quarters for immediate attention, while the others were given dry, warm clothes and refreshment (usually alcoholic – rum or brandy) while awaiting transport back to their airfields.

'This work I found very rewarding in itself, and I was many times invited to USAAF bases for generous hospitality, but my biggest reward came at a time of billeting problems when I was accommodated for six wonderful weeks in the ATS quarters in Great Yarmouth, one bloke amongst 350 females, and the first time in nearly two years that I had a proper bed with sheets – and tea in the morning! What luxury!'

The Mediterranean

We hold, in our pockets, no comfortable return ticket:
Only the future, gaping like some hideous fable.
The antique Mediterranean of history and Alexander,
The rattling galley and the young Greek captains
Are swept up and piled
Under the table.

Charles Causley: Conversations in Gibraltar

CHASING *VITTORIO VENETO*

Illustrious, badly damaged by Stukas, left the Mediterranean for repair in the USA. *Formidable* relieved her. On 27 March 1941 she joined the Fleet at sea to follow up a report of three Italian cruisers in the Ionian Sea. The next morning Swordfish from the carrier reported three enemy cruisers and four destroyers south of the west end of Crete, steering south-east, while Cunningham's cruisers sighted three enemy 8 in cruisers to the northwards. Out-gunned, out-ranged and slower, they retired towards the battleships. The enemy cruisers turned away, having succeeded in luring the British cruisers towards the big guns of the battleship *Vittorio Veneto*, steaming down from the north. Swordfish sent from *Formidable* to attack the enemy cruisers sighted *Vittorio Veneto* and attacked her, turning her back. The chase was on, with the Italians having the speed advantage.

Warspite was now flagship of the Mediterranean Fleet, with Swordfish floatplane 'Lorna' and two of her crew from the epic Narvik sortie. PO Ben Rice was still her pilot, Maurice Pacey her TAG, but Brown had been promoted Commander and had left the ship, to be replaced by the Fleet Observer, Lieutenant-Commander A. S. Bolt, DSC. At 1215 'Lorna' was launched as Action Observation, her duties to obtain a visual link between the two fleets and report on the tactical situation.

Bolt reported that the Italian Fleet showed no signs of pressing on to the south-east after the Fleet Air Arm torpedo attack. By that time he was worried about his fuel state. 'The endurance of my aircraft was about 4¾ hours, though we had on occasion achieved 5 hours under favourable circumstances. My routine reports of fuel state evoked no response from HMS *Warspite*, until I reported only 15 minutes of fuel remaining. Suda Bay was over one hour's flying away, so a decision had to be made to recover or destroy the aircraft although the Fleet was in hot pursuit of the *Vittorio Veneto*, having been slowed as we thought by a torpedo hit from an aircraft from *Formidable*.' (The ship hit and slowed down was actually the heavy cruiser *Pola*.) 'My aircraft was ordered to alight ahead of the *Warspite* in the grain of the Fleet. With the crane swung out on the starboard side, the plan was to hook on as the ship steamed up to overtake the aircraft, taxi-ing on a parallel course.

'The sea was calm and my pilot, PO Rice, made a good landing about two cables ahead of the ship, turned on to a parallel course and taxied at about 10 knots with the ship coming up fast astern. We had never practised this method of recovering and were a good deal disturbed by the bow wave. However, I was able to con PO Rice to a position under the grab hook and Lieutenant-Commander Copeman, with whom I had a good understanding in the recovery operation, hoisted us quickly clear of the water as soon as I gave the hooked-on signal. The aircraft was put on the catapult and refuelled while I went to say my piece on the Admiral's bridge. The ship lost only one mile through the water during the recovery and I do not believe she was doing less than 18 knots through the water at any moment during the operation.' *Formidable*'s second torpedo strike had been led by Lieutenant-Commander Dalyell-Stead, with Observer Cooke and TAG Blenkhorn, all of whom were killed.

At 5.45 p.m., less than an hour after they had been recovered, Bolt and Rice were catapulted again, with PO Pacey as their TAG. 'The last thing I did', said the latter, 'before take-off was to grab three flame floats as I realized that we were going to have to alight at night on the open sea with no organized flare-path.'

Bolt sighted the *Vittoria Veneto* at 6.20 p.m., and Pace made their first report by W/T direct to Alexandria W/T Station at a distance of some 400 miles. 'We had', says Bolt, 'carried out a great deal of practice with this station during dawn anti-submarine patrols from Alexandria and it was very satisfying that PO Pacey was able to clear some dozen Operational Immediate messages in a matter of minutes'. These were repeated to Malta and Gibraltar and received immediately in Whitehall, so that the Admiralty had them nearly as soon as the C-in-C in *Warspite*. These reports told Winston Churchill that the enemy was still some 50 miles ahead of Cunningham, making a speed of 12–15 knots on a course of 300°, which meant that the British Fleet had an advantage of some 7–10 knots. The chasing destroyers anticipated going in with torpedoes, and *Formidable* had high hopes of a dusk torpedo attack. The Italian Admiral could see eight of her Swordfish circling astern of him in the dying sun.

At 7.50 Bolt was relieved and ordered to return to Suda Bay. 'The night was clear and moonless and I expected that the alighting on the water without a flare path would present my pilot with some difficulty. Suda Bay was steep too and narrow, and with all shore lights blacked out was not the sort of place to take liberties with on a very dark night. The entrance to the harbour was protected by two booms watched by patrol craft. As the sea was calm I decided that we could land outside the harbour and, after doing a low-level run, to put down a line of flame floats, we turned and made a good landing. PO Rice deserves great credit for this achievement as we were landing towards the shore, it was pitch dark and there was no suspicion of any horizon. Furthermore, as there was a shortage of spares we had surrendered our instrument flying panel to the carrier squadron and the aircraft was fitted only with a primitive turn and bank indicator. We identified ourselves to the patrol vessel on the boom and then proceeded to taxi into harbour – a distance of about 5 miles, which seemed interminable. The Aldis lamp was most useful as a headlight and eventually we met a motor boat which guided us to a mooring for the night. I went to HMS *York* and reported to Captain Portal and it was on board that ship that I heard reports of our night action.' (The Italians had in the end lost three cruisers, but the *Vittorio Veneto* returned to port.)

'*York* had been attacked by explosive motor boats a few days earlier and I shared Captain Portal's regret that his wine store had been flooded. We had been airborne for more than eight hours and had had an exciting and eventful day. However, we were used to night and dawn flying operations and, though the aircraft was not radar-equipped, the open cockpit of the Swordfish enabled us to do many things which were impossible from an enclosed cockpit. Above all, as a crew, we had been together for more than a year and were able to rely on a competent maintenance team which kept the aircraft serviceable through all difficulties with a minimum of shore support.'

YORK'S WAR

It was in HMS *York* that we left Scottish AB Chris Buist steaming flat-out for Halifax from the sunny West Indies on the outbreak of war. With one of her three 8 in turrets still out of action she escorted a convoy to Britain. In the Norwegian Campaign Chris spent all his time down in the 8 in magazine supplying cordite to 'B' turret, and was there again on 12 October 1940 when *York*, covering an eastbound convoy from Malta, sank the Italian destroyer *Artigliere*, one of the three which had attempted to intercept the convoy; the other two were destroyed by *Ajax*. In the early part of 1941 *York* was in various actions in the Mediterranean, and on 25 March during the Allied retreat from Greece entered Suda Bay, Crete, for topping up with oil. Following closely in her wake so that the ship's Asdic would not pick them up was an Italian 'explosive motor boat'.

'I was below decks when we heard these engines revving outside in the Bay. We fuelled from the oiler and there was this bump followed by a mighty bang and a flash of flame right through our messdeck. The ship lifted up in the air, then down with a crash, all the lights and power went dead and it was black as Hell. We went up on to the fo'c'sle where all the rest of the ship's company were assembling. The ship was pulled on to the beach bows-on. As the quarterdeck was under water we lost all our stores, rum, etc. We were real chokka, I can tell you.' It was estimated that five months would be needed to render her fit for towing, but from 22 April there were incessant air attacks on the ship and she was further damaged. She was finally abandoned on 22 May, two days after the Germans had begun their assault on Crete.

While they unloaded the ship her crew lived in Army tents, ashore. 'About three weeks after the ship was hit I was unloading one of the cutters when the Germans came out of the sun with bombs and machine-guns blazing. I dodged behind a rock but a bullet grazed my steel helmet. After the raid I was shaking like a leaf, my nerves were shattered, so I was sent to the Army Hospital up in the hills.

'When the buzz went round we were getting off the island, the Colonel in the hospital said that all those who wished should try to escape to Egypt. I and several Army chaps left the hospital and made our way over the hills to a little cove where we knew we might find a boat. We pinched a Greek caique and set out for Egypt after several attempts to get the old diesel engine to work. We ran out of fuel half-way there and floated around until we saw a destroyer in the distance, which came alongside with her guns trained on us, but we were picked up and taken to Egypt.'

Malta Strikes Back

Look! Malta spun on the sea, shaping to sight
Fragilely as a promise, framed by metal
And the deft handling of airmanship.
Nudge. Nod. That's there all right. A petal
Yellow, all veined with green in the sea's hard
Flooring of other elements, of timeless running.
Malta, upon the blood-invested water, cactus, nettle-
Leafed, old prickle guard.

John Pudney

TARGET LIBYA

When on 16 October 1939 twelve Heinkels and Dorniers attacked the Forth
Bridge and ships below, it was finally decided that Donibristle was no place for a
training squadron, so Nos 767 and 769 Squadrons were moved by stages to the
French military airfield at Polyvestre, in the south of France, with HQ at Hyères,
four miles away; they continued working with the old carrier *Argus*, which
carried on the deck-landing part of the syllabus just off the French coast.
Trainees were mainly junior officers of the new RN (A) Branch, the RNVR (A)
Branch, with some RN rating pilots. On *Argus* a pupil made one supervised
landing in a Tiger Moth, then soloed in a Swordfish. This continued until 10 June
1940 when Italy entered the war. The next morning Italian fighters strafed
Polyvestre, and it was time for the trainees to leave. Before they did so the
instructors staged a token raid on Genoa, using improvised bombs made from
12 in shells. On the morning of the 18th they received the signal: 'Fly to England
via Bordeaux but if fog precludes proceed to Bône'.

On ringing Bordeaux for a weather report, they were answered in German,
so that night in the light from burning equipment on the airfield eighteen
Swordfish, manned by instructors and pupils, took off for North Africa, and
arrived at Bône 4 hours 20 minutes later, almost out of fuel. There they waited
for further orders from Whitehall, and on 20 June the CO, Lieutenant-
Commander Howie, sent for rating pilots Charles Wines and Freddie Parr and
said, 'I've been ordered to form a front-line squadron to go to Malta. I've been
told to take ten officer pilots, but I'm taking you two as well.' Six aircraft flew
west to Gibraltar, twelve to Hal Far airfield on Malta. From there, as No 830
Squadron, they began a long, stubborn assault on Axis convoys carrying supplies
and men from Italy to North Africa and also on Tripoli, the receiving port.

It was Tripoli again on 18 March 1941. Just before midnight nine Swordfish took off, two of them flown by POs Wines and Parr. The weather across to Africa was good, with some low cloud as they neared the target. Bomb flashes from the attacks by six RAF Wellingtons guided them to the target, and five aircraft dropped mines off the harbour entrance.

It was Wines' job to divert guns on the harbour mole from attacking the mine-droppers. 'When I arrived over the harbour I couldn't believe the sight below me. There were no searchlights, but the whole place seemed covered with exploding fireworks, as guns of all descriptions blazed away, their glowing trajectories converging on the centre of the harbour.' Wines, like most rating pilots, felt he was always on test in combat. The Lower Deck aviators were not intended for operations at all, but shortage of officer pilots had given them the chance to prove themselves, at first in fighters only. Now Frankie Howie had given him and Freddie Parr an opening as bombers, and he had proved to be the squadron's best. But he had to keep up his reputation.

He turned inland away from the lethal pyrotechnic display and, gliding back from the desert with his engine off, dropped a bomb straight across a seaplane hangar near the eastern mole, and saw a whoosh of fire behind him. The bomb destroyed the hangar and the nine seaplanes inside it, as well as a fuel storage dump. But he climbed again and looked for further targets.

Through the Gosport speaking tube TAG Nat Gould heard him yell, 'Look at that beautiful ship in the middle of the harbour – I'm going after it!'

From 4,000ft Wines threw the 'Stringbag' into a near-vertical dive. Gold hung on grimly. Something big hit him in the stomach. He gasped with pain and thought 'I've been hit!' Then he saw that a spare drum of ammunition, resting on the gun ring, had slipped off and hit him. He hooked his arm over the side of the aircraft, heaved himself up and looked down over the nose of the plunging Swordfish. 'The sight nearly made my heart stop. It was like daylight, tracer racing up from all directions, swishing and cracking. Right below us the ship looked enormous. I clung on as we straddled her with our remaining bombs. I heard them all explode, then we were turning away. Charles threw the aircraft about in evasive action, the ack-ack ceased, and we were clear.'

Wines and Parr really thought that progress was being made when Howie said to them, 'You will go down to Kalafrana and carry out a torpedo course.' Rating pilots in a first-line torpedo squadron! What happened to the 'Lack of moral fibre'? What next – an invitation to briefings, perhaps? It was not a popular decision among some of the true-blue 'Darts' in 830. 'A torpedo costs £1,500, you know,' one of them said to Wines dubiously.

Down in Kalafrana Bay, Wines performed reasonably well in practice, but Freddie Parr dropped his first tinfish much too close to the Range Commander's boat and had its crew running about like frightened rabbits as it practically scraped the side, then carried on into the Bay. Out there three flying-boats were moored, a Sunderland, a Catalina and a French aircraft. The torpedo raced straight for the Sunderland and was almost on it when it turned to starboard and headed across the Bay towards the Catalina. The Swordfish turned in tight circles above, Parr and his passenger, Nat Gold, watching its progress in fascinated horror. It nearly touched the hull of the Catalina, then veered away again and made for the French flying-boat. As it approached the aircraft it gradually lost speed and finally stopped with a gentle nudge of the hull.

CAPTIVES IN THE SAHARA

At 3.33 p.m. on 12 April 1941 Squadron-Leader Whiteley's RAF Maryland reported a convoy of five merchantmen escorted by three destroyers south-west of the island of Pantelleria. One Swordfish went off first with flares to search for and shadow the reported ships. Behind him the CO led five torpedo-droppers, including Charles Wines, with L/NA Edwards as his TAG, and Freddie Parr as the dive-bomber.

At 6.20 p.m. the shadower saw them – one merchantman of about 8,000 tons and four of 6,000–7,000 tons, escorted by three zigzagging destroyers and one smaller craft. At 8 p.m., when the shadower thought the striking force must be near, he dropped a flare ahead of the convoy. Another flare in the empty moonlit sky was answered by a soaring Very light to the south-east. At 8.37 the aircraft of the striking force had the enemy ahead of them in the path of the moon, and against the light of more flares dropped down for their attacks against heavy and accurate flak.

Wines came in second, at what he thought was the right height, and let go his torpedo, becoming as he did so the first and only RN rating pilot ever to drop a torpedo in anger – the anger, in fact, considerable when he realized he had missed. In fact he had held on too long. As he cleared the target ship his Swordfish was hit continually and he was covered in oil. He flew on, heading towards the beach at Hammammet. Edwards got off a hasty signal to say that they were forced-landing, which was picked up in a mutilated state by Howie's aircraft. Then the Swordfish hit the sand – where in future years British tourists, including Wines himself and his family, would recline in their Ambre Solaire skins – ploughed across the wide beach and jarred to a stop. Vichy French police came running out to meet them. An Inspector said, 'There is an English lady in Hammammet. Perhaps you would like to see her?' and they were taken to Miramar, the big house owned by the Hensons, an American expatriate and his English wife, who gave them dinner before the police finally took them away to captivity.

Meanwhile the others had made their attacks. TAG Alan Todd hung on as his pilot, Sub-Lieutenant Dawson, dropped his fish amidst 'some very smelly flak. Then the engine stopped. I thought: It's Norway all over again. We hit the water short of the shore, splashed our way on to the beach and were picked up by gendarmes.' After a few weeks in the local Prisa Prison Camp at Aumale, where they met Wines and Edwards, they were transferred to the big camp at Laghouat, deep in the desert in Algeria.

There they met about two dozen RAF fighter pilots who had ditched when trying to reach Malta from a carrier and run out of fuel or had pump trouble. 'Rations in the camp were Latin – pasta in olive oil, and bap-type loaves, harsh wine from the bottom of the vat, which would stain the floor as well as any varnish if you spilled any. There was not much in the way of recreation, though

Charles Wines organized some boxing. Hardly any Red Cross parcels made their way across the Sahara. There was constant talk of escape, though we were 300 miles down in the desert, and all efforts to do so failed, as bounty-hunting Arabs simply waited at all the water holes to collect their 1,000 francs a head.' A tunnel was dug, and about 30 of the men headed north with the vague plan of wandering along the coast until they found a fishing boat to sail to Gibraltar. It was a 'Catch 22' dream. They were out for four days, then armed Arabs picked them up. After a while men from the destroyer *Havock*, which had gone aground, joined them (including Jack Dodds, who had worried that joining another destroyer would be bad joss after his narrow escape from the rammed *Duchess*). With them were the survivors from the destroyer *Legion*, whom they had previously rescued, and survivors from the cruiser *Manchester* also came in. They were all released after the successful Allied landings in North Africa, and made their way to Gib.

MALTA CONVOYS

Stoker and former engine driver Mark Wells saw plenty of action in Mediterranean convoys in the cruiser *Arethusa*.

'So began the Malta Convoys. It was the end of sailing right through the Med to Suez. That could not be done with such superior air power on both sides of the sea. We were committed solely to Malta convoy work, from the Gibraltar end, with Force H, made up of fast ships like *Ark Royal* and *Renown*, and the minelayer *Manxman*, which, it was said, could do 40 knots.

'We ourselves had not suffered much so far in the way of air attacks. Now, as Admiral Somerville said, we were going "To taste the quality of the ice-cream." Italian ice-cream was palatable, but the German variety was bitter. Sixteen hours into our first operation a spotter plane was seen, and a few hours afterwards the sky was full of "bandits". Bombs rained down everywhere. On rare dashes up on deck the blue sky was full of tracers. Once a gunner waved me to get down, I looked up and right overhead was this bomber. He near-missed us, thanks to the Skipper's skill at throwing the helm hard over just as the bombs left the aircraft.

'It was Action Stations most of the time. We struggled to get some sort of hasty meal in the lulls, but the respite was always short-lived and always the alarm went, and we sang "There's a bomber overhead" to the notes of the bugle which sounded the alarm to make it clear that this was an air-raid. Down below we plodded on with our duties as the raid went on. If only the 6 in or 4 in were firing, trouble was a little way off yet. When you heard the Oerlikons and pom-poms the bombers were getting closer to the ship. Then you would wait for the crunch of the bombs, some right alongside. More speed would be called for, the ship would heel right over, the revolutions telegraphs would clang "Ting Ting Ting" as the pointer dropped for lower revs.

'We were very tired and all over the place men lay on deck, sleeping in the shade, out of the sun. It was very hot. Once I was sleeping on the upper deck not far from the ship's gangway, lying in just a boiler suit and with my head on my lifebelt. I awoke to the sound of a bosun's whistle which meant someone important was coming aboard. I nodded off again as did others lying in the shade, but woke suddenly as someone tripped over my foot. I looked dazedly to see who it might be, and was horrified to see the Admiral, Sir James himself, standing there. I scrambled to my feet, but he said, "Don't get up, you'll need all the rest you can get. I'm sorry I woke you." So I lay down again and went off.

'Malta was being starved out, not only of food but ammunition and fuel for the few aircraft defending it. One day at Gib we started to load ammo and aviation spirit. The boxes of aviation cans were stacked on the upper deck aft, as high as the gun turret, with hoses laid over the top directing a steady flow of water over the cargo. Ammo was crammed into every available space below, alleyways, locker rooms, bathrooms, we became a floating ammunition dump.

'We were told of the utmost importance of this convoy, which included *Manxman* in the lead, *Arethusa*, and the cruiser *Euryalus* and one other cruiser. This was to be a make or break effort, made at high speed, in line ahead. We left in the dark (we had never left in the dark before) to give us a good start. The second night at sea I was in the engine room when there was a sudden thump right under the keel, followed by a few small rumbles. It wasn't an explosion. We looked at each other, puzzled. Then we learned that *Manxman* had struck an Italian submarine pretty well dead centre as she lay on the surface in the dark charging batteries. There was no question of stopping, our convoy was too vital for that. We sailed into Grand Harbour, Valletta, to cheering thousands of Maltese. At last a convoy had got through, and unscathed. *Manxman* still had part of the submarine she had hit hanging round the bows. The main body of the sub had rolled over under our keel and then under the following cruiser with no time to come to the surface again. We all wondered what the return trip would be like, but we reached Gib safely, where all the crews lined decks and gave us three cheers. We dry-docked for a quick check of the hull after many near-misses, and had a bit added to the rudder to make us a bit quicker in the turn.

'After this series of convoys it was decided to try convoys also from the Suez end of the Med, and it wasn't long before we were rounding Africa, via Freetown, Capetown, Mombasa and Aden and up to Suez and Port Said. There we saw the cruiser *Orion* and a couple of destroyers. There were precious few ships left here at the eastern end of the Med. A few convoys were attempted but so intense was the bombing that they were turned back, destroyers running out of ammunition, one with none left at all.

'Admiral Vian – Vian of the *Cossack* – took over in the Eastern Med, with his flag in the cruiser *Cleopatra* (appropriate in her Egyptian base), and we set sail with her to bombard Rhodes island. Back in Alex the boss had us hard at it, exercising damage control and abandoning ship – with us all jumping into the harbour – and cutting down the time to go to Action Stations. If a gunner was having a bath when the alarm sounded, said Vian, he would dash to his post just as he was. "These practice routines are for your survival," he said. "There are only two kinds of people out here – the quick and the dead." Another convoy was arranged, and we put to sea.

'On the third day we had fought off the bombers and were settling down slowly for what we hoped would be a quiet night. I had just relieved my opposite number as Leading Stoker in the engine room. I did my usual check round and came back to the Control Platform. It was about 1809. There was a sudden huge explosion and the ship listed over to port, sloping down for'ard as well.

'We had been hit by a torpedo somewhere below the bridge area, and the fore deck was awash on one side. There was a big fire forward of No 7 boiler room. By the merest chance the sea had got into the forward magazine before the flash, but our shipmates had suffered serious losses, a whole detachment of Marines, many seamen. There were many serious burns, and many died afterwards from shock. Many stokers off watch also died, including the man I had just relieved. The flash had flown right down one side of the upper deck and no one in its path there had survived. Boats crashed to the deck, their falls burned through, trapping others. The air was black with smoke for a long time and was sucked down the vents. The worst smell of all was the smell of human flesh.

'The night dragged on, portable pumps working frantically. At dawn we were rolling about, engines slowly turning. We tried to steam stern-first but we would never have reached Alex that way. Eventually the destroyer *Petard* arrived and towed us in, with the tow rope breaking over and over again, and we were harassed by bombers. Those of the dead who could be found were buried at sea. Every able-bodied man, led by the First Lieutenant, turned to to move the anchor cables by hand to the stern to get it down in the water a little. Down below there was only the stokers' messdeck bulkhead holding back the sea. It was shored up but the pressure behind it was terrific, and it bulged out like a bow. The messdeck itself was awash with oil, some of the tables still with cheese and pickles on them. We lost all our clothes.

'The trip to Alex took about three days and we lived on the odd sandwich and one or two good tots of rum. We comforted our burned and wounded mates as best we could, but some were unrecognizable. When we got in we were put into lorries, and spent the night in King Farouk's stables. I remember seeing the Captain being helped along the deck with most of his clothes burned off, badly burned and in obvious pain in legs and arms. One thing always remains in my mind, the quietness over the ship. No shouting, just a quietness. Just the odd senior rank calling "Lend a hand here, anyone able" and such like. We were sent to a transit camp on the edge of the desert somewhere. A PO met us and said, "There's a pile of tents over there. Grab one and pitch it somewhere."

'We had no money so we walked into Alex and saw some senior officer who arranged cash for us, and we paid a final visit to the old ship. I asked if anyone knew what was to happen to us. My two friends thought it would be the UK. Me, I really didn't care where as long as I got a ship. I hated being stuck on land even though it was an easy-going life where we were. You came and went as you pleased and no one asked where you were going, so we strolled out each day and made our way to the first cafe that had steak, eggs and chips. Love for the sea was strong inside me, as ever. None of us, strangely enough, ever mentioned the old ship. It wasn't until after the war that I realized that I never spoke of the happenings in *Arethusa*. I mention this because in civvy life people can't wait to tell you about some drama or other. Was it the same in the Army or Air Force? *Arethusa* was the only casualty in the convoy, and it was the first convoy from the Eastern end of the Med to reach Malta for many, many months.

Beneath the Waves

The ships destroy us above
And ensnare us beneath,
We arise, we lie down and we move
In the belly of death.

However terrifying the rage of a high sea can be, the dangers in its depths are more spine-chilling – nameless terrors of darkness, shadows of childhood fears. When I arrived in Malta as an Ordinary Seaman we were quartered in Verdala Barracks under a big half-Maltese leading hand who was also a diver. Under the sun-bleached colonnade on the edge of the small parade ground we used to sit and listen to his tales of the deep.

'Mate of mine,' he told us, 'big, tough bastard, just before he went down he says "Don't forget – one tug on the line, bring me up nice and slow, I don't want no bends. Two tugs – haul me up faster than that! That means I'm in trouble!" Well, down he goes, and after a couple of minutes there suddenly comes this terrific tugging on the line – not one, not two, but a whole lot of panicky jerks! We hauls him up at the double, and, you won't believe this, when he went down he had thick, jet-black hair – and when he come up it was *white* . . . and he never spoke another word . . . What had he seen down there, eh? Just think about it.'

'Have *you* ever seen anything really horrible down there, Hookey?' someone would say – anything to delay a return to square-bashing. 'Ah, now,' he would say darkly, 'there's things *I* can't even talk about . . .' 'What about octopuses, Hookey, and giant squids? And manta rays, and barracudas?' 'Hold on, hold on, my sons, or I shall think you're taking the piss! Octopuses? Nothing to 'em. If you ever meets an oc-toe-puss down there, and he grabs you, don't panic, stay cool. Before he can finish you off proper, he has to sort of spring off, to get his full strength, like, before he finally crushes you . . .' '*Reculer pour mieux sauter*' murmured a dipped CW . . . '*that's* when you whip our your old Pusser's dirk, and stick it right in his optic – he's only got one, and that'll put him right off you!' We sat there in the still air, mind-boggled.

DANGERS OF THE DEEP

From the light cruiser *Curacoa*, Bill Filer, ex-Barnado's Boy from the Watts Naval Training School, went in 1937 to HMS *Excellent* to qualify as a Diver III, but in the same year the Rating Pilot AFO came out and he volunteered, winning his wings in 1939. By the beginning of war someone in the Admiralty had thought better of the Rating Pilot scheme, and Bill was one of those returned to General Service against their wishes, which in his case meant dropping back from PO to Leading Seaman. Others similarly treated transferred to the RAF and obtained comparatively accelerated promotion. But Bill still had his non-substantive qualification, and in 1941 found himself in the battleship *Queen Elizabeth* at Alexandria as an L/S Diver.

While he was there the ammunition ship *Churukka* was sabotaged and scuttled at her moorings. The ship contained the only 15 in bombardment shells available to Admiral Cunningham, which, in view of Rommel's close proximity, made this a serious situation, and the C-in-C ordered a 24-hour continuous operation by divers of the Fleet to recover the shells so urgently needed to stem the Afrika Korps' progress in the desert.

'The holds of the *Churukka* were packed to capacity with the 15 in shells, each one weighing a ton, with the grab for picking them up of a similar weight. The first problem was that they were packed so close together that it was impossible to get the grab on them, and it needed considerable seamanship using strops and tackles and a lot of muscle to coax a shell into a position where the grab could be properly fixed on it – all this to be accomplished using the old helmet-type diving equipment with its limited mobility. Nevertheless it had to be done, and we got on with it.

'There were four holds packed with the urgently needed monsters, and a diving team worked one hold, six hours on, six hours off. From this system developed what turned out to be a somewhat unhealthy Fleet Regatta type competition, with each team of divers from the different ships trying to outdo the others in the number of shells recovered in a 6-hour session.

'This brought about Problem No 2. In their eagerness to outdo one another the divers took the easiest way out and grabbed the shells lying in the centre of the holds, which could be reasonably accurately plumbed by the crane. This was all right to start with but eventually resulted in the diver standing at the bottom of the hold with shells towering above him to his right and left in a V formation. The worst of this situation was that the uppermost shells which then had to be removed were well and truly hidden, tucked away under the coaming of the hatches, hard up against the ship's sides, and in no way could the grab be positioned to extricate them directly.

'Thus it was, on one never-to-be-forgotten morning about 0400 that I was struggling with these problems in the after hold when I was instructed over the intercom to return to the surface immediately. "Why?" I ask. "Don't argue" says Bill Scudder, and with a CPO Light Heavyweight Boxing Champion you didn't. Something traumatic was clearly afoot.

'I spindled my way back up to the surface to learn the worst. A Chief Electrical Artificer was trapped down below in No 2 hold which was being worked by the team from the destroyer depot ship HMS *Woolwich*, and his surface support team could neither communicate with him nor pull him up to the surface. Without bothering about our normal check tests, I was dropped down swiftly to find and recover the missing diver.

'Down in the flooded hold I gathered up his air hose and "breast rope" communications cable, which led me to a very sad sight. There was the diver, with a ton-weight 15 in shell right across his chest, the weight of which had driven him back so hard that the nose of a shell immediately behind him had penetrated his helmet. He was trapped, drowned and dead when I reached him. Although I had never met him, a diver was a diver and not just somebody else, so understandably I had a second or so of grief. You can't wipe your eyes inside a copper helmet, so I set about relieving my feelings by getting "Steve" to the surface as soon as possible just in case he had an outside chance of survival.

'First I had to remove the 15 in shell off his chest, which, with topside co-operation, I did as expeditiously and tenderly as possible, following which I extricated him from the shell penetrating his helmet, through which the sea had entered. Drowning like that must have been a terrible experience, while still conscious. I still shudder at the thought. With signals to my surface support team, he was carefully hauled to the surface in his waterlogged tomb, with me guiding his body clear of the numerous obstructions which are always there in any wreck.

'His untimely death was unofficially ascribed, by us divers, to the fact that he had not succeeded in getting the grab secured to the shell correctly so that when the shell had been lifted some six feet clear of the water it fell out of the grab and landed up on the diver's chest. The shell which had opened up his helmet and drowned him had let the water in at some 15–20 psi. It didn't take long to drown him, but instant death in action would have been so much kinder. He just had to lie there, pinned down, and wait until he drowned. What a horrible way to go! We also felt that someone who was a top-class artificer should not have been used on this type of job, where seamanship and muscle were essential and not exactly commensurate with a "Tiffy's" skills. Also our team exercised a discipline whereby prior to a shell being hoisted clear of the water, we made sure that the diver had taken cover under the hatch coaming. Had the *Woolwich* team followed this rule the tragic loss of life would have been avoided.'

SUBMARINE SERVICE

British submarines played a big part in Mediterranean operations. New, smaller boats of the 'U' and 'T' classes took over from the old 'O', 'P' and 'R' classes which had been so out of place in these shallow waters. In the new *Tactician* (P314) was ex-Canvey Island Sea Scout, late of destroyers *Keith* and four-piper *Lincoln*, Iain Nethercott. Chock-a-block with the grinding monotony of Atlantic convoys, he had volunteered for the Submarine Service. After a course in 'demolitions, torpedoes, electrics, mines and other peaceful pursuits', at 'H Majesty's Girls School, Roedean', he 'abandoned gymslip, hockey stick and tiara' and reported to Ford Blockhouse, HMS *Dolphin*, feeling rich with an extra 6d a day, and positively plutocratic when he received his submarine pay of 2/- a day. From Roedean it was 'a mile down the social scale' to the former reformatory of HMS *Elfin*, the submarine base at Blyth, Northumberland, for operational training, which consisted of day runs to sea in the old *L23*, doing every job in the boat, grateful for a duty-free canteen and beer at 2d a pint. *Thunderbolt*, formerly the tragic *Thetis*, was alongside, back from the Med.

Finally qualified, Iain was drafted to the Clyde Flotilla at Rothesay, running from the old *Cyclops*, a coal-burning depot ship. 'The Flotilla consisted of the remainder of the old H-boats, built in 1917–18, the *Otway* and a couple of old American boats – "State Express" and "The Reluctant Dragon", so called because she often refused to dive.' They operated out of Campbelltown, Londonderry, Tobermory and Rothesay, acting as clockwork mice in training the escort groups and new ships in Asdic attacks. 'I joined *H43* as LTO, in charge of all the electrics and main batteries – and the motor room, from which the main motors were controlled when dived. This was the life! I had two AB LTOs under me and we made a good little team.'

'There was only one bunk on board, and that was the Skipper's. We kipped on cushions on the deck. We had a crew of about twenty and three officers. Our First Lieutenant was RNR, a former entertainments officer with the Orient Line, an Adonis who had a way with women, and chased them with every opportunity, though married to a red-haired virago who followed the boat around like a bloodhound. We had a succession of captains, all lieutenants who had just passed the CO's course and were getting a taste of command. One was Menzies, the Menzies of Menzies, the clan chief, uncomfortable in Tobermory and Ardrishaig among the fierce Campbells, and dubious of me as I was born in Caithness and am a member of the Gunn Clan, who used to fight alongside the Mackays, hereditary enemies of the Menzies, but a good captain. I made a good submarine brooch for him out of a silver spoon and gave him some of my tot, which he repaid with whisky in the wardroom.

'We spent a lot of time at Londonderry, where we had two narrow scrapes with American "cans" in training, which came zooming in as we surfaced, intent on ramming practice, and we scrounged a huge Stars and Stripes ensign and lashed it all round the conning tower to show the next lot we were friendly. An Aussie navigator gave us some scary moments too, when he tried to trim the boat, and sent her plunging down at 60°, thankfully straight into mud – it could have been rock. The coxswain was highly indignant as he climbed back up out of the periscope well. Another bind (literally) was our toilet, the contents of which had to be blown outboard by low-pressure air, but owing to faulty valves sometimes blew back and covered you with confusion. I once had to save our Jimmy from a vengeful husband from a Free Norwegian sub by holding him off at the gangway with a burst from a Tommy gun, like in *The Godfather*.

'But my Scottish holiday came to an end and suddenly I was available for world tours or sunshine cruises. What I got was the T-class *Tactician*, *P134*, being built at Barrow. I was glad to see some familiar faces aboard – Jack Coss, gunlayer off *Rorqual*, Les Etichnap, Killick fore-endman off *Unbeaten*, Ian Dunbar, PO LTO off *Unison*, and lots more. I was in good company. Our Skipper was Lieutenant-Commander Mainwaring off *Unruly*, who had just got a bar to his DSO. We could expect some action.

'At Barrow we lived in lodgings in the town, and went down to the dockyard every day to watch everything being put in place, though we spent more time in the pub. The super T-boats were well designed, though their diesels were never as good as the German engines. The boat was fitted with eleven tubes (six internal with reloads, and five external – two for'ard, two midships and one in the tail). The latter five were all mine, in addition to my motor room job, the TI owned all the others. In harbour I and my crew used to pull all the fish out, reload, check the horizontal and vertical rudders and the gyros, charge up with air, then strip down the pistols and detonators. When the Skipper scored a hit with one of *my* fish, it went off with a bang!

'Mainwaring went sick, and we got a new skipper, Lieutenant-Commander Collett from *Unique*, a great friend of the incomparable Wanklyn, and a good skipper who understood submariners. During the two years aboard the boat, from commissioning to paying-off, we had no defaulters and no real trouble. We all knew that in an operational boat any punishment would send us back to General Service, the worst disgrace the Admiralty could think up. Ashore we were a wild bunch, but naval authorities in all the ports abroad kept well clear of stirring up trouble with submarine crews.

'We were in good company at Barrow and later at Dunoon. *P313* was just ahead of us, and her crew mutinied, refusing to sail under the number 13. The Admiralty gave her new pennants – *P339* – and she sailed. *P311* had been sunk off Italy, and after she had gone they called her *Tutankhamen*. *Traveller* had also been lost with all hands, and we were due for the Med.

'First we did a shake-down patrol from HMS *Forth* up to Norway. The weather was terrible, tremendous seas, hurricane winds and about 20° below freezing. God knows what we were looking for – the Germans weren't daft enough to put to sea in weather like that. Conditions on the conning tower were so appalling that the skipper decided that all seamen should help do lookout duties, which included a one-hour spell for me. Although wearing many sweaters and trousers with an Ursula suit over all, within five minutes you were saturated. We wore safety belts with steel chains and dog clips to hold on to the rails on the inside of the cab as we were totally submerged in huge waves half the time. One great roller of hundreds of tons wrenched away my handholds and crushed me against the Vickers gun stand. I felt three ribs crack before my head came clear of the water. The cox'n strapped me up later. A new U-class submarine was on the next billet to us, and when we both withdrew from patrol and worked our way to Lerwick, she sailed into the harbour with all her conning tower gone, together with her gun. We returned to *Forth* at Dunoon, and eventually sailed for the Med, where we did our first patrol in the Gulf of Lions, with *Taurus* in the next billet.

'Here we made our first sinking, and ran up our Jolly Roger, but when we came up to fight a gun action with an auxiliary schooner the gun seized up. We returned to Algiers and our depot ship *Maidstone* to find that Tubby Linton, VC, and his *Turbulent* had gone, *Thunderbolt*, with all my mates, had gone, *Splendid* and *Sahib* were missing. It was a bad week for subs. The only good part of it for me was my flannelling my way through my PO's board and being rated up.

'We carried on with patrols from Algiers up the west coast of Italy and Sicily, and built up our sinkings, though counter-attacks by the Italian frigates were very accurate.

'Once we had sunk a merchant ship in convoy and were being attacked by three escorts. We were down at 200ft with everything shut off for depth-charging, and at Silent Routine. Some of the depth-charge patterns were so close that you could hear the "click" of the pistols just before the charge exploded.

'One string of charges exploded just over the boat, and one right over the engine room hatch. I was on the switches in the motor room. Poor old Shiner Wright, the Chief Tiffy, was standing under the hatch, which had its strongbacks fitted. The explosion and consequent implosion sheared the hatch clips right off and it lifted momentarily. About a ton of water shot in, most of it on poor old Shiner, who wasn't used to sudden baths in his own engine room.

'When the Germans surrendered in North Africa we were based at Malta doing patrols up the eastern coast of Italy and Yugoslavia. We had all swapped cigarettes for Afrika Korps uniforms with the Eighth Army, stuck our badges on them, and the King must have had a shock when he saw us all lined up on the casing as he passed by in review on a cruiser. Except for going up to the Palace for my DSM, I hadn't seen him since Dover in 1939.

'As an LTO, after an attack I used to be very busy with my crew, first replacing all the shattered electric light bulbs, then checking the main batteries. The cells in a submarine's batteries stood about 4ft high and held about 30gal of acid each. On a T-boat they were split into three batteries of 112 cells each, which gave a total voltage of 240–350. They were strapped together with six large lead straps and bolts in a voltage-increasing configuration in the separate battery tanks inside the floor spaces between the control room and the torpedo stowage compartment. The floor boards in all the messes and wardroom were, in effect, the steel tops to the tanks, and had to be lifted up to examine the cells underneath, which lay with the straps only 18in below the tank tops. Unfortunately, a lot of the cells lay underneath steel cross-sections between the messes and the gangway and could only be sighted by lying flat on the top of the battery and picking out the tops of the cells with a torch. Once a month every cell had to be topped up, just like a car battery, with about 3gal of distilled water, and the boat was always in a state of complete chaos while this was being done.

'After a depth-charge attack it was always possible that some cells might have been cracked. Me and my crew would have to sight every single cell in all three batteries to check that the acid level was up over the plates. If the cell casing had cracked, the acid ran away into the bottom of the tank and the cell became dead, but still in circuit, with the danger of it catching fire during charging.

'Consequently, having sorted out the numbers of the cracked cells, I would have to draw up a cutting-out plan, to disconnect the dead cells and to pass cutting-out straps over the tops on to the next good cells. The final result gave a reduced voltage but a safe one. The problem was that the cutting-out straps were as thick as your arm and working underneath the steel floorboards and lying flat on the battery straps meant that an LTO had the full voltage of the battery passing through him, especially when his overalls were soaked in sweat and acid. Every time he moved, his arse came up against the steel deckhead and he got a huge kick of about 250 volts and several million amps. No wonder we LTOs had curly hair! I've put my freedom from rheumatism in my advancing years down to the fact that my body has been so highly charged.

'We, together with all available submarines, were sent to patrol off the Italian naval ports during the Sicilian invasion, and were then routed, after *Maidstone* was sunk, to the Eighth Flotilla at Beirut. Here we lived ashore, when not on watch aboard, in an old French colonial barracks, full of fleas. All the other boats were here, *Trooper*, *Taurus*, *Tally Ho* and the rest of the boys. In addition, Captain (S) had commandeered a first-class hotel and its staff up at Aley in the mountains of Lebanon, a luxury resort run by submarine cox'n "Brigham" Young, who had set himself up as the local potentate. Here we all went after a patrol, to go skiing up in the mountains and join in the night life. Good French wines, beautiful girls – and willing. Paradise.

'Down in the harbour was a Greek submarine depot ship together with a brood of half-a-dozen Greek submarines, crews on full pay and provisions. They never went to sea. The Admiralty guessed that they would immediately return to Greece and join the Germans. The town was dangerous for matlows, some of whom had been knifed and slung into the sewers, to appear in the harbour after a few days. Ashore, I always carried a revolver, an Italian Beretta, and a Commando knife. The place was full of disillusioned Arabs, who had expected to be liberated now that the Vichy French had been so soundly beaten, but the only scraps we got into were with the French Foreign Legion. Down in the harbour a 10 ft-high fence topped with barbed wire protected the sub pens, guarded by the King's African Rifles, who did not hesitate to shoot any Arab who tossed one of their home-made cocoa tin bombs over the wire. At night the boats were enclosed in a floating boom, patrolled by two matlows in a small rowing boat who dropped made-up 1-pound demolition charges over the side every quarter of an hour.

'Every day a huge queue of ragged little Arab children used to form up outside the warehouse gate, overseen by a big fat brutal Arab who kicked and clouted these poor little waifs and sent them on board the boats for work. Our cox'n, "Fearless Fred" Fleming, would then pass the kids on to the various messes where they were immediately stuffed full of bread and jam, and given a little bit of dhobi-ing to do.

'We were very close to *Trooper*'s crew, and used to have wonderful sing-songs with them in our bar down in the French barracks. She was due to go home to pay off very soon, and we knew that we were going east. We were all operating up the Aegean now, but since the Italian surrender targets were getting short. We came in from one patrol on which we could find only caiques to sink and do a few shore bombardments.

'*Trooper* was due in a few days later, just after dawn. Down on the jetty Captain (S) had the usual welcome ready, the long tables laid out on the quay with dozens of Arab servants bringing on more and more beautiful food and fruit.

'All was ready. We were up on the casing to exchange our usual rude remarks with her crew. Captain (S) was pacing the jetty with the base staff.

'We waited and waited, but she never came home. The Arabs ate the feast, and we went back down the boat. *Taurus* had slipped and sailed for Port Said, and a week later we followed through the Canal and from Aden took the long road to Colombo.'

Beachhead Sicily

Roll on the *Rodney*,
Nelson, Renown,
This one/two/three/four-funnelled bastard
Is getting me down.

Scribes at Salerno

Naval Writer Cliff Smith in *Nelson* fancied himself as 'a devil-may-care Jack-my-Hearty manning an Oerlikon gun', even though 'We Writers and Supply blokes were kidded that we were non-combatants. This was far from the truth. My action station down in the 6 in shell room lugging projectiles weighing 90 to 100 pounds was no sinecure, and being in the bowels of the ship battened down wasn't very pleasant. However, after nine months at sea, surviving a torpedoing during Malta Convoy "Halberd", and repairs and refit, I was transferred to the 4.7 in supply party, a vast improvement on my last station. At least I could smell fresh air.

'However, it wasn't that much of an improvement. During other convoys in the Med, particularly the big "Pedestal" of August 1942, we all experienced some hair-raising moments. Jerry's dive-bombers were heart-stopping. It was frightening when the Air Defence Officer up on the bridge reported some 20 Junkers 88s approaching the ship. I'm sorry to have to say how relieved I was when they ignored us but dive-bombed the carrier *Indomitable*, astern to starboard. I went on the 4.7 in gun platform and saw a pall of smoke issuing from one of her gun turrets which was hanging over the side. Prior to this drama I remember hearing what I thought were depth-charges being dropped, but it turned out that HMS *Eagle* had been torpedoed and I saw her go down in about five minutes.

'We just had to take it, until the tide turned in 1943 when we invaded Sicily. I well remember when the old *Nelson* escorted a huge convoy of ships, stretching as far as the eye could see, 10 July 1943. My oppo and I were off duty on the upper deck watching this remarkable armada. "Musso is in for a shock," he said, and so it proved. *Nelson* was flagship for the invasion forces, which successfully put our armies ashore. I didn't know that my best pal was among those Pongoes, and was killed on the beaches which we were attacking. I remember him every Armistice Day, and all the other brave lads who died. Later during the battle for Sicily we and sister *Rodney* were pounding hell out of some 11 in shore batteries commanding the Straits of Messina, and all we could think about was how much damage our great 16 in shells were doing to our own messdecks. When we were stood down we rushed below, to find every piece of crockery shattered, and chaos everywhere.

'The final engagement in the Italian campaign as far as I was concerned was the Salerno landing on the eve of my birthday. A buzz went round the messdecks that Italy had surrendered and we thought we would have no opposition. How wrong we were! That evening and night of 8/9 September 1943 was the most harrowing experience I'd had during my service. *Nelson* was in the bay to soften up the defences with her big guns, but Jerry, who had withdrawn into the Alban hills inland, threw everything but the kitchen sink back at us. Our own AA guns were working overtime and we slaved to provide the guns of all calibres with ammo. After a hectic hour or so the guns were firing faster than we could supply them, and the Gunnery Officer ordered the hatches to be opened so that ammo could be drawn straight from the magazine. This meant that there was a lift shaft from the main deck down to the magazine and any flashback or shell hit could blow us all to kingdom come. We didn't need urging on, and wasn't I glad to see the last pom-pom ammo box come up!

'One of the proudest days on board ship was in Grand Harbour, Valletta, Malta, when the surrender of the Italian Fleet was taken by General Eisenhower. Mind you, a lot of us felt a bit mad when the Italian Head of Staff, Field Marshal Badoglio, was also allowed to inspect *Nelson*'s Royal Marines. I suppose it was a common courtesy, and the Italians were now our allies, but the niceties were a bit overdone in the eyes of the Lower Deck, and most of Jolly Jack's comments were unprintable. Not that 90 per cent of us even saw the ceremony – we were banished to the depths where we could not see or be seen or blow raspberries.'

Combined Ops Isle of Wighter Dave Satherley was also at the Sicilian beaches in his beloved, now battered *LCI 127*.

'We landed our troops at Cape Passaro at dawn on invasion day, then went back to Malta for more troops. On passage back to Sicily we were ordered to proceed to Syracuse harbour as word was that the port had been captured; and we, with some LCIs and LCTs, plus a Fleet 'sweeper, headed there, passing a merchant convoy and escort under heavy air attack by extremely brave and determined Jerries, attacking mast-high, passing over our small group of landing craft low enough to see the pilots clearly. As our troop spaces were packed, plus the deck crowded with squaddies, we left them alone and they ignored us on their way to the fat prizes. An ammo ship actually blew to pieces and debris crashed around us, a piece striking my hand as I stood in the Oerlikon pit gripping the gun handles, cutting my wrist and bleeding.

'Then, as we were about to enter Syracuse harbour, an Italian sub surfaced in the harbour mouth, trying to make it to base, no doubt. It was immediately fired on and the Fleet 'sweeper's forward 4 in struck the conning tower. *127*, being only yards away, went alongside, and AB Wiggy Bennett and myself jumped aboard, armed with Lanchester sub-machine-guns (posh Sten guns), and he stayed in the conning tower while I went down below to take the surrender. This was not so brave as it seems as many Eytie crew had come on deck from various hatches with white handkerchiefs, sheets, etc. First thing I saw was a young man's head and shoulders on the first "level" on the ladder going down, the rest of him had been blown away. The sub was the *Bronzo*, and the crew received me like a hero, offering cigarettes and lovely peaches. The sub was filthy, as were the crew. At that moment German aircraft appeared and machine-gunned and bombed us, and not exactly wishing to go down with a sunken sub I beat the Eyties *easily* getting the hell up the ladder to the conning tower. There Wiggy was kneeling and firing his Lanchester at an aircraft, and as my head came out the hatch his bullets missed my skull by inches.

'We took the sub in tow and entered the harbour, then went alongside the Hotel Salvatore Firenze, where our troops climbed over the guardrails to join the fight instead of wading ashore. The hotel was being looted by dozens of Sicilian peasants who were tossing sheets and pillows, clothes, mattresses and anything else to their friends below, while our Oerlikons were blasting away at Jerry aircraft passing overhead! When things quietened we nipped across the quay and investigated the hotel ourselves, liberating hundreds of dinner plates to save the washing-up problem that had brought us to punch-ups in the past. They lasted till after D-Day over a year later. I also got a Harold Lloyd straw hat which I wore with pride, and we stood to the guns in harbour with a grand selection of hats: an Italian general's worn by Wiggy, Taffy Jones in a lady's hat that would have done for Ascot, a top hat worn by Eddie Gunn, bowlers, fedoras – for the posh hotel had rooms vacated in a hurry, the wardrobes still full of clothes. I saw one Sicilian stumbing from a toilet bleeding badly, having pulled the chain and set off a booby trap. The local people certainly risked life and limb to get at some goodies.

'Wiggy and I, as gunners, were then ordered ashore into town as hordes of Italian soldiers with the inevitable suitcases were trying to surrender and getting in the way of our lads getting at Jerry. So for three days we "captured" hundreds and marched them to the railway station, which served as a gathering point. At night Wiggy and I kipped where we could, begged food, dodged shells, bombs and bullets, and enjoyed ourselves as only British matelots do when getting a spell ashore. We actually slept one night in a rather fancy brothel which had a courtyard, paying with cigarettes. Oh, and Montgomery spoke to me, asking if I were with a rifle regiment, as I had on shorts and black (Navy issue) stockings.

'We raided the Italian (Adriatic) mainland and Yugoslavia, based in Barletta, doing the run to Vis and Yugo creeks, mainly with supplies and Special Service troops, returning with wounded partisans, from October 1943 to April 1944 with occasional runs back to the other (Naples) side of Italy for landings. Our matey ship on the Yugo runs was *LCI(L) 124*, captained by Lieutenant Alec Guinness (now the famous actor). Number *124* was wrecked in a storm on a trip to Yugo and we picked up the crew. Otherwise, with the collapse of Italy and many Allied PoWs, roaming about, we often took agents behind the lines up the Adriatic coast and returned days later hoping to find British escaped prisoners waiting on the assigned beach. We never did, just plenty of Italian men and women wanting to be taken south, and the women were *very* appreciative for being rescued, so much so that we hid four of the best-looking young ones in the mess-deck for a week after returning to Barletta harbour!

'After landing troops at Termoli, up the Adriatic leg of Italy, we were attacked by a couple of Dorniers. A cannon shell blasted a rum jar in our tiny store, and Leading Stoker Gilbey, rum bosun and fully paid-up alcoholic, reckoned that the blast could easily have destroyed the other nineteen jars, which were wicker-covered stone jars. These were duly smashed with a hammer and replaced when we returned to Malta, leaving us with a surfeit of rum which we sold, greatly watered down, to US Navy landing craft we often tied up alongside. Even then we had rum in every kettle, saucepan, dixie, overflowing from lockers. Christmas 1943 was such a "rum" do that the turkey we had been supplied with was still on the messdeck table days later, cooked and untouched. Talk about cold turkey.

'In May 1944 we sailed for home and the D-Day Normandy invasion, our great little flat-bottomed LCI doing her stuff again, a record, I think, you can match with any Fleet ship, albeit we were the "Hooligan's Navy". Later, I saw *127* at Singapore. She's probably now in the Taiwan Navy or some such!'

Me and Mine

Now you take the port side
And I'll take the starboard,
We'll both paint the ship's side together,
And when Jimmy comes along
We will sing the same old song –
Thank Christ we didn't join up forever!

When I passed the Pillars of Hercules in 1944 aboard the troopship *Volendam* as one of a draft of Ordinary Seamen for Malta, not only had 'The antique Mediterranean of history and Alexander, The rattling galley and the young Greek captains' been 'swept up and piled under the table', but Malta and Matapan, Oran and Algiers, Sirte and Salerno and many young British matlows had joined them in the dust of history. All that was really left of the war was the mopping-up.

As we steamed on for Malta, Africa was distant in mist to starboard. Yellow Malta – 'Isle of honey' to the ancients, 'Island of bells and smells' to Jolly Jack – rose out of the sea like a railway buffet rock cake. After a short stay, with heart-pounding visits to The Gut of evil legend, The Egyptian Queen and Lucky Wheel, Caruana's Bar, where the distant heroes of 'Faith, Hope and Charity' once drank, I got a draft to a ship called *Antares*. The only *Antares* I knew was a red but feebly glowing star out in distant space – which was where this unknown ship might as well have been, as no one knew anything about her except that she was not a stone frigate and was believed to be somewhere in the Tyrrhenian Sea.

A Mast To Climb

To Naples I went, aboard the light cruiser *Black Prince*. As dusk came on I kipped on the upper deck with bag and hammock. I dropped off but woke up almost at once, shivering. Some men of the draft had lit up. Their fag ends glowed like campfires in the dark. I got up, strolled around the humming, vibrating ship, spoke to one or two of the men on the guns, scrounged a cup of kye from the galley. The cruiser steamed on through the night, seemingly invulnerable, a symbol in steel of irresistible power, though now and again the oily, supple sea would suddenly punch her thin, bare flanks, and the whole great structure would jump and quiver, suddenly turned to a jelly of mad atoms, rivets jarring and dancing in their holes, the skin of metal trembling as if under the whip, a ripple running right through the ship.

I stretched out again and watched the masthead as it rolled in drunken parabolas from star to star. One star did a formal dance with the lofty truck, like someone trying to fix a silver doll to the top of a swaying Christmas tree with its roots in water . . . 'And a star to steer her by' . . . The ship became a rocket in space, revolving eternally in fixed orbit, and darkness rushing past. I thought of that other mast . . . I was a *Ganges* boy, too, I had had to face that daunting ascent. The mast had been the first thing I noticed when I jumped down out of the draft truck. The mast was manned, and right at the top, balanced on the swaying Button, a boy was standing, semaphoring into the empty sky. What was he sending – his name, so that the world would notice him? Then came that fateful forenoon, when we had to make our own attempt on Everest . . .

We lined up facing the lower shrouds, three at a time.

'All right,' sang out old Harry Brown, 'First three – up you go!'

Well, the first stretch wasn't so bad, no harder than shinning up a rope ladder in the school gym, though the shrouds tapered as you rose, until you reached the point of decision, The Elbow. There, the shrouds disappeared backwards over your head out to the edge of the maintop. Of course, you could simply carry straight on and go up through the Lubber's Hole, but both old Harry, who had been in the Boxer Rebellion, and could still go up and over like a chamois, and the ancient CPO Duckmanton, whom we called the Squadron-Leader, for some reason, both these Ancient Mariners had let it be known that *their* class was expected to go over The Elbow, like *real* sailors.

I rather prided myself on my head for heights, on the strength of some rock-climbing in Cheddar Gorge, but this was worse than the overhang in the 'Easy' Knight's Climb, or even the 'Severe' Pinnacle Bay.

Then, with a panicky lunge, the lad to my right scrambled straight on up through the Lubber's Hole.

I stared after him. It was an ugly performance. A new feeling surged up in me, a boiling flood of anger at my own weakness. I took one hand away and grasped the ratlines which soared away dizzily over my head. I shifted my other hand, then my feet, and started to climb, upwards and outwards.

I seemed to be climbing forever, under the roof of the maintop. Then all of a sudden I could see daylight and the edge of the platform. Then I was reaching over the edge, gripping the thin brass rail running round just inboard of the rim. A few heaves and I was sitting on the edge, dangling my legs, looking down at the blank white faces, feeling good. In fact, so euphoric did I feel that when it came to coming down the other side I hung by one hand from the rail for a few giddy seconds before tucking my feet in and scrambling down, and old Harry's whispered 'Good lad' was music to my ears.

It never occurred to me to climb further, let alone right up to the Button. Perhaps I knew my limitations, even then. I dreamed about the mast often afterwards . . . I was back on that tall, grim tower, symbol of strength, of iron manhood, swaying with all its great spars and sails through a lashing gale, but holding firm with the massive fortitude of the Royal Navy, and suddenly I was falling, down towards that surging, howling sea, slipping, screaming . . .

I woke up sweating and trembling. Around me the scene had changed. Moonlight had broken through, silver on the sea. I went and looked down at the rushing foam as the ship shouldered forward into a wide world to be explored . . .

NINEVEH IN NAPLES

Naples was a Nineveh in late 1944, a babel of sound and lights, roaring Jeeps and soaring voices, where little *raggazzi* pimped for their clean, virgin, schoolmistress sisters, and sold rotten apples in paper cornets. We were quartered in an old castle, the Fort Dell'Ovo, down on the seafront, sleeping in the dungeons on a damp stone floor, where I quickly developed tonsillitis and was whisked off to the big white 52nd General Hospital on the hills above that famous bay. There I had a fortnight of eating melons, followed by another two weeks' recuperation on the island of Ischia, where I became happily up-homers with the Lollo look-alike who owned the small trattoria near the rest camp. Big eats, Jack, steak and chips and vino every day. *La dolce vita, bella fanciula.* My oppo there was a tall, stooped, hollow-cheeked stoker who looked like one of the living dead from a Bela Lugosi film. Once a Chief, he confided in me that he had had 22 doses of the clap . . . 'I've been out here five years, but I can't go home, not like I am . . .'

Back in Napoli I found that all my kit was gone, bought some more from shops with a 'casual', flogged the lot in a little cafe on the Via Roma, not far from the old Royal Palace, which was now a huge NAAFI, with facilities unheard of before by Jack-my-Hearty. In the wine bar was a swarthy waitress who stroked my hand as she served me . . . 'Cor!' said the Cadaver, 'The old green light! You're in there, mate. Fill yer boots!' I heard that you could even have art lessons, and had just turned into the art studio when there was a power cut. I stood rooted to the spot and when the juice came back I was standing facing a slim, dark girl, who turned out to be Tullia Matania, daughter of the famous artist. Under her guidance I brushed up my drawing, and once persuaded Tullia to use the wine-bar Sophia as a model, and there I was in heaven with lead in my pencil . . .

Another rare treat which Naples had to offer was a trip out to Pompeii, by lorry from The Palace every morning. The Cadaver knew the barrack guards, who were all from his old ship and let us come and go as we pleased, and I took the lorry every morning, to visit with the Vettii brothers, laze in their atrium, study the naughty frescoes, shout Shakespeare (I didn't know any Aeschylus) in the theatre, studying the positions on the walls of the brothel, still instructive though faded. One sunny morning I was sitting counting lizards in the Forum and listening to *L'Après-Midi d'un Faun* in my head when an Aussie voice said, 'Hey mate, how do you do this house of the Tragic Poet?' Quite without thinking I said, 'Straight down the Forum, under the Arch of Caligula, first left and it's the fourth house on the right. You can't miss it.' It was as if I was in Bath, my home town, directing some tourist to the Roman Baths or Sham Castle.

I nearly got caught. I returned to the 'Fort of The Egg' one day to find that the Tannoy had been asking for me all morning. My draft to the distant *Antares* had come through and in short time I was on passage to Taranto, this time in the huge, empty *Queen of Bermuda*, just six of us matlows in the whole of that floating hotel. We berthed at Taranto in the dark, and I was rushed off in a jeep to HMS *Antares*, lying alongside, gangway light glowing.

COMING OF AGE ABOARD *ANTARES*

She turned out to be a Fleet minesweeper of the *Algerine* class, built by Montreal Shipyards in 1943; one funnel, one 4 in gun for'ard in a shield like a telephone box, and all her real business gear aft on the quarter (or sweeping)-deck: huge drums of wire for sweeping contact mines or shiny black electrical flex for the magnetic variety, 'kites' for holding the sweep wires at the required depths, Dan buoys for marking a swept channel. The radar was my concern – one Type 271 10 cm surface warning set, with the old vertical handle (very useful to hang a bucket on) to turn the aerials and the old A-scope screen with horizontal trace. Back in RDF training at Douglas, Isle of Man, we had been told that the 271 could detect a surfaced U-boat at 8,000 yards, thanks to a fiendish device invented at Birmingham University called the Strapped Magnetron. There were still one or two U-boats in the Med, and I had no desire to be the hero who picked one up. The set was sited at the rear of the compass platform, with its distinctive 'lantern' containing the scanner above.

The next morning *Antares* and the other ships of the 19th Minesweeping Flotilla left Taranto and steered round the heel of Italy into the Adriatic and some very nasty choppy seas, which had us corkscrewing all the way up to Ancona, a God-forsaken wasteland of a place with one sordid cafe in a sea of mud and ruins. From here we were to sortie across to Yugoslavia to sweep the Hun mines laid all along the coast.

There, within easy range of German 12 in guns ashore, our ships would sweep in echelon. The Radar Party consisted of myself and AB Johnny Hayes, a large genial youth who had been studying for the priesthood when war broke out; later young OD Brothers was added. Johnny and I formed a kite block team on the sweeping deck as well. The 'kite', which really looked like a boxkite in steel, had to be fixed by a block on to the sweep wire, which had the cutters attached. While one man swung out backwards over the ship's wake holding up the kite block, his team mate reached over from the stern and clamped the block on to the sweep wire. The kite was then streamed, and slid down the wire to its selected depth. We had some good weather, and then the sweeping deck was a fun place to be. I took boxing lessons from Leading Stoker Lightowler, a former Navy champion. But it could also be a highly dangerous place. Old hands could tell if there was too much tension in the sweep wire, first from the change of pitch in the perpetual humming sound which it gave off, then by sitting on the wire, bouncing up and down as it transmitted danger signals. When it seemed at breaking point he would leap off . . . 'Take cover!'. . . and everyone rushed forward to find shelter from the lashing, berserk wire which would leap over the stern, its jagged end looking for a matlow's tender body, or wrapping round him and cutting him in two. This never happened while I was aboard *Antares*, but we had one or two false alarms.

Another potentially dangerous job was to hold the wire with sinkers attached which also held the wires down. This had to be wound round the holder's forearm and released extra smartly when the weights were streamed, or he either got dragged overboard into the foaming wake or lost his arm. I was doing this job one day when the First Lieutenant, who was also Sweeping Officer, neglected to tell me he was streaming the weights, and I just got rid of the wire, which was doing a boa constrictor on me, before I was smashed against the after rails prior to serious injury and probably worse. I have often pondered on that little episode. I did not get along with Jimmy, who was known as 'Tojo', from a physical resemblance, but then neither did anyone else. I expect his mother loved him. He liked to keep me on the set, reporting the positions of the other sweepers in broad daylight, when radar's magic all-seeing eye was really redundant.

The ship was Canadian-built and quite comfortable. Most seamen slept in the lower messdeck, which was battened down and no-go during operations, when a mine or torpedo could have turned it into a graveyard; some, including myself, slung our hammocks in the upper messdeck, over the dining tables. There was one officer (who shall be nameless, as I don't fancy seeing him in court) who had the habit of wandering round at night (we were usually tied up by nightfall), peering and groping in men's hammocks, and I was cautioned to turn in with my hand wrapped round some form of weapon to repel boarders. The galley opened on to our upper messdeck, and food was usually hot and plenty, potmess being very popular. I have always loved my grub, and I became known as the ship's gannet. Anyone who left any of his meal always scraped if off on to my plate automatically. My particular oppos were Johnny Hayes, Chris the Asdic, and Ray Sadler, a rather bitter dipped CW candidate, who spent most of his off-watch time on a correspondence course on architecture.

I came of age, which in the Navy was 20, aboard *Antares*, and was able to draw my tot of Nelson's Blood at last, though I had been enjoying 'sippers' for some time as the price for small favours like the loan of a station card for a run ashore or a sub till pay day. It was 'grog' of course, watered rum, but very welcome as dished out by Scouse Palfrey. I was given the traditional ceremony, which included sippers from all the rummies in the mess. I passed out in the course of this orgy, and was lashed into my hammock and slung in the Lower Power Room. When I woke up with all the machinery thrashing round me, I thought I was in some sort of technological hell.

Sometimes home-coming to Ancona was less than warm, like the bitter winter night when we clawed our way in through a literally blinding snowstorm, Aldis lamps blazing, butting again and again into the boom before creeping into the harbour and crashing into our trot mate, the scruffy *Arcturus*. Once in it was cosy enough. The lads soon settled down, and the foul air of the lower messdeck was once again loud with 'Mazaire-a-vair', 'Crafty miz', 'Stick', 'Bust', and 'I'll go a bundle'. Jumper Cross would get out his guitar and try once more with his truck-driver's hands to pluck a recognizable tune from the sullen catgut. Ray Sadler thumbed his *Life of Christopher Wren*; myself my notebook, well filled by now with examples of the priceless lower deck argot and the occasional poem. While based on Ancona we fed a deserter from the Queen's Regiment who lived in the centre of a huge American Spam dump left behind by Mark Clark's overfed doughboys; he tapped on the scuttle every night with a sack of tins in exchange for white bread, bacon, butter and anything the cook would spare. Where are you now? Did they shoot you after all? Other 'rabbits' were brought aboard by the Radar Mechanic, an ex-policeman who had nothing to do on board, as the set never broke down, and had become ship's posty. His mail sack was always full.

YUGOSLAVIAN CAPERS

We received no more thanks from the Yugoslavs for our services in freeing their coasts of mines than did our lads on Russian convoys from the citizens of Murmansk and Archangel. They were all Tito people, not the Fascists of Mihailovic, and they did not like to see us ashore. Split was the nearest port, its streets so full of 'partisans' you wondered who was fighting the Germans. Offering a cigarette to a youthful *partijani* I was angrily stopped by a beautiful girl in uniform, and was about to object when I realized that, like the Venus de Milo, *she had no arms*. What damp and the vandals had needed centuries to do, a German grenade had accomplished in ten seconds. Johnny and I were invited to the home of a former professor of English and his two daughters, who wept when they confessed that they had only acorn coffee and black bread to give us, and two cabbages to take back to the ship.

More usually we tied up at a fishing village just north of Split called Kastel Sucurac. On our first stay there one watch went ashore, and I was climbing the ridge above the village when I heard a 'ping' quite close by, which sounded like a bullet to me. And so it was. No one had told us that the Germany Army had vacated the place only two hours before we arrived. While there we heard a buzz that a certain partisan leader had designs on the ship. The Skipper, a rotund, jolly Dart, took this seriously enough to ride with only two easily slipped wires – and me with a Sten gun (no bullets) on bridge watch. Irish Paddy said, 'If they pinched the f★★★★★g ship you'd never notice.' The lads got their own back on our sullen allies in a spectacular way. On the hills above the village stood the huge sign TITO in white letters. As we steamed away and left the golden shore of Kastel Sucurac (hopefully forever), the final 'O' was conspicuous by its absence.

We oftened wondered idly why the German shore batteries never fired on us, as we were a gaggle of sitting ducks, and put it down to their not wanting to ruin a good thing for themselves, having lived the *dolce vita* for years in something like a big Butlin's – with vino. Then, one day, the inevitable happened.

We were carrying out an orthodox Oropesa sweep in echelon, and the fine, sunny day had been marked by a phenomenon – our revered flotilla leader HMS *Rinaldo*, had actually appeared to lead us. Where she got to on the bad days we had no idea, but we hardly ever saw her.

Anyway, there she was, just ahead of *Antares*, on our port bow, sweeps out, float bobbing, every bit as if she knew what she was doing, when suddenly she swung away off course. A few minutes later aboard *Antares* there was an almighty bang . . . and the ship's 1,000 tons leapt into the air. Below, in the upper messdeck the cook was showing some of us one of his vast collection of dirty postcards. He thought the wrath of God had hit him and dropped the pictures all over the deck. We all thought it was a shell which those moribund batteries had at last decided to throw at us, and waited, suspended in horror, for the next round, which would surely blow us all to hell among the Chief Stokers.

None came, but a leading wireman staggered across the for'ard door, his face bleeding – as it turned out, from being hit by an attaché case falling on him. We rushed on deck, and the first person we saw was the Buffer, an unpopular man, blood streaming from his mouth and down his white shirt front. 'Buffs, Buffs,' we cried in our grief, 'What have you done?' He opened his mouth just long enough to snarl, 'I bit me f★★★★★g tongue!'

This rather set the tone of the whole drama. We had, mercifully, not been hit by a shell, but by a mine which our leader had put up – and had then got out of the way quicker than shit through a goose, instead of moving over to cover us from the rest of the assumed minefield. The mine was an 'O' type, the smallest in Doenitz's armoury, not big enough to sink us, but big enough to bite a big hole out of the bottom of the ship, and all the NAAFI stores fell out, which for some reason made the Canteen Manager very happy.

I reached my action station on the bridge just in time to pick up the buzzing phone and hear one Ordinary Seaman Metcalfe (of whom more later) report, from right aft, 'Mine exploded for'ard sir.' I repeated this to the Captain, who by now had reached the bridge and was giving a crisp series of orders which showed plainly that he, at least, knew exactly what he was doing. He listened gravely and said, 'That man is sucking up for promotion.'

Everyone was shaken, except the Captain, who was delighted at the blessed relief from the boredom of being all dressed up with nowhere much to go. The worst injury was a broken leg, and we slowly made our way down to Malta, with myself and young Brothers doing watch-and-watch in the absence of Johnny, suffering from bottled tot.

As we manoeuvred to approach our berth we contrived to go astern into the cliffs below Bighi Hospital, which did no significant damage to Malta but did *Antares'* already shaken structure no good at all. In Dockyard Creek we moored astern of the huge American light cruiser *Savannah*, and came in for some up-to-date movies on her quarter-deck, not to mention loads of tinned food from her cornucopia of goodies. She had just come in from the States, and Jack returned her kindness by exchanging for her lovely US dollars a sackful of counterfeit lire which had been dumped on us in Italy, but which the Yankee gobs and grunts seemed eager to collect, as they were heading up that way. After the dockyard men had taken a cursory look at our damage, we set sail for Ferryville, North Africa, praying fervently that we never, ever, met the *Savannah* again.

DESTINATION FERRYVILLE

Steaming slowly up the narrow canal to Ferryville, we eventually berthed. That night the starboard watch went ashore – and did not come back. We sat around well into the small hours speculating on what could have happened. Then, about half-past three, a very agitated and distraught Metcalfe, OD – the one who told the Captain all about the mine – struggled up the gangplank, with a truly epic story to tell . . .

'We all go into this knocking shop, see? There's a lot of French matlows in there, and we have to take our turn. Then some bloke rushes in and tells us the Patrol is outside. Them Frog dabtoes is very friendly and lend us bits of their uniforms, see? We're all sitting there trying to look French and that, and a dirty big PO of the Patrol comes in. He goes all round us, looking us up and down, and stops in front of Palfrey (the Rum bosun, a small, thin Scouser) – 'he's got one of them flat hats with a red pom-pom on, and says, "Well, *you* don't look French!" An' Palfrey says, "Well, I f★★★★n' am!" An' they cop the lot, except me, I dodged out the door at the back . . .'

Bit by bit the rest of the story came out, how starboard watch carried out a fighting retreat towards the ship, reminiscent at least of Moore's men at Corunna, with Leading Stoker Lightowler outdoing Leonidas of Sparta and Roland at Roncevalles rolled into one bringing up the fighting rearguard, but going down at last to heavy reinforcements of the local gendarmerie and being dragged off to 'le clink', where they still were, sad, sore and homesick.

When Metcalfe repeated his story in the wardroom, it was reported by the officers' steward that the Skipper laughed right through the dog watches. Collecting his battered lads from the local Chateau d'If with the promise of dire punishment for all – and a special example to be made of the valiant Lightowler – he led them back up the gangplank still grinning all over his face, gave out a few minor restrictions of leave – which didn't mean much in Ferryville anyway – and sentenced Lightowler to tend bar at the ship's dance.

Leaving a Care and Maintenance Party behind, the rest of us took passage in the floating slum of an 'Allied' Italian destroyer to Malta, and I was drafted to HMS *Kimberley*, a survivor of Mountbatten's *Kelly* class, a Med fixture known as 'Cunningham's Taxi'.

Kimberley's beat was the Dodecanese Islands, still German-occupied. Here we patrolled uneventfully, except for a bombardment of Rhodes with our 4.7 in popguns, cut short when the somnolent Germans fired back with their 12 in, and we left in a hurry.

We were back in a short time to receive the German surrender by their General Wagner. He stumped red-faced up the ladder, followed by his aide, a Goebbels look-alike, who gave us a stiff-arm Sieg Heil job. There was a growl from the lads, and the Skipper waved them brusquely below, following which we steamed through the harbour entrance once bestridden by the Colossus, and gave the new Governor, Archbishop Makarios, a 21-gun salute as he sailed in, black beard blowing in the wind.

The Eastern Fleet

Come to the Spare Crew, make no delay,
Come to the Spare Crew – two bob a day,
Sweeping up the messdecks, nothing else to do,
Come to the Spare Crew, do.
Joyful, joyful, joyful we will be
When the boats are shoving off to sea,
We'll be sweeping up the messdecks,
F★★k-all else in view,
Come to the Spare Crew, do.

HEAT AND THE RISING SUN

In Trincomalee harbour, Ceylon, in the trot alongside the submarine depot ship HMS *Wu Chang*, an old Chinese river steamer, was Iain Nethercott in *Tactician*, which had made the trip from Beirut.

'*Taurus* had left on patrol down to the upper parts of the Molucca Straits. It was the monsoon season. Filthy greeny-black skies and sheets of warm rain. We went on patrol. As we pushed on south it got hotter and hotter in the boat, and more and more humid. The only thing to wear was a towel round one's waist, and nothing else. When dived, the temperature went up to 120°–130°, and we just streamed with sweat. First of all it was prickly heat and sweat rash. The skin peeled off between our legs and from under our arms. We had no air-conditioning in these older T-boats, but Vickers had fitted us with a wonderful specimen of technological ingenuity called a Dehumidifier. Although this box of tricks used many precious amps from my battery, the Skipper decided to try it out. After a lot of work the Outside ERA got it going. It made a tremendous din, and after a couple of hours' running when dived it had wrenched about two pints of dirty water out of the atmosphere. We never used it again.

'Conditions on board after a few weeks at sea were appalling. The food was all wrong. The bread had turned to green mould after a few days, so the cook had to bake bread every night. The flour was full of weevils and had to be sieved before use. We had jars of salt tablets and "Sunshine Pills" (Vitamin C) in all the messes. For a long time these had been mistrusted by Jolly Jack, as someone had spread the buzz that they dampened his sexual ardour, like *Ganges* bromide; then it got around that in fact they had just the opposite effect, and were swallowed by the handful. I've often wondered when they'll start to work.

'Water was very short, only to be used for drinking and cleaning your teeth, and the Chief Stoker had it turned off most of the time. The boat was infested with rats and cockroaches, and before long most of us had a dose of crabs, and as we had nothing on board for that kind of trouble we tried white spirit, with its ensuing rash.

'The waters we were operating in were smooth and oily, with countless uncharted mudbanks and small islands which at night looked just like ships. The Japanese were active but the targets were not really worth all the effort. The American subs in the Pacific were getting all the good targets, and only in Sabang, Penang and Singapore, all naval bases, was anything happening.

'We finally withdrew from patrol and headed for Trinco. Thirty miles out we were escorted in by *Eritrea*, an Italian naval sloop which a few months earlier had been fighting us. This time we went alongside *Adamant*, a spotless, gleaming brand-new depot ship which, till we tied up alongside her, had never seen a submarine, having been operating bloody cruisers off the East African coast. She was all brass and bugle calls, and her paintwork shone in the sunshine. We soon changed all that when we scraped alongside in our dark-green and rust-red motley, the officer of the day and attendant side-boy with telescope glaring down at us. The splinter holes we had received in the Med had never been patched up, we had our Jolly Roger up, and the casing party made an effort and lined up in their Afrika Korps uniforms. The *Adamant* shower tied us up and just left us. No welcome, no mail, it was uncanny.

'I wandered up the gangway, wearing only my pair of greasy khaki shorts, with six weeks' beard, crabby and filthy-dirty. As I crossed the immaculate well-deck to look for their duty ERA to get the shore leads down our conning tower and belted on, I was pulled up short by a hysterical shriek. An immaculate, overfed little subby was yelling at me. I drifted over and received a king-sized bollocking for the state I was in . . . "Why aren't you in the rig of the day? Look at the mess you're making! Stand to attention! Get your hair cut!" etc, etc. I strolled back on board *Tactician* leaving my trail of greasy footprints over his white deck.

'The Coxswain tried to calm me down with a tot. The Skipper was next door entering up all the lies in the log before going inboard, heard me doing this tremendous toot and came in to ask me why I wasn't my usual smiling self. I gave him both barrels . . . Rig of the day – when all my kit was somewhere between Beirut and Colombo, and probably lost forever? And a shampoo and set was difficult on a patrol submarine, and short of jumping over the side with a giant bar of salt-water soap and bathing every night of the week, how the bloody hell do you keep clean – especially when you've been crawling about under the engines to repair the ballast pump? Etc, etc . . . Cocoa Bill – so called because anyone in the boat who made up a mug of kye at night found the Skipper at his elbow asking for a cup – had an evil sense of humour, told me to stop my almighty drip, took me to the wardroom where we both had a whisky, and away we went up the gangway. The Skipper sought out my little commissioned friend and explained to him very forcibly that submarine crews at sea did not spend their time sitting on deckchairs on the casing drinking Martinis.'

'For month after month,' says Nethercott, speaking for all the East Indies Fleet submarines, 'we carried on patrolling, sinking Marus in the Straits of Malacca, and many junks, with Japs in the water trying to kill any Malays swimming towards us, spies and raiding parties, picking up half-clad men from the jungle. We laid mines at dawn off Singapore, creeping right in under their patrols. We could fight a gun battle in our sleep. We were harried by small Jap sub-chasers, which at times were very persistent. We even had to surface one night, having been kept down overlong, till we were literally blue in the face and gasping for breath, and take on the chaser in a gun action. It was a short but bloody action in which they all finished up dead. *Stonehenge* and *Stratagem* had gone by then, and most of *Stratagem*'s crew had been executed.

'D-Day in Europe came and went, our boat was getting more and more cranky, all our batteries suffered from sulphation, the Engineer Officer was nearly in tears over the state of the main engines, the stern glands had slow leaks, the rifling of the gun barrel was worn smooth, and, worst of all, we were getting overtired. With one or two exceptions we still had the original crew from Barrow, and it was now the middle of 1944.

'The terrible heat in the boat, especially down on the Equator, gradually made us more and more ill. We lay on rush mats now, as we found that we stuck to the locker cushions when we lay on them. We wore sarongs made out of curtain material, the Skipper sporting the gaudiest. He allowed the stokers up on the conning tower at night in pairs, but nothing could really be done. At night when we were forced down in the middle of a battery charge, the engines were red-hot and the batteries overheated.

'All ventilation had to be switched off as we were hunted, and wave after wave of terrific heat built up round you. Men collapsed with heat stroke, but nothing could be done for them till we were able to open up the hatch again and vent the boat. We took a naval surgeon lieutenant to sea on one patrol to report on conditions. He collapsed in the second week and nearly died in his bunk. The temperature was 140°, beyond which they reckoned men couldn't survive. We did.

'At night when we were on the surface we had our dinner and our rum. We left most of the dinner but drank the rum. The gash buckets were always slopping over with all the dinners chucked into them. These buckets had to be hauled up the conning tower at night using a hook rope, and ditched over the leeward side of the bridge. When the boat was rolling the buckets collided with the sides of the tower on their upward journey and often half the contents finished up either in the tower or in the Control Room beneath. Once the klaxon sounded off in the middle of this operation. The gash party up top and the two lookouts leapt for the conning tower hatch as she started to dive, with about 30 swilling gash buckets lined up under the Control Room ladder. The Skipper and Jimmy were dancing around in the Control Room, leaping in and out of buckets while all of us who had to run the length of the boat to get to our Diving Stations got caught up in the general mêlée, skidding around on spud peelings and lumps of fat as the boat plunged down.

'On one patrol we were so desperately hot and sick that the Skipper took us out 20 miles from the coast and allowed "Hands to bathe", twenty at a time at 0300 in the morning, cheerfully telling us that he would dive and leave us if he was surprised by a patrol boat. It was wonderful until one of our ABs got bitten in the leg by a barracuda and let out a yell of "Shark!" We cleared the water in about ten seconds.

'Once we sailed to rendezvous at a creek in the jungle on the Malayan coast to pick up a spy who had been landed by *Telemachus*. The Skipper had checked it through the periscope during the day, and we crept inshore that night and waited for the light signal so that our SBS folboat men could creep in and fetch the agent. We got light signals all right, but they were coming from the wrong place and were not correct. While the Skipper was thinking we suddenly spotted a Jap patrol boat coming round the headland. We opened fire with the 4 in and charged out to sea and dived away out of it. The spy had been captured and tortured and the whole thing was a trap.

'When we sailed on patrol from Trincomalee we used to fill the boat up with green tropical fruit which was hung in every available space except the Engine Room, Control Room and Motor Room. Looking through the boat into the fore-ends looked like the Tropical House at Kew Gardens. The trouble was that it all went rotten after a couple of days, and made the ship stink more than ever. 'Admiral "Slim" Somerville came aboard just before we went on a particularly hazardous patrol and gave us a boost-up speech and walked through the boat. When he arrived in my Motor Room and looked aft into the stokers' mess, all he saw was a mass of greenery, with one of the killick stokers stark naked looking for his seagoing sarong. "Like Tarzan of the bloody apes," said the Admiral.

'One thing about the life was that you never knew till you got to sea who you were likely to find in the mess or fore-ends. You would stroll up to the torpedo stowage compartment and in the dim red patrol lighting you would find a gang of Chinese cut-throats cleaning their guns, or strange parties of Aussie soldiers with dozens of packs of explosives and Tommy guns. We had Chinese spies in the mess; half of whom probably fought against us later on in the Malayan troubles. Men we picked up from the jungle were sometimes dying of fever, some were wounded, and we carried no medical aid other than the cox'n had, who had done a week's course at Haslar Hospital. Intelligence back in Ceylon were very eager to get hold of some live Japs, and two captains, Red McKenzie (Rufus) and the Black McKenzie were in competition to get one. They never succeeded, though not for want of trying – a great relief to us as the idea of one of those fanatics on board, possibly getting loose, and pulling every valve and lever in sight before we could recapture him, filled us with dread.

'The Japanese submarines operating out of Penang, on the Malacca coast of Malaya, were committing terrible atrocities on merchant ship crews, many of whom were ordered out of their lifeboats and hacked to death on the submarine casing. *Taurus* had sunk *I.8*, a big ocean-going submarine which had sunk an Allied merchantman, killed the crew and thrown some of them back into their lifeboats. The Captain had survived – with his hands chopped off. Yes, we were definitely after those bastards.'

UNDERWATER RESCUE

'We were detailed off at the end of one patrol to be crash boat off Sabang, Sumatra, to cover an Anglo-American carrier raid on the port. *Saratoga* was operating with *Illustrious* in a dawn dive-bombing attack on the oil tanks and other military targets.

'We surfaced off Sabang about 10 minutes before zero hour and patrolled slowly in towards the harbour, trimmed down. The Skipper had detailed Frankie Mustard, a killick stoker, and me as swimming party, as we were the best underwater swimmers in the boat. Just as dawn broke we heard the roar of aircraft coming in from seaward, Hellcats and Wildcats. In a flash they were over the port. We blew the boat right up and speeded up, and sailed in towards the harbour. A section of three American fighters flew alongside at sea height covering us. The whole harbour area was alive with explosions, the bombing was very accurate. Suddenly the first shells from the shore batteries arrived, and the Skipper started weaving the boat about.

'A patrol boat appeared inshore, coming out of the harbour towards us. The Skipper yelled "Up with the guns' crews!" and "Break out the Ensign!" to Scouse, the bunting-tosser. The 4 in opened up as we sailed in towards the shore. Our three aircraft were shouting to us and each other over the R/T and streaked towards the patrol boat and riddled it with fire. It stopped, and under another attack, caught fire. A Hellcat was down in the water close-in, and Air Escort and others were calling us on R/T while others circled the downed plane.

'We steamed as fast as we could towards the sinking aircraft, and the shore batteries were getting very close (afterwards the starboard lookout swore that one shell went between the periscope standards). The plane had practically sunk now, with only its tail showing. As we smashed alongside, Frankie and I jumped in from the starboard ballast tank and swam down. We could see the pilot inside, desperately trying to open the canopy, and it seemed to have flooded up inside. I tried pulling the canopy back but it wouldn't shift, when suddenly Frankie, who was on the other side, found an emergency release lever of some kind and we pulled the canopy back. The chap was OK and had already undone his webbing. We dragged him out and swam up with him. McNally of the casing party dived in and grabbed him, and he was dragged aboard. Our air escort gave us the all-clear and we dived away and made for the open sea.

'After a bit of medical attention our friend was walking around the boat. He was a US Navy officer, and I don't think he had ever seen anything like our boat and crew. We must have looked like pirates to him, with our scruffy beards and sweaty bodies, and the last time they had seen a sarong was on Dottie Lamour; but he was friendly enough, as we all knew that if we hadn't picked him up he would have been dragged ashore and executed.

'When we came into Trinco a few days later we had our flier up on the bridge to show him off, and the whole Task Force cheered ship. The *Saratoga* was dressed overall for us, and as we made fast alongside *Adamant* we were invaded by dozens of American launches full of boxes of cigars, crates of Coke, ice-cream and cameramen. They completely ignored the *Adamant*'s protocol and swarmed aboard and were down in the boat snapping us in every conceivable position. Eventually I managed to get aboard *Adamant* and got my hot bath and shave.

'That night we were all invited aboard *Saratoga* for films and big eats. Their Admiral had Frankie Mustard and me out in the front and gave a big speech personally thanking the Skipper. Some time afterwards Captain 'S' sent for me and told me that the Americans had wanted to give some of us a medal, but that the Admiralty had declined the offer, stating that we were only doing our job. This was true.

'We had a succession of young lieutenants and subbies sent to the boat for patrols to give our chaps a break. We had Aussies, New Zealanders, South Africans and Rhodesians. One very pink and proper South African subby came to the boat in immaculate whites to join us for a patrol. After a couple of weeks, like the rest of us he got a huge dose of crabs. He came along to Fred the Coxswain for advice. He'd never even heard of crabs and was appalled. Fred was in one of his funny moods and told him to go to the wardroom, take his shorts down and squat over a bucket of water. The human crab, he said, was a strange creature that suffers from dizziness. It would see its reflection in the water moving about, get giddy and fall off into the bucket and drown. The Springbok swallowed all this, went along to the wardroom, where everyone was turned in, and squatted down over his bucket. The Skipper came out of his box and caught him at it, laughed his head off and told him the Coxswain was taking the mickey. He explained that the proper treatment was to rub in a mixture of rum and sand. The crabs got drunk on the rum and threw rocks at each other until they were all dead.

'At Trinco the number of surface warships grew bigger every time we came in. It got crowded ashore. The Fleet canteen was built of thatch, with just Australian canned beer and long tables. The Aussies set fire to it and destroyed it, and that was that. We were still sent up into the hills to recuperate, but it was bloody boring.

'At long last we were told – one more patrol and we were going home. *Adamant* and her T-boats were sailing for Fremantle in Aussie, to be followed by *Maidstone* and the "S" boats. All submarines were to come under American command and work up in the islands.

'*Taurus* sailed for home on one engine, and we went on our last patrol. It was a difficult one. How many of our submarines had been sunk on their last patrol due to their crews being overstressed and suffering from fatigue? Wanklin's *Upholder* may well have gone that way. However, we made it, although most of us were at the Skipper's elbow almost willing him to be cautious and not take any chances.

'When we arrived back off patrol we just couldn't take it in. We were going home! In submarines you never thought beyond the next patrol. Personally, I never thought that I would survive, and now, with a bit of luck, I was going to live.'

Illustrious Goes East

Death is not an adventure for those
who stand face to face with it.
Erich Maria Remarque

Here they were, a veteran ship, but with, for the most part, an untried air group whose principal experience so far was of crash after crash, of doubt and death. They were young, the youngest only schoolboys, none of them yet masters of their temperamental machines, their new leader only a 'Temporary' VR with no combat experience. Most were newly trained men from the US Navy's Miami Fighter School, young men from all parts of the Empire, with different backgrounds and accents: 'Bash' Munnock, a tough ex-Marine from Middlesbrough; Johnny Baker, a big husky Canuck; Gordon Aitken, a colonial public schoolboy born in Ceylon, where his father, a planter, still lived; Eric Rogers, very young and very noisy, from Birmingham; Neil Brynildsen, a quiet New Zealander . . . all ordinary young men.

ENTER *SARATOGA*

Admiral Nimitz, USN, Allied Naval C-in-C in the Pacific, wanted operations mounted against the East Indies which would be both directly damaging to the Japanese war effort and draw men and material away from the Pacific, where his great offensive was in full swing. The first of these targets was to be Sabang, an island close to the northern tip of Sumatra, where oil storage tanks, an airfield and a submarine base were concentrated. HMS *Illustrious* was to mount an attack on these, in co-operations with the USS *Saratoga*.

The two veteran carriers met on a bright blue day in the Eastern Indian Ocean, *Illustrious* bringing with her Taranto, Salerno and the Malta convoys; the great *Saratoga*, the glory of Guadalcanal and the Solomons, Rabaul and the Gilberts and Marshalls. She and her prancing destroyers *Fanning*, *Dunlap* and *Cummings* came up with *Illustrious* at 1145 on the morning of 27 March 1944. Admiral Moody flew to *Saratoga* in a Barracuda, which caused one US pilot to comment 'Gee, the British'll be inventing airplanes any day now.' '*Sara*' sent over her Air Group Commander, 'Jumping Joe' Clifton, to lead tactfully the inexperienced British air group into practice for Sabang. In Jumping Joe's group some of the lads recognized a number of their former instructors from Miami Fighter School. There were big gin parties, with Norman Hanson, 1833 Squadron's VR

Co, at the piano; although PO Mechanician Con Shiels from Tyneside complains that the attitude of the officers, in the otherwise reasonably democratic regime which prevailed generally in *Illustrious*, showed itself when 'all cooling machinery for the rest of the ship was shut off so that they could have ice in their drinks – and we were in the Indian Ocean!' The Americans greatly improved British creature comforts, offering the use of their washing machines, cartons of Lucky Strike or Camels, T-bone steaks, Mom's Apple Pie – all free.

Sabang was scheduled for 12 April. Specific targets were the huge oil storage tanks, the airfield, tankers, supply ships and submarines in the harbour, as well as the radar station and power station and sundry targets in the town, the whole to be co-ordinated by a hovering Jumping Joe in his Hellcat, while the rest of the Fleet bombarded from seaward. It was the Corsair boys' first real op. They were excited, as before an important rugger match, but death was not in their eager minds.

'We sailed early in the morning,' says Leading Wireman Dennis Bond in *Queen Elizabeth*. 'The sea was lovely and blue and we had the company of flying fish. We steamed east for a couple of days, the Fleet looking splendid spread over a wide area of sea, with *Illustrious* on the horizon. But the heat below was stifling. Then came "Hands to Action Stations!" We had arrived. The shore didn't look very far away. It was funny to think of the Japs so close. I went down to my action station with the Leading Stoker, and, boy, was it hot down there! We sat down near the switchboard and tried to make ourselves as comfortable as we possibly could under the circumstances. Then over the intercom we heard the order "Fire when guns come on target", a routine by now as familiar as it had been in the *Whitshed*. But the next thing that happened was not at all familiar. With a gigantic roar we let go a 15 in broadside. The whole ship sank down on the recoil, and we below decks could hear the water gurgling up the side as the ship was pushed down.'

Meanwhile *Illustrious*'s Corsairs and Barracudas had taken off. As they approached the target Sabang came up, 'a little green tropical island rising from the silver water against the silken curtain of the pale-blue early-morning sky', wrote Norman Hanson. 'When the first dirty black mushroom of flak began to blossom silently above the island it seemed like sacrilege.'

No fighters came up to meet them. They nosed over and went down with the 'Barras'. '*Now*, Hans!' said Forde crisply over the R/T, and the Corsairs shot ahead. Norman, in the lead, 'aimed at gun flashes appearing above the leading-edge of the wings, too excited to notice details!' They joined up again. There was a barrage of chatter on the R/T. Norman gleaned from it that Jumping Joe's wingman, Dale 'Klondike' Kahn, had been shot down in the sea. 'He must be saved!' shouted Joe. Down below, HMS *Tactician* had seen the Hellcat go down and headed straight for it. Four Hellcats strafed an awkward shore battery into silence, the submarine reached the sinking plane and after a brave and successful rescue act, *Tactician* headed seawards and submerged.

The next targets were Jap installations near Surabaya. *Saratoga*'s Dauntlesses hit the oil refinery at Wonokromo, *Illustrious*'s planes the Braat Works, the biggest engineering unit in the Indies.

The raid was a success, and '*Sara*' departed for the Pacific. In July aircraft from *Illustrious* beat up Port Blair, South Andaman Island, a big staging post for Jap forces in Burma, and its airfield, where tiny figures tried to out-run the 'Whistling Death', as the Japs called the Corsair. Yammering 0.5s tore into parked planes, setting them off like giant fireworks. Young Londoner Reggie Shaw raced down the side of the field, knocking petrol bowsers into blazing wreckage. Then it was the radar station on Mount Harriet, target for their AP and incendiary. 'Watch that bastard with the machine-gun up on the mast!' shouted Norman.

The cruiser *Suffolk* – *Bismarck*'s bloodhound – was blasting away with her 8 in guns when a Seafire came in low on their starboard side. 'We could see he was in trouble,' says Bill Earp, still on his 4 in AA gun, 'but the destroyer on our beam began firing at the poor bugger, who was obviously trying to ditch alongside the ship firing on him. In spite of all this, the pilot got out as he hit the water and was hauled aboard the destroyer safely. We all cheered like mad but what was said when he got aboard is not hard to guess. It was unfortunate that in the heat of battle Seafires and "Zeros" tended to look alike, and it took a lot of self-control to hold fire until the order was given.'

Vian had them exercising on Christmas Day. Says Norman Hanson, 'One of our guys missed the wires and slammed his Corsair into the barrier, covering the deck with flaming oil and petrol. A fierce wind swept this aft. The kid in the cockpit jumped out on to the wing but instead of jumping down for'ard, where he would have been safe, leapt off the trailing-edge right into the fire, with sleeves and trousers rolled up and no mask or goggles – strictly against instuctions – and suffered massive third-degree burns.'

In January 1945 they struck the refineries of Pladjoe and Soenei Gerong at Palembang in south-east Sumatra.

Norman's Flight flew into a circus of 'Tojo' and 'Oscar' fighters over Pladjoe, and when they returned to the ship they were all weary, nerves shot, reflexes ragged.

Norman came in to land: 'Wheels and hook down, on to the downwind leg at 500 feet. Flaps down . . . Christ! She's not slowing down. I've been hit . . . But Bats is signalling "Roger". . . Fast let-down on to the deck . . . Suddenly the ship is blotted out (another Corsair cuts in ahead of him). Stall . . . the sea races at me, a great blinding crash . . . The world goes black . . . I come to – underwater . . . *I'm drowning* . . . hanging upside-down in my harness . . . scrabble with one gloved hand . . . There's a narrow opening between hood and windscreen . . . Somehow I rip the harness off and drag myself out through the gap. Looking up I see the lighter green water near the surface . . . A violent jerk to get free and reach that wonderful light, so near, half-drowned, gagging and swallowing water, remembering to blow up my Mae West with the CO_2 bottle . . . burst up into blinding sunlight . . .

'I lie back in the water gasping for breath, choking on salt water every time a wave swamps me . . . I see a smoke float which the ship has dropped, about 300 yards away . . . It's burning well but I can't make it . . . No thought of sharks or of getting rid of my revolver or jungle machete – no use here . . . Then, unspeakable delight, there's a destroyer coming up . . .'

AVENGER BLUES

'Three days later', recorded Sub-lieutenant (A) Eric Rickman, RNVR, of *Illustrious*'s No 854 Avenger Squadron, 'Admiral Vian came aboard to talk to the aircrews. He said that Pladjoe had been extensively damaged, and was considered out of action. That left Soenei Gerong, next door, and we were to attack each dawn until that too was destroyed. He returned to *Indomitable*. We pilots studied the model refinery Intelligence had provided, our Flight of six being allocated the pumping-house, which brought up the oil, a pin-point target about as big as the average semi.'

Eric, who shared piano duty in the frequent evening singsongs with Norman Hanson, had completed three years of art school training before being called up, and had successfully sat the entrance exam to the Royal College of Art – 'to be followed up if we won, and if I survived the war'. Eric had also been interested in aircraft 'from the age of eight, but since my father came from Cowes, and his father had sailed the world in a two-masted schooner, plus an uncle of mine was a PO, RN, I opted for the Fleet Air Arm rather than the RAF'.

Pladjoe was comparatively trouble-free, in spite of the forest of balloons surrounding it from 2,000–6,000 ft.

'Next day, about 0445, we approached Soenei Gerong at 12,000 ft. I could see the target ahead and the balloons, then the CO called "Line astern – go!" and we dropped back to 100-yard intervals. I had just opened the bomb-bay doors when Vick, my TAG, called on the intercom "There's an Oscar on our tail!" "Open fire then!" I shouted. I heard Vick's Browning chattering, the target was coming up just ahead, slightly to port, just right. "Gun's jammed, Skip . . .' Vick's voice was tense. "Well, unjam it fast, you twit!" I screamed, tension showing. "Never mind, I'm going down now." The refinery was almost below me, and as I trimmed the Avenger for the dive and put the stick forward, I could see the three aircraft ahead of me, and the balloons, and . . . yes, there was the pump-house, just like the model.

'Luckily the Oscar broke off. We were now below balloon height, and I could see one particular balloon cable between us and the pump-house, almost vertically below. Charlie will go round it I thought . . . but he didn't – to my horror, he hit the cable with his port wing, shearing off two-thirds of it as clean as a whistle, the rest of the Avenger going into a vicious one-wing spin, blowing up on impact seconds later.

'The Senior Pilot, Gerry Connolly, rounded the cable and was making his attack, and behind him and just ahead of me was Roland Armstrong. I could hardly believe my eyes when he hit the same cable, just as the CO had done, with exactly the same result. I felt sick and angry – how could they not have seen that cable? . . .

'Time to bomb . . . I jinked round the cable . . . The target was obliterated in a huge rising smoke cloud, black with flashes of flame in it. I pressed the button, started pulling out, realized I couldn't avoid the smoke cloud, so went straight into it. The Avenger bucked in the turbulence, and emerged from the smoke on its side at 500 ft. I levelled out, went down to tree-top height, and headed round for the coast, blasting away with my front guns at horn-locator sites, lorries, huts, anything worth firing at. Approaching the coast I started to climb, looking round as I did so for Jap fighters – none. Then I saw another Avenger, away down to starboard. It looked all right, wasn't trailing smoke or anything, but as I watched it I realized it was in a shallow dive, and it blew up as it hit the sea. Result of attack – 18 direct hits. We did not need another dawn at Palembang.'

The next day they refuelled at sea and steamed for Fremantle and the Pacific. Australia did its best for them – movies, night clubs, bars and bathing beaches, two dozen oysters for lunch swilled down with champagne at five bob a bottle. Vian himself was seen with a big blonde in a night club. They were all chasing the golden hour, as the future sidled stealthily closer.

DEADLY SAKISHIMAS

Some replacement pilots joined the ship and they put to sea – just in time for Operation 'Iceberg'. This was the invasion of Okinawa. As Task Force 57, the BPF (British Pacific Fleet) would be part of Admiral Ray Spruance's Fifth Fleet in this grim task – a small unit compared with Admiral Marc Mitscher's famous Fast Carrier Force, Task Force 58.

From China to Okinawa itself was a chain of airfield stepping-stones formed by Formosa and the Sakishima Islands. When the attack on Okinawa began they would try to fly in planes from this chain of airfields. It was the job of the British carriers to stop them. 'They've given us the dirty work,' said Vian privately.

On 11 March 1945, with the carriers in the Solomon Sea, Hanson wrote in his diary: 'Scenery wonderful; the islands vary from massive outcrops of rock to green, flat reefs with lovely golden sands. Just like a fairy tale.'

Manus, the great fleet anchorage in the mouth of the Bismarck Sea, dispelled the image. Says Con Shiels, PO Mechanician in *Illustrious*, 'The Yankee matlows called the place "the asshole of the world" and quite rightly. I had to queue up at the RN canteen for one bottle of beer, though when I was made up to Chief I would be invited to the USN canteen, where we were given a book of tickets which entitled us to 20 beers. I still have one of those books, empty, of course.'

On the night of the 14th the four British carriers crossed the Equator, and on the 20th entered Ulithi lagoon, the US Pacific Fleet's main advanced base, a great, smooth stretch of blue water enclosed by rough, rocky atolls. On the 23rd the assault on Okinawa began.

Three days later they took station 100 miles south of the Sakishimas, and their part of 'Iceberg' began. Logbooks recorded: 'Strike on Sakishima Gunto: airfields.'

For the first time of many they flung themselves down from the eye of the bright, hot sun upon those criss-cross runways, deadly with thick ack-ack – and returned several planes and aircrew short. Runways were blasted out of action, aircraft shot up on the ground.

The next day they went to Ishigaki, the boot-shaped island with the fiercest flak of all. Eric Rickman sat in his Avenger, ready for take-off. This was not a day to be celebrating his birthday. 'Rick', said the voice of John his observer in his headphones, 'have you looked out to starboard?' 'I turned my head. The orange sun was just clear of the horizon, and scattered clouds in the east caused the sun's rays to form a huge radial pattern in the sky, like a celestrial Japanese flag! Some omen!'

'However, the raid on Ishigaki was straightforward, apart from the flak, which even as we had approached at 12,000 ft had been smack-on for height, and too close for comfort. It seemed the nearer one got to Japan itself, the more accurate the flak became. Not surprising, perhaps.

'Next day, Hirara airfield on Miyako Jima. I got two direct hits on the radio station, and saw the large wireless mast collapse. Away at tree-top height as usual, I made for the rendezvous area, climbing. "Do you know where we are, Johnnie?" I asked.

"Near enough. How's our petrol?"

"It's OK."

"And how's the starboard aileron?"

I'd forgotten about that. Light flak had removed half of it, but it seemed to work all right, but for how long?

"Seems OK. Call the ship."

'We reported, and flew back to *Illustrious*. A mile away the ship called us. "Stay clear, we're being attacked by Kamikazes." I glanced at the petrol gauge – enough for half an hour, perhaps more. Fifteen minutes later we landed on.

'Two Fireflies, carrying a larger dinghy, had been sent to find Notts, without success. Hours later a submarine just happened to surface a few hundred yards from his dinghy. It was, I am happy to say, American.'

Now the pattern was – strike and rest, strike and rest, blast craters in the airstrips, then come back when the Japs had filled them in – on and on in a hazy chain of hard action and reaction, with losses mounting and men getting steadily more and more weary and twitched: '. . . bags of flying all day. Wrote a few letters tonight. *Bloody* tired.' . . . so that every deck landing became a thing of jarring nerves and churning guts.

KAMIKAZE

Then the pattern changed, and there was a new word for fear – 'Kamikaze'. It meant 'Divine Wind', a reference to the great storm that smashed 4,000 Mongol ships which had come to invade Japan in 1281. It was also known as 'Tokko', the 'Special Attack Force', created by Vice-Admiral Takijiro Ohnishi in October 1944 to combat the mounting force of the American offensive. 'In my opinion', said Ohnishi, 'this can be accomplished by crash-diving on the carrier flight decks with Zero fighters carrying 250 kg bombs.' This was of course a suicide mission. 'It is better to die with honour than to live without honour,' said Kamikaze pilot Lieutenant Yuko Sehi. From the battle of Leyte Gulf onwards it was a major weapon. US Navy carriers had 'soft' flight decks of Oregon pine, and many were knocked out, as well as destroyer radar pickets.

At half-past seven on the morning of April Fool's Day 1945 a 'Divine Wind' hit the BPF when a 'Zero' struck *Indefatigable*'s bridge island. There was some damage but she was operational again in the afternoon. Meanwhile the destroyer HMS *Ulster* took a 'Kamikaze' right through her Iron Deck and into her boiler room. Then a 'Deadly Johnson', as the British matlows called the suicider, to deflate some of its mystique, scraped *Victorious*'s bows.

Five days later it was the turn of *Illustrious*. 'We heard in the engine room', says Charlie Shiels, 'through the Tannoy, the Commander, who always kept us informed of what was going on up top, warning us that a "Kamikaze" suicide plane was coming straight for us. It was my fifth wedding anniversary, and I kept saying "Please God, not today, don't kill me today. Tomorrow if you must, but please, not today!" It would have hurt my wife enough to have me killed, but on our wedding anniversary it would have made it much worse.'

The gunners had seen him coming, diving towards the for'ard part of the ship. He may have been following the usual 'Tokko' practice of aiming for the forward lift. Whatever he had in mind, the Bofors gunners changed it for him, knocking him about so much that he exploded over the side.

He left some souvenirs behind. His starboard wing had actually crashed into the bridge about nine feet away from Captain Lambe, and pieces of plane and pilot were scattered over the flight deck. Bob Ellison bent down and dazedly picked up two eyeballs and a piece of skull. He was looking stupidly at them when New Zealander Don Hadman of 1830 Squadron dashed up and grabbed the piece of skull from his hand . . . 'That's my mascot from now on!' Don was carrying his mascot when he took off and stopped the breath of the next 'Divine Wind' to appear over the Fleet; then, with bitter irony, returning alone, badly shot-up, he was fired on by his own gunners in mistake for a 'Kamikaze'. A Seafire on the tail of a 'Deadly Johnson' was hit by the barrage intended for the Jap and shot to bits.

At Okinawa the 'Kamikazes' inflicted the greatest losses ever suffered by the US Navy in a single battle, killing almost 5,000 men.

SHUTTING UP SHOP

On 13 July there were two strikes on Formosa. By now nothing Japanese was to be seen in the sky over their airfields, and nothing visible intact on the ground. On the 14th somebody stuck their head round Norman Hanson's door and shouted, 'Wakey, wakey, get up and look what's on our starboard bow!'

It was *Formidable*, fresh out from England – their relief. Every man, HO or Regular, aboard felt the great, unimaginable lift of spirit. 'The Admiralty thought we had had enough,' says Con Shiels, 'which I could not deny, and sent us home.' 'We simply shut up shop,' said Norman Hanson.

The other 'cast-iron carriers' of TF57 carried on digging holes in the Ryuku runways, with trips to the replenishment areas 'Cootie', 'Midge' or 'Mosquito' on 10, 14, 18 and 22 May, when the US escort carrier *Sangamon*'s TU.52.1.3

relieved them. After Okinawa finally fell, the Allied Fleet prepared for Operation 'Olympic' – the invasion of Japan. On 17 July the BPF joined Halsey's Third Fleet off Tokyo for strikes on the area and ships in the Inland Sea, and was refuelling again on 6/7 August when the BBC and Sydney Radio reported the atom bomb attack on Hiroshima. On the 9th the second atom bomb was dropped on Nagasaki, and the Japanese sued for peace.

Warrant Officer Alf Barlow in the escort carrier HMS *Stalker* relates, 'After many fruitless exercises and operations we were at the surrender of Singapore when the Jap generals were (as thought) going to commit suicide after seeing Mountbatten at the big parade, but of course they did not. I remember our Lieutenant-Commander (Flying) and the COs of squadrons having great difficulty in getting a flying programme to take effect after the Jap surrender. Our young, keen RNVR pilots were most reluctant to fly in peacetime; the interest in flying evaporated completely as they considered it a waste of time.'

Eric Rickman, the former art student turned Avenger pilot, considered staying in the Service, 'having much enjoyed most aspects of my four and a half years service. But I had found, in common with many FAA personnel, that the higher echelons in the Navy tended to be unimaginative, and lacking in individuality, consequently this was not for me.' Most regulars were put ashore so that HOs with low demob numbers could sail the now redundant ships home.

Also serving in *Stalker* was Tom Bailey, now a PO, who had joined in far-off days for 'three square meals a day', and discovered that he loved the Navy. Today, from his house outside Newcastle-on-Tyne he writes, 'God Bless all my old shipmates, God Bless all our present Servicemen, especially Navy – we may not have the biggest navy, but we have still got the best.'

Birds of a Feather:
The Wrens

This book is about sailors – *men* who fought at sea (or loafed ashore) – but it cannot be thought in any sense complete without mentioning the *women* who made this possible, the Women's Royal Naval Service, the WRNS, the Wrens.

We never knew much about them – they were dismissed as officers' perks – and most matlows never got beyond the stage of admiring them as sex objects, of which we were so cruelly starved. Indeed, my own immediate memory of them is of attending gramophone recitals of classical music at *Ganges*. These genteel happenings were thought to be the proper pastimes for ladies in blue, and hairy matlows willingly endured a Beethoven quartet, even a blast of Bartok, just to be near them. I had a cousin in the Wrens who, as a Second Officer, referred to Fleet Air Arm pilots, whose ranks I was then desperate to join, as the 'dirty-fingernailed type'. I have never seen or spoken to her since. There was also the vague idea that Wren boats' crews were the cream, all debs and hockey-playing Honourables (Wren officers being all grammar school girls). The reality took some time to appreciate.

The wartime Director of the WRNS, Dame Vera Laughton Matthews, identified three stages in the appreciation of her 'gels'. 'First, the shock period; one admits that it must have been a shock, and many were the seafaring ancestors who were said to have turned in their graves. To the same period belongs the "Every nice girl loves a sailor" attitude on the part of the matelots (and Vivian Ellis's "Up with the lark and to bed with a Wren").

'Then came the period of astonished admiration: the Wrens were a success – in fact they were Wonderful. They could work hard . . . they could do not only the jobs expected of women, but all kinds of technical and mechanical work; they could run boats in the black-out and when it was blowing half a gale; they were calm and cheerful under bombing and shelling ("Deserving of the highest praise", said C-in-C Portsmouth in 1940). Next came the stage which is the greatest compliment of all – we were taken for granted. More and more Wrens just fit into the picture and are an integral part of that wonderful organization which is the Royal Navy . . . On D-Day there were WRNS Signal Officers and Duty Officers; Wrens received and sent wireless messages to the ships; they coded signals and plotted ships – the greatest plot ever; they serviced sea-craft and aircraft and guns and torpedoes; they saw that Jack got his mail, that his pay was in order and that he left shore well fed; they transported supplies and medical stores and ammunition to the ships.'

Today no one should be surprised that girls could run tenders, picket boats, mail boats, hospital boats, boarding drifters and skimming dishes, ceremoniously twirl a boathook and belay a rope with the best foretopman in the Fleet. It was certainly the most romantic category of women's wartime service (Monsarrat's heroine in *The Cruel Sea* dies, pregnant, in a boating accident), but entailed a tough seamanship training after a Probationer Wren had completed the General Service Training – knots and splices, swabbing decks, elementary navigation, boxing the compass, climbing ropes (in trousers of course), and leaping in and out of boats without falling in the water. Their less glamorous sisters in Motor Transport handled staff cars, supply vans, draft lorries, boat trailer tractors.

Wren Wireless Telegraphists and Visual Signallers needed a quick brain and good powers of concentration – to read and transmit by Morse buzzer, Aldis lamp or flags as fast and fluently as in a chat with the hairdresser or dishing the dirt with the girls. Wrens intercepted Morse commentaries on naval battles, the tense, terse reports from a beleaguered convoy, or sometimes the news of a husband's or brother's loss – to be kept secret from family for long, cruel weeks. V/S Wrens were closer to the ships, wagging urgent flags like racecourse tictac men from gyrating boarding craft, passing sailing instructions for take-off; Wren W/T spoke to test pilots, and received their calm relays of disaster.

The Masters of many a convoy of US Henry Kaiser Liberty ships lying-to off an English shore after battling Atlantic gales, wallowing deep-laden with urgent cargoes, gaped astonished as a young woman with blue rings on her sleeve climbed nimbly up the swaying Jacob's Ladder with complex orders which she proceeded to explain patiently in detail. Boarding Officer was the only commission most Boats' Crew Wrens would accept, as the only one which could give them the movement of a ship beneath their feet and the salty tang of spindrift.

Fleet Air Arm Wrens measured the arcana of wind speed and direction by theodolite and pilot balloon, the plotting of the weather on the 'actuals' board, rearmed guns, repaired airframes, serviced engines and radios. Some packed parachutes – 'I'd rather a woman did it than some dozey matlow,' said one Seafire pilot. Wren 'torpedomen' worked on the electrics of tinfish and depth-charges. Some griped that they were not allowed to *fly* the aircraft – fast fighters, bombers, even sleepy Swordfish. The Women's Auxiliary Air Force did, didn't they? The lucky, or crafty, ones got to test equipment in the air. Others did the same things for ships, wielding the acetylene torch, forging chain cable links, straightening bent davits, re-planking stove-in ships' boats; operated lathes and milling machines, polished lenses for submarine periscopes, qualified as riggers (how many seamen could make an apple-ring fender?).

Base of the pyramid were the Housekeepers, doing the jobs men knew they could do – the cooks and stewards, in galleys big and small, making hot meals for exhausted men just in from the Battle of the Atlantic; survivors gaunt from days in open boats; for new entries, many with the thin, starved look of poverty about them; packing rations for night-fighting ML men ('What is it tonight? We had *grapes* with the last lot . . .'). Wrens were much preferred to male stewards ('A bit like home'). Wrens learned hairdressing and made careers of it after demob.

Wren Stores Assistants handed out books and bell-bottoms, nuts and bolts, even the sacred rum ration. Wrens of the Fleet Mail Service channelled those longed-for letters to matlows ashore and afloat, took them out to them at anchor – and wrote some of the replies.

In spring 1941 the first Wrens went overseas to the East, to SEAC; others went to Normandy; many were lost in transit at sea.

Men *and* women won the war. After all, 'ODs? I've spit em!' but Wrens? 'Our lives would be misery without them', said Flag Officer, Dover.

Epilogue

'Memories . . . the *tiredness*, a continuous and overwhelming tiredness I have never known since. Even in harbour . . .

'But it was at its worst at sea, exaggerated then by the discomfort, the constant motion, the conscious physical effort of even standing upright at times – all this going on for day after day after day. And how the last few minutes of a night watch dragged by. It's 0345 and you're coming towards the end of a tiring middle watch – and going down below to shake your reliefs. Down all those ladders, through all those hatches, along all those flats and passageways, dodging over hammocks, stepping over sleepers in semi-darkness and in thick fog, then right down to the forward lower messdeck, with still-sleeping, half-awake, half-dressed, weary figures everywhere, then off back to the bridge to finish off the watch, trying hard not to give in to tiredness (not yet anyway). But I sometimes weakened – so tired that I couldn't resist the temptation to sit down, just for a few seconds, on one of the stools on the upper seamen's messdeck just to rest aching bones and muscles. And in that few seconds I have fallen asleep, only to be quickly awakened with a jerk as my elbow slipped off the mess table or I fell off the stool.

'And so back to the bridge, hoping that your reliefs really are awake and that they will put in a timely appearance. And then, glory be – they appear . . .

'Sleep . . . A hammock was a lovely, comfortable bed – snug and reasonably warm in spite of one blanket only. The pillow a rolled up jersey. All hammocks jammed together, and the ever-present muttering and movements of people coming and going underneath or alongside you – a late card school, men going on watch, returning from shore leave, sometimes bumping into you but in spite of it all you slept well – and in spite, too, of the joker who would wake you up in the middle of the night and ask "What time is it?"

'Sleep at sea was different – in fact that is just about all one did at sea (other than duties and meals, etc) where you would be so utterly tired and weary that very often one just slumped on to a bench or a table or in the hammock netting, fully clothed, and fell asleep within seconds. Many never slung their hammocks at sea. It *was* a hard life, at sea in wartime – even ignoring the ever-present danger from the enemy. Two watches (sometimes three if you were lucky), the endless heaving motion of the ship pitching and rolling, the coldness, the rain and the gales, the seasickness, the sea blowing inboard and soaking everyone even up on the bridge, the eternal tiredness from lack of sleep and effort of doing nothing more than putting up with your living conditions. And then, at last, going off watch for that precious sleep, only to find the messdeck swilling in seawater as it had been for days, thanks to leaking seams and inefficient ventilators and Atlantic weather . . . all this for day after day after day, months on end, till a spell in dock brought relief – and the sight of those molly-coddled dockyard maties swarming onboard to "work", to repair your ship by spending half their time playing poker in the forward clothing store hidden away from the foreman. These, the men who mostly lived safely at home in houses that stayed still, who slept all night in comfortable beds without the ever-present possibility of a torpedo and who awoke fully refreshed next morning and ready to spend half the next day loafing. We resented them.

'And so – hurry below to the blessed relief of your hammock or to slump, fully clothed, on to the mess stool or the table or even the deck – if it is not swilling in three inches of seawater. Only to be awakened a couple of hours later for dawn action stations which lasts just long enough for it not to be worthwhile turning in again.

'In spite of the dangers and the tiredness and the physical discomfort and everything else, if you look at it one way it could be said that we were thoroughly molly-coddled. All you had to do was do your job properly (and you were trained for that), and keep the messdeck clean and your place of work. And that was all. No rent, no rates to pay. No maintenance or repairs to see to – if that electric light bulb, or this fan, or that heater stopped working, someone came along (eventually) and saw to it, for nothing. All your food was provided free, in bigger ships without even the necessity for you to make a decision as to what colour shirt or tie or suit to buy next time you needed new clothing – those decisions were all made for you. No need to worry about money – you could spend the whole lot on drink ashore, knowing that you would manage to live without starving till next pay day. No fear of redundancies, of the firm going bankrupt or being taken over. Plenty of companionship, plenty of card games on the messdecks on evenings onboard, free cinema shows, free postage for letters (and free French-letters if you wanted them), free medical treament, free trips to all those wonderful and exotic places in the Mediterranean and the east, free heating, free lighting, the advantage of living only a few yards from your place of work. I could go on and on. Put that way, what a cushy way of life it seems to have been. Yet I don't suppose that, quite understandably, any man who ever went to sea in wartime ever thought that he was being molly-coddled. We would have thrown a dozen fits if anyone had ever suggested that to us.

'Really of course, sailors were in far more danger than were the majority of airmen and soldiers.

'Most airmen spent their war being in very little danger at all back at their airfields. Only those who flew on ops were in danger (though, obviously in *great* danger) and then only for a few hours at a time.

'Same with the Army. Only the fighting men – infantry, tank corps, etc – were in danger, and that was only when there was actual fighting taking place. And it's surprising how often, during the war, there was very little actual fighting taking place.

'All the higher-ups in both services – Group Captains, Colonels and above – usually stayed somewhere at the back in a place of comparative safety.

'But in the Navy *everyone* went into action – cooks, stewards, writers, marine, bandsmen, supply assistants, admirals, the whole lot shared the dangers equally. And there were quite a few admirals killed in action. Nor was it only in a battle that there was danger. At *any* moment throughout all the hours and days and weeks that ships spent at sea there could be that torpedo on its way towards you, that mine ahead of you, those bombers suddenly appearing from over the horizon – almost non-stop from the beginning to the end of the war the sailor, from boy to admiral, lived in danger!'

List of Contributors

Edward Baggley
Thomas Bailey
Alfred Barlow
A. S. Bolt
Dennis Bond
A. G. 'Murgy' Brown
Christopher Buist
Christopher Burston
Ivor Burston
Jack Copeman
Eric Craske
Michael Dale
Geoffrey Denny
Jack Dodds
William Earp
Douglas Ellliot
William Filer
S. France
Frederick Hall
Norman Hanson
Jack Harker
William Harman
Jackie Heath
'Pusser' Hill
Norman 'Blondie' Hollis
C. P. O. Hunt
Kenneth Illingworth
William Jeffery
Ben Kennedy
Dame Vera Laughton Matthews
Frederick Lee
Frederick Longman
Ronald Lunberg
William McCall

B. S. McEwan
Colin Malcolm
Burt Male
Alan Mathison
Neville Milburn
Eric Monk
George Monk
C. P. O. Neal
Iain Nethercott
Ernest North
Dennis 'Vic' Oliver
Maurice Pacey
Geoffrey Penny
Bert Poolman
Kenneth Poolman
Ben Rice
Sir Ralph Richardson
Eric Rickman
David Satherley
Leslie 'Ginger' Sayer
Brian Seymour
Geoff Shaw
Con Shiels
Jack Skeats
Alfred Slocombe
Christopher Smith
Jack Smith
William Thomas
Alan Todd
Peter Trant
Mark Wells
Len Wincott
Charles Wines

Index